Understanding Post – Covid -19 Governance Challenges in India

C K Mathcw
A. Narayana

Indian Institute of Public Administration

Prints Publications Pvt Ltd

Published by

Prints Publications Pvt Ltd
Viraj Tower-2, 4259/3, Ansari Road,
Darya Ganj, New Delhi-110002
Tel.: +91-11-45355555 Fax: +91-11-23275542
E-mail: contact@printspublications.com
Website: www.printspublications.com

Prepared by:
C K Mathew and A. Narayana
Understanding Post – Covid -19 Governance Challenges in India

Edition: 2024

ISBN 978-81-19972-58-6

Price Rs. 995/-

Published and Printed by Mr Pranav Gupta (Managing Director) on behalf of Prints Publications Pvt Ltd, New Delhi.

Understanding Post-Covid-19 Governance Challenges in India

Table of Contents

INTRODUCTION

Ever since Covid-19 began its marauding journey, starting from Wuhan in the People's Republic of China, to every nook and corner of the globe, the planet has become a battle ground to defeat this common international enemy. Peoples and their organizations, countries and their myriad agencies, scientists and pharmaceutical companies, medical and para-medical staff, political parties, non-governmental bodies and philanthropists— all came together to defeat the pandemic. When the crisis is over, we will be celebrating the achievements of scientists from all over the world who collaborated to manufacture effective vaccines in the shortest time possible. We will have praise for governmental structures who brooked no barriers or impediments in achieving their goal. We will have the deepest admiration for the frontline workers and the doctors and nurses who gave their everything to quell the pandemic everywhere. And most of all, we will thank the ordinary citizens of the globe who struggled through adversity and challenges to overcome this insidious, invisible and implacable enemy.

One thing that the pandemic proved is that the virus recognized no boundaries of political ideology, national identities, race, sex or economics. It struck out equally at all humanity with terrifying speed and crushing impact. In a world that boasts of interconnectedness and simultaneity, it appeared that the virus was demonstrating the truth of these present-day universal characteristics in its own behaviour. As we write this in the last week of November 2021, about 26 crore persons have been infected by the virus worldwide and there have been 51.8 lakh mortalities. India, even ignoring charges of underreporting, has to this day recorded some 3.46 crore cases of Covid infection and the burden of some 4.67 lakh deaths.

Entire sections of the economy were adversely affected in all countries. In its early days, school education was at a standstill, with over a billion and a half children suddenly deprived of the very means to equip themselves better for a prosperous tomorrow. Health and wellness institutions were overwhelmed by the sheer numbers of the infected. Entire countries were almost brought down to their knees. Small businesses and labour, more so in developing countries, were suddenly deprived of their means of livelihood. Those at the lower end of the labour market, lost their employment and migrated back to their homes to eke out whatever sustenance was possible from their meagre rural assets. Public finance took a beating as all available resources were diverted to saving people from the disease. The travel, tour and hospitality sectors were virtually devasted. Real estate created across the globe, at such a massive cost, was now vacant and empty, as the work force returned back to their rural homes and to manage work from the safety of their own four walls.

Yet, there were certain sectors that showed a surprising resilience. Agriculture and some elements of rural economy were largely intact, and the rural labour force ensured that food production did not suffer. Industries based on information technology and communications thrived and became the backbone of the spread of evolving medical knowledge as well helping in the setting up of the required infrastructure required to tackle the menace. They also helped the retail market to metamorphize and reshape itself so that the people, who were trapped within the four walls of their homes, were not left lacking for any supplies or resources. The boom of electronic industry stand testimony to that innate strength of the sector and its ability to service the requirements of the time. The prowess and determination of the medical and health sector demonstrated that a sense of commitment and devotion can overcome almost insurmountable odds. Governments, normally accused of red-tapism and delay, refashioned themselves to meet the challenge and delivered results through sheer dedication and innovation. The massive challenge of vaccination of the general population of a planet with seven billion souls—no ordinary task—is now going ahead smoothly, despite a few initial hiccups.

Why this Compendium?

It is in this context that the seed of this compendium of essays was sown. It was during certain casual discussions held between members of the Constitution Conduct Group (CCG) and the faculty of the Azim Premji University that the idea was first put forward. It is necessary to introduce CCG here: The CCG is a group of retired officers of the All India and Central Services who, in the course of their careers, have worked with the Central and State Governments. The members of the Constitutional Conduct Group believe in impartiality, neutrality and commitment to the Indian Constitution and in safeguarding its values. The vision statement of the CCG states that it draws its inspiration from the values embodied in the Constitution and that it stands by the principles enshrined in the Constitution of India. The group is firmly committed to pluralism in all its forms – gender, religion, ethnicity, class, caste, language, or otherwise as well as adherence to the ideal of non-violence in conduct, both word and deed. The Group is deeply concerned with what it perceives to be as increasing departures from the rule of law and the decline of robust institutions. It emphasises need for internalisation of the values of justice, liberty, equality and fraternity, which underpin the Constitution. The CCG is non-partisan in nature and is not aligned to any political party. It believes in the motto of "Speaking Truth to Power" and periodically raises issues of public interest to persuade the governments of the day to faithfully abide by their oaths to the Constitution of India.

The Azim Premji University arises out of the Azim Premji Foundation which works in the non-governmental space towards a just, equitable, humane and sustainable society with a focus on India. The Foundation was begun by Azim Premji in 2001 and over the years he has transferred a significant part of his financial assets for philanthropic purposes. The work of the Foundation spans from education to other important areas of equity and human well-being. The Foundation works on improving the public-school education system in India, with a focus on the more disadvantaged areas of the country. At present, on the groundwork spans seven States and work with government schools The work involves every aspect of school education, including capacity development of teachers, head teachers and functionaries, curricular improvement, text-book development, assessment reform, and education policy. The Foundation has set up field institutions and also runs eight demonstration schools in some of the most backward areas of the country. The Foundation works closely with the Central and State governments on matters of policy and curriculum. For example, it has contributed significantly to the development of the National Education Policy 2020. The Azim Premji University in Bangalore was set up in 2010: Its mandate is to run teaching programmes and conduct research to contribute to the social sector in India, and to be an exemplar higher education institution with inclusion and quality. The Universities' focus is on education and other domains of human development, for example, livelihoods, governance and policy, public health, and sustainability. At the undergraduate level, they offer a broad-based liberal education, across the physical and biological sciences, humanities and social sciences, integrated with interdisciplinary studies in fields of human development. There is also a separate Philanthropic Initiative that provides financial support for not-for-profit.

The premise behind bringing out this publication jointly was that even as international organisations and countries are working together to control and eradicate the deadly virus, there is an urgent need to look at how the pandemic has adversely affected important sectors of the social and economic fabric of the globe, with special emphasis on India, and how these institutions would need to rethink and reconstruct themselves in order to continue with their work once the pandemic is under control. In a way this collaborative effort, where practical wisdom gained over a lifetime in administration, met and worked together with the academic rigour of professors and researchers, is an ideal combination to address some of the governance challenges that this international crisis has engendered.

There are some common features of the impact of the pandemic that are really universal in nature. That is to say, irrespective of the geography or the demographics of the affected swathes of population, there have been some common attributes that the virus has left behind in its wake. In all countries, the impact on education, and especially school education, has been extreme. Across the globe, it is apprehended that some billion and a half children, predominantly in schools and also in tertiary education, may have had to face disruption in the acquisition of knowledge. For those children coming from deprived social and economic backgrounds, the impact would be even more disastrous. It is anticipated that there would be severe learning deficit and even a regression in learning capabilities that is likely to set them back to a level that may be difficult to overcome. In effect they may become factors that retard the overall long-term growth of the country and the capabilities of its work force.

Another critical area that has suffered is small and informal businesses. Deprived of active consumer behaviour that in normal times would have ensured the continuance of their business activities, a large share of these entrepreneurial efforts have dwindled away, leaving them without a reliable and dependable means of livelihood. Their stories are largely undocumented and untold. In any city or town, the sight of closed shop shutters and the absence of shoppers bear testimony to this inescapable fact. Even below this rung of the economic ladder are the casual and migrant labourers who, almost overnight, were deprived of their labour market forcing them to resort to reverse migration to go back to the villages from where they had come to the urban labour markets to earn a living. The shock of seeing on our TV screens the millions of workers moving back home on foot immediately after the first lockdown in India at the end of March 2020, must have horrified many of us. But the lack of data, as confessed by the government of India, only highlighted the appalling tragedy unfolding on our screens, rather than diminishing them. Yet, today their plight remains hidden from public view and we are not aware of how they may have survived or succumbed to the tragedy that suddenly had befallen them.

On the other hand, the health sector has been continuously in the public eye. As ordinary citizens, we have admired and applauded the courage and determination shown by doctors and nurses and paramedics, and frontline workers who have stood firm in the face of overpowering odds. All over the world, and especially in developing economies, the pandemic revealed significant gaps and weaknesses in the medical infrastructure that almost threatened to overwhelm the hospital facilities in virtually every country. The pandemic revealed, especially in a country like India that the investment made in the sector over the last three-quarters of a century is woefully short and inadequate. Even as countries are now investing in the much-needed medical infrastructure, it has become painfully clear that a sizeable share of the public finances in the near and mid-term future will have to be invested in the health infrastructure, and trained personnel to prevent the kind of havoc we have seen reign in most parts of the world.

Not much study has been done on the pandemic's impact on the people who are at the south end of the economic scale and are, by definition, invisible and uncounted. There is a need to study and appreciate the difficulties that they have been going through in this time of crisis. Women and children from weaker social groups, the Scheduled Castes and the Tribes, the differently abled, those living below the poverty line, etc. require to be given utmost attention in these critical times to keep them afloat. The governments, State and Central, must be forced to acknowledge the nature of the difficulties that these vulnerable sections of society face, and put in place supportive mechanisms to sustain and protect them in these difficult times. It is also unsettling to realise that the country may have been hugely under-reporting the fatalities of Covid-19, because there is no robust, reliable and uniform state -supported systems to record deaths across the country. All these may pose significant challenges that the government will have to address in the days to come.

It is with this as the background that an effort was made to compile these essays to act as pointers to highlight important issues, analyze the implications on society and to make recommendations to correct aberrations and to put in place more reliable and supportive practices that will address these lacunae. A brief overview of some of the essays in this compilation will give us an idea of the vast canvas of subjects that have been impacted by the virus and which require corrective action. All the writers have practical experience in administration or have the necessary academic expertise that make them competent to address these varied issues and suggest modalities for the future.

Organization of the Compendium

Following this Introduction, the essays in this compendium are organized in two parts. Part-I is titled 'Health, Education and Environment in the time of Pandemic: Lessons on Development and Welfare.' As the title suggests it covers some of the crucial sectors affected by the pandemic. Restoring normal functioning of these sectors after the pandemic and to keep them ready for facing any future crisis of this scale would require enormous administrative imagination and care. Five essays in this section cover a wide range of issues that are crucial as India imagines governance for post-Covid times.

The first paper titled 'Recording Deaths – With or Without Covid-19' by Narayanan Unni and G Balagopal focuses the Civil Registration System (CRS) in India in the context of the pandemic. Covid-19 raised a lot of questions on the ability of India's existing system to record deaths due to the pandemic accurately. It is estimated that more than 10 percent of births and 13 percent of deaths are not registered in India. This is despite the presence of a legal framework to do so.

This paper provides a detailed analysis of the existing mechanism for reporting deaths and births. The analysis extends to the issues present in the existing structure. The authors identified variations in the organizational structure of CRVS across the States. Civil registration related responsibilities are vested with Panchayat Secretaries in various States. Since the power devolved to panchayats varies, efficiency of the system also shows variation across the States. The process of reporting also has some flaws. The system lacks consistent mechanism to capture the cause of death at the time of registration. Mostly, the cause is verbally informed by the relative of the deceased. Medically Certified Cause of Death (MCCD) is not registered along with death registration in many cases in India. This is due to inadequate systems in place. The authors point out that some of the analysis done by researchers on Covid-19- related deaths in India could be flawed due to potentially bad assumptions made on the sample data.

The authors provide detailed suggestions on improving the command control structure of the reporting organizations, including the use of a centralized identity management system to track birth and deaths, regular audit of birth and death records and a state-wise action plan to revive the process and systems. This paper cites the example of Africa Programme for Accelerated Improvement of Civil Registration and Vital Statistics systems (APAI-CRVS) as a best practice to address the problems that plague the registration system in India.

The second paper in Part I, by Shreelata Sheshadri, takes the debate on the governance of health sector in the wake of Covid-19 crisis ahead by a wide range of relevant issues. The paper titled 'The Covid Pandemic and the Health Sector – What Have We Learned' focuses on the health policy related suggestions to improve pandemic response. It recommends that we should form guidelines along the lines of Pandemic Influenza Preparedness Framework (PIPF). This framework proposes the setting up of surveillance centers, prediction mechanisms, laboratory networks and deploying trained personnel. The current pandemic response relied heavily on National Disaster Management Authority's policies which were not a health-specific policy formulation. Even crisis management in the National Health Policy 2017 does not have much with respect to a pandemic outbreak.

The paper brings out some of the lessons we learned in the aftermath of the pandemic. The first lesson is that there is no alternative to primary healthcare. Covid-19 exposed issues in our primary healthcare network. Kerala and Karnataka serve as good examples. The second lesson tells us that the existing health system should be equipped and ready to apply the science that is fast evolving. Third being the importance of achieving the National Health Policy target for health sector investment at 2.5 percent of GDP. Fourth lesson is about the need of a regulatory framework to ensure that private sector pitches in to support the Government whenever there is a need. Such regulatory authorities can prevent the private sector from charging heavily from patients especially during crisis situations. Fifth is about the focus on the Union government's schemes like Ayushman Bharat which covers for hospitalization benefits. Policy emphasis on such schemes do not strengthen primary care. There must be transparency in communication with the public and a policy framework that goes beyond the health sector. Above all these things, there must be an effort to improve the data that is required for evidence-based policy making in the health sector, the paper concludes.

The third paper in Part I focuses on post-pandemic governance challenges that the education sector faces in India. C.K. Mathew's paper titled 'School Education in the Post-Covid World', terms post-Covid scenario in education as a leapfrog moment with various organizations coming forward to support building remote learning facilities for children. The Brookings Report which is discussed in the paper suggests leveraging public schools and improving engagement from parents. Technology remains at the core of improving education infrastructure as well as improving content delivery. The paper reiterates that online education should not be seen as an alternative to conventional education and should be used as a support mechanism.

The paper recommends the constitution of National and State level committees which will have experts from various fields to oversee things from school re-openings to resuming education. The promotion criteria for children in schools need to be set objectively, considering the loss in learning. There must be an effort to bridge the learning gaps. Teacher training in future must be designed keeping these demands in mind. Identifying children without access to digital infrastructure and identifying students with lacking knowledge are both important. There must be an effort to engage with parents and guardians. There is a need to do a psychological evaluation of children who are impacted adversely by the pandemic. There must be a special focus blended learning which is going to be the future of education, this would also mean ensuring adequate digital infrastructure in schools as well as homes. The education system must look at recalibrating the curriculum by keeping the focus on learning outcomes. The paper concludes that a collective will to make these changes is the need of the hour.

The next topic is environment. The paper titled 'Post-Covid Economic Challenges and Environmental Regulation' by Kanchi Kohli and Manju Menon provides an analysis of regulations related to environment in India with a specific emphasis on what happened during the Covid-19 pandemic. Covid-19 restrictions in India exposed the poor living conditions in many parts of the country. While the lockdown that followed the pandemic had a positive impact on the environment, it had a disastrous effect on the economy. To revive the economy though, Government relaxed environment regulatory restrictions on industries.

Environment Clearance, Forest Clearance, Wildlife Clearance and Pollution Consents are at the core of the Central government's decision making for the conversion of natural resources for economic development. Ministry of Environment, Forests and Climate Change and various boards are expected to oversee the implementation of these processes in accordance with the existing norms. However, in recent years these processes have weakened considerably. The paper details the weakening of these processes post-Covid. During the lockdown, poaching and illegal activities damaging forests grew multiple times. Industrial activity resumed without proper checks to ensure that pollution norms are adhered to. This resulted in at least three large-scale industrial accidents, and it took a while before the regulatory mechanism swung into action to curb violations. This period also witnessed weakening of approval processes for developmental projects. This included exemption from environmental approvals, approval meetings conducted online and for shorter duration, extension of pollution clearances and environmental clearances, cancellation of public hearings or moving them online.

To aid the V-shape economic recovery, further easing of environment regulations were brought in. Some of the projects that were approved were damaging for environment. Amendment to Mineral Laws were done to encourage commercial mining. Paper points out that increasing coal mining would result in more carbon emissions which will be damaging for the environment. The economic revival plans also included exploiting more ecological fragile regions like the coastal areas of Lakshadweep and Andaman and Nicobar Islands. This is in continuation of the vision document that was presented by NITI Ayog in 2019.

The authors propose a slew of measures to strengthen environmental regulations. They stress the importance of bringing back transparency and encourage public participation in environmental policy making. Preventing deforestation and rejecting projects that damage environment could go a long way in protecting environment so that there is no habitat destruction that could cause a rise in zoonotic diseases. The focus must be on public health and safety than economic recovery at the cost of health and environment.

The fifth paper in Part I, by Aditi Mehta, shows how the pandemic accentuated the problems faced by certain vulnerable and marginal sections of society. This paper titled, 'Covid-19 and Vulnerable Groups' attempts to understand the intersection of caste and poverty keeping the pandemic-induced stigmatization in mind. The analysis is based on the study conducted among the population of De-Notified Tribes (DnT) inhabiting peri-urban areas adjoining Udaipur city and in a mofussil town called Dabok. The paper looks at the material condition prevailed in various DnT communities which made it virtually impossible for them to follow public health advice. The gendered impact of Covid-19 is also explored in the paper. There has been a general impact on women and children. Caste and class added to the woes of Dalit and tribal women apart from the issues that they faced along the gender lines. Access to food and nutrition, access to essential commodities, access to basic healthcare also suffered during the pandemic. The increase in child abuse cases, domestic violence cases were alarming throughout the pandemic days which saw intermittent regional shutdowns or state-wide lockdowns. While listing out the issues specific to the marginalized communities in India, this paper brings out how different factors like caste, class and gender have played a role in their suffering. Digital divide also added to the misery of the vulnerable groups.

The paper lists out a set of measures focusing on what local self-governments can do in terms of providing basic citizens' rights to the DnTs and other marginalized communities. Need for the government to focus on protecting livelihoods of the marginalized communities is stressed in the policy suggestions. Addressing gender gap issues, providing sexual and other healthcare services during crisis are suggested.

Three papers in Part-II titled 'Pandemic, Cities and Technology: Governance Questions,' looks at the post-Covid challenges from the perspectives of life in cities in an emerging technology dominated world. The pandemic has once again highlighted the need for taking urban planning seriously. Despite the massive reverse migration seen during the peak of the pandemic, rural to urban migration is a reality in India. The lessons learnt during the Covid-19 crisis should inform the future planning of cities. The pandemic also enhanced the dependence on technology leading to innovations and massive changes in lifestyle. Governance in the future needs to be alert to this new reality.

The first paper in this section by P. Joy Oommen emphasizes the need for an inclusive approach in urban governance and planning in post-Covid India. The paper titled, 'Urban Development and Pandemic: A Time to Reset the Priorities,' says that while some administrators want their cities to be more resilient, it can be achieved only by making the poor and vulnerable sections of the population more resilient to unanticipated shocks. Providing a cleaner and more hygienic environment, adequate and safe housing, access to reliable and affordable healthcare for them should form the core of this effort. This in turn will call for an all-out effort to regularise and upgrade slums and other illegal colonies where the economically or socially weaker sections live or provide them alternate accommodation.

Increasing the stock of affordable rental housing is another priority identified in this paper. Availability of land is often mentioned as a constraint, but many Government departments and PSUs are making plans to monetise the 'excess lands' in their possession. This, the paper says, should stop and all excess lands should be handed over to Local Governments with a mandate to use them primarily for developing civic amenities and housing for the weaker sections. A reliable and efficient public transport system with coordination among all players - public and private- is surely a priority for any city. It would help the cause of a cleaner environment while saving money and time for the commuters. Helping more people to get jobs and livelihoods is another major challenge. Ease of doing business is best achieved when local governments facilitate investments and new enterprises. Special efforts would be needed to help those in the informal sector to get their jobs and livelihoods back. Targeted skill development and retraining, setting up of orderly and well- maintained markets, facilitating bank loans and ensuring support of civil society organizations are needed to achieve this. Overall, it is the opportune time to reset our priorities and move forward.

Continuing the urban planning debate in more specific terms, Champaka Rajagopal's paper titled, 'Misaligned Goals, Policy Opportunism and Planning' for Bengaluru draws attention to how Covid-19 pandemic has exposed the inequities that inhabit Indian Cities. Focusing particularly on the case of planning in Bengaluru, the author highlights the misalignment in values and goals across various organizations - public, private as well as hybrid - which are involved in urban planning. Apart from the concerns related to institutional arrangements of urban planning, the paper also points to far reaching changes that the governments introduced to the relevant laws during the pandemic. Amendment to section 109 of the Land Reforms Act in Karnataka, for example, allows the acquisition of agricultural land with an approval period of 30 days reducing the previous timeline of three years. In October 2020, there was an amendment to BBMP Act. The easing the acquisition process could increase the urban sprawl. This paper concludes by suggesting a slew of measures that can be taken up to improve urban planning in Bangalore as well as cities of similar size and governance complexity in the light of lessons learnt during the pandemic. One important proposal is to reinstate municipal corporations at the center of urban planning as envisioned in the 74th constitutional amendment. The importance of a five-year tenure for the mayor and more power to the municipal corporation in terms of aligning planning goals across various organizations is proposed. The paper identifies an outcomes-led approach as the best measure in ensuring the triumph of public interest in urban planning.

The third paper in Part II by Krishna Mohan, titled, 'Opportunities and Challenges to E-Governance During Covid-19 and After' focuses on how technology emerged in a big way in the operations of the state and the lives of the people. Society's dependence on technology is only going to grow. Since the pandemic hit the country, technology adoption has increased to a new height not only by Central Government but also by State & Local Governments and tech-savvy citizens and by many who were not active technology users earlier. It has been a slow movement towards a contactless world. Thus, the author says, it is important for the Government to proactively plan for the new reality and emerge stronger from the crises by further accelerating the digital transformation of Governments service delivery and engagement through e – Governance. If leveraged correctly this situation can help India attain new heights in terms of e- Governance adoption and utilization.

The eight papers in this volume together give a wide and critical view of the governance challenges facing India in the post-Covid times. Neither the issues covered, nor the policy measures suggested here are comprehensive, but they do highlight how some of the key lessons learnt in important areas of governance can inform future policy decisions.

Editors:

C K Mathew: former IAS off cer, 1977 batch, Rajasthan

A. Narayana: Associate Professor, Azim Premji University

PART I

Health, Education and Environment in the time of Pandemic: Lessons on Development and Welfare

1

RECORDING DEATHS — WITH OR WITHOUT COVID-19

K Narayanan Unni and G Balagopal[1]

Abstract: *There have been many discussions about the number of deaths due to Covid-19. Several researchers conclude that the numbers given out by the government are gross underestimates and that they are not consistent with the excess mortality during the peak months of covid infections over the corresponding periods of the previous year. This has brought the Civil Registration system in the country into focus. This article looks at the systems for recording deaths and compiling data on deaths and cause of deaths and identify their weaknesses. It suggests some measures to improve the system so that data are available without delay and the quality of data on cause of death is improved.*

Key Words: Civil registration, vital statistics, births, deaths.

Introduction

The second wave of Covid-19 resulted in a larger number of deaths in India. There have been serious doubts about the veracity of the number of deaths reported by state governments. In some cases, the numbers got revised after audits. Increase in deaths due to all causes have also been used to prove that a large proportion of deaths due to Covid-19 are not included in the official count. This brought into focus two issues - (i) correctly identifying deaths due to Covid-19, and (ii) getting accurate data on mortality due to all causes.

Registration of births and deaths has been compulsory in India since the implementation of the Registration of Births and Deaths Act, 1969, from April 1970. It is unfortunate that even after 50 years more than 10% of the births and 13% of the deaths are not registered[2].

The Infant Mortality Rate (IMR) in India stands at 32 per 1000 births in 2018 while the latest estimate of Maternal Mortality Ratio (MMR) is 113 for 2016-18[3]. We have missed the target of reducing IMR to 30 and MMR to 100 by 2010 set by the National Population Policy 20004. But we do not know the districts or sub-districts of the country with higher levels of IMR or MMR so that appropriate actions can be planned to bring them on par with other areas.

Cause profile of mortality is important in public health planning. The World Health Organization (WHO) says, *"It is important to know why people die to improve how people live. Measuring how many people die each year helps to assess the effectiveness of our health systems and direct resources to where they are needed most. For example, mortality data can help focus activities and resource allocation among sectors such as transportation, food and agriculture, and the environment as well as health.*[5]"

An efficient system for registering deaths and recording the cause of death is the only source that can provide data for estimating IMR, MMR and other mortality indicators for any desired geographic level. While it provides the numerator and denominator for estimating IMR, MMR, etc, it can also provide the numerator for estimating several indicators required for monitoring the progress towards the Sustainable Development Goals[6]. The main sources of data on the number of deaths and causes of death in India are Civil Registration and Vital Statistics System (CRVS), Medical Certification of Cause of Death (MCCD) and Sample Registration System surveys including Verbal autopsy.

The CRVS system is unable to cater to the need for providing periodic data on deaths and causes of death due to various reasons. This drawback is more pronounced at the time of a pandemic when data are required at short notice and at frequent intervals. Reasons for this are discussed later in detail.

Civil Registration in India involves the registration of births and deaths under the Registration of Births and Deaths Act (RBD Act), 1969. MCCD scheme is an offshoot of the same Act and requires the medical professionals who attended the deceased before death in notified areas where facilities exist, to prepare a certificate of cause of death to accompany the report of death made to the Registrar of Births and Deaths.

The Sample Registration System is a sample survey operated by the Registrar General, India in all states with the purpose of estimating vital rates at state level. A verbal autopsy of every death recorded in the system provided the cause profile of mortality in the country. Though not as detailed as in MCCD, these estimates from a representative sample also cover deaths not attended by medical practitioners.

A vision for data on deaths and causes of death

- Availability of data with least time lag at low administrative levels like Subdivisions. Municipal towns, panchayats and other local self-government institutions - if possible, within a week to identify occurrence of spikes.

- Data by age and sex being available on a monthly basis in normal times and the system having the ability to generate such data for any given period at any point of time.
- Data for all institutional deaths being based on the standard cause of death certificate recommended by WHO. Wherever possible, deaths outside medical institutions have standard medical certification of cause of death and data on such deaths are based on them.
- Sufficient number of non-institutional deaths being subjected to verbal autopsy to provide cause profile of such deaths at sub-state level.

This paper examines the current status of the CRVS system in some detail. It dwells upon the major issues that hamper its development into an efficient system that caters to the need for statistics on deaths and causes of death. It is pertinent to note here that several of the organizational issues discussed later apply as much to registration of birth as to deaths.

Data systems and related issues

At the national level, 'Registration of Births and Deaths' and 'Vital Statistics' are the responsibility of the Ministry of Home Affairs under the Business Allocation Rules and are handled by the Office of the Registrar General, India (ORGI). The Civil Registration System collects information on cause of death for every death that is registered and is designed to provide data on causes of death for any geographic level of the country. Another source of data on causes of death is based on verbal autopsy for the deaths occurring in sample areas where the Sample Registration System, operated by the ORGI, is implemented.

The Civil Registration System and MCCD

Civil registration is defined as "the continuous, permanent, compulsory and universal recording of the occurrence and characteristics of vital events pertaining to the population, as provided through decree or regulation in accordance with the legal requirements in each country[7]".

In India, the Registration of Births and Deaths Act, 1969 (RBD Act, 1969) implemented throughout the country provides for establishing a system at the state level for the compulsory registration of births and deaths with the Registrar General, India (RGI) appointed by the Central Government at the nodal position. The State level organization, established by the state government, is headed by a Chief Registrar and supported by lower-level functionaries. Only a small number of functionaries in the CRVS system are handling the work on a full time basis.

The Act itself is in need of a revision as 50 years have passed since it was enacted and several developments, like use of information technology, large proportion of births taking place in hospitals, etc. has made some of the provisions of the Act outdated. The maximum penalty for violating the provisions of the Act is Rs 50 (about US$ 0.67 at the present exchange rate, down by about 90% since the law was enacted) and it has lost its value as a deterrent.

Legal provisions

Some of the legal provisions that are of interest in the current context and are discussed below.

Under the RBD Act, Registrar General, India is required to coordinate and unify the activities of the Chief Registrars and is empowered to give general directions to them8. It is important to note that the RGI does not have supervisory powers over the Chief Registrars who are appointed by the state governments under Section 4(1) of the Act. S/he is required to submit two annual reports to the State Government - one on the working of the Act and the other being a statistical report on the data collected during registration of births and deaths.

Under the provisions of the Act, the registrar required to take steps to collect information about every birth and death taking place in his jurisdiction9. This provision indirectly mandates that the births and deaths are to be registered at the place of occurrence and not where the mother/parents reside or the deceased resided.

It casts responsibility on certain persons to report births and deaths for registration[10]. For births/deaths occurring in a hospital, reporting them to the Registrar is the responsibility of the Medical Superintendent. For those occurring at home, it is the responsibility of the head of the household or an adult member.

Sub-sections 2 and 3 of Section 10 of the Act11 provides the legal basis for the compulsory medical certification of cause of death in places where the state governments consider that facilities exist. It also provides that the State Governments may prescribe the format of the certificate. Currently the formats proposed by the RGI, based on WHO recommendations, are in use.

Challenges and issues

According to the Annual Report on Vital Statistics for 201812, only about 89.3% of the births and 86.0% of deaths of the estimated number of these events in 2018 have been registered. Though significant improvements have been noted in these percentages during the last two decades, there is still a large gap to be covered. Further, there are large interstate variations in the level of registration. This can be seen from Table 1 categorising the major states into various classes based on the level of registration of deaths which is of interest in the context of this article. In view of the uncertainties regarding the estimated number of deaths in smaller states, they are not included in the table.

Table 1: Distribution of major states by level of registration of deaths, 2018

Percentage of deaths registered	States
More than 90%	Andhra Pradesh, Gujarat, Haryana, Karnataka, Kerala, Maharashtra, Odisha, Punjab, Rajasthan, Tamil Nadu, West Bengal
80-90%	Chhattisgarh
70-80%	Madhya Pradesh, Uttarakhand
50-70%%	Assam, Jharkhand, Telengana, Uttar Pradesh
Below 50%	Bihar

Note: Data are not available for other states. The table has been prepared using the table 3.13 in the Annual Report "Vital Statistics of India Based on Civil registration system 2018"

This situation is the result of several factors with the organizational set up for birth and death registration having a major contribution. There are several challenges and issues in reforming the registration system to cater to the needs of a modern public administration. These are examined below.

Organizational structure of CRVS

One of the major issues relating to the CRVS organization is that it spans multiple Departments of the State Government without a unified command and control structure. Table 2 provides details of the functionaries appointed as Chief Registrar, District Registrar and Registrar for Rural areas in the states.

In addition to those shown in the table, there are Additional Chief Registrars in many states appointed from the Departments from which the Registrars have been drawn. Sub-registrars have been appointed to support the Registrar of Births and Deaths in some states. However, in many cases the Registrars and Sub-Registrars are from other departments and the Registrar may not have any control over the Sub-Registrars.

Table 2: Registration Hierarchy in the states

State	Chief Registrar	District Registrar	Registrar in rural areas
1. Andhra Pradesh	Director, Health	District Medical and Health Officer	Panchayat Secretary
2. Arunachal Pradesh	Director, Health	Dy. Commissioner	Extra-Assistant Commissioner/ Circle Officer
3. Assam	Director, Health	District Magistrate	Medical Officer of CHC, PHC, State Dispensary, etc.
4. Bihar	Director, Economics and Statistics	District Magistrate	Panchayat Sevak
5. Chhattisgarh	Director, Economics and Statistics	District Planning & Statistics Officer	CEO Janpad Panchayat
6. Goa	Director, Planning, Statistics & Evaluation	Additional Collector	Secretary of Village Panchayat
7. Gujarat	Commissioner of Health, Medical Services & Medical Education	District Health Officer	Talati-cum-Mantri/ Mantri
8. Haryana	Director General Health Services	Civil Surgeon	Medical Officer in charge of PHC
9. Himachal Pradesh	Director Health Services	Chief Medical Officer	Panchayat Secretary and Panchayat Sahayak of Gram Panchayat

10. Jharkhand	Secretary, Planning & Development	Dy. Commissioner	Panchayat Sevak, M/O in-charge of Referral Hospitals, Medical Supd. of Sadar Hospitals /Subdivisional hospitals
11. Karnataka	Director, Economics and Statistics	Dy. Commissioner	Village Accountant
12. Kerala	Addl. Director Panchayats	Dy. Director Panchayats	Panchayat Secretary
13. Madhya Pradesh	Director, Economics and Statistics	District Planning Officer	CEO Janpad Panchayat with Panchayat Secretary / Karmi as sub Registrar
14. Maharashtra	Director of Medical & Health Services	District Health Officer	Gram Sevak/Asst Gram Sevak
15. Manipur	Director of Medical &Health Services	Chief Medical Officer	BDO for CD Block areas, SDOs/ MO in-charge of PHCs of hilly areas
16. Meghalaya	Director of Health Services	District Medical and Health Officer	Medical and Health Officer in charge of PHC
17. Mizoram	Secretary/ Commissioner Planning	Dy. Commissioner	Primary School Teacher
18. Nagaland	Director, Economics and Statistics	Dy Commissioner	Head Teacher of Primary school
19. Odisha	Director of Health Services	Chief Medical Officer	Medical officer in charge of PHC/ CHC
20. Punjab	Director of Health Family Welfare	District Civil Surgeon	Multipurpose Health Workers (Female) Sub-Center, ANM
21. Rajasthan[23]	Director, Economics and Statistics	District Statistical Officer	Gram Sevak Group Sachiv Head Master of Primary, Middle School

22. Sikkim	Principal Director of Health & Family Welfare	Chief Medical Officer	Medical officer in charge of PHC/ CHC
23. Tamil Nadu	Director, Public Health and Preventive Medicine	Collector/District Revenue Officer/ Additional Collector	Village Administrative Officer Medical Officer in-charge of PHC
24. Telengana	Director Public Health and Family Welfare	District Medical Officer	Panchayat Secretary
25. Tripura	Director of Health Services	District Collector	Tahsildar (in TTAADC area) Panchayat Secretary (in Non TTAADC area)
26. Uttarakhand	Principal Secretary/ Secretary, Medical, Health and Family Welfare	District Collector	Gram Panchayat Vikas Adhikari
27. Uttar Pradesh	Director General Medical & Health	District Collector	Gram Panchayat Vikas Adhikari
28 .West Bengal	Director, Health Services	District Magistrate/ Dy. Commissioner	Block Sanitary Inspector MO In-charge of BPHC/ PHC

The Chief Registrars of births and deaths in 17 States are from the Health Department and in 10 States they are from Planning, Economics & Statistics Department. In Kerala s/he is from the Panchayat Department. In Gujarat, Jharkhand, Mizoram and Uttarakhand, Commissioner/Secretary/Principal Secretary have been appointed as Chief Registrar.

The district level authorities are mainly divided among District Collectors/ District Magistrate/Deputy Commissioners (12 States), Chief Medical Officers/ District Medical and Health (12 States), District Statistical/ Planning Officers (4 States) and Deputy Director of Panchayats in one State.

In rural areas, Registrars are appointed from the Panchayat Department in 14 States and 3 UTs; Health Department in 10 States and 4 UTs; Departments of

Revenue and Education in 2 States each and Police Department in the erstwhile State of Jammu & Kashmir.

In most of the urban areas the Municipal administration handles the birth and death registration with the Health Officer being appointed as the Registrar of Births and Deaths. In smaller towns, normally, the Executive Officer of the town administration functions as the Registrar. In large hospitals in many states either an official has been designated as a Registrar or Sub-Registrar or some sort of an extension of the Registrar's office have been established for providing better service to the citizens.

Chart 1 provides a diagrammatic representation of the hierarchy in the registration systems in two states - Orissa, with the same Department looking after the work at all levels and Uttar Pradesh with different departments involved in the work at various levels.

Where the people in the hierarchy come from different Departments, in most cases, the work is not integrated with that of the departments. The staff always feel that they are doing some additional work which is not that of their department. This view can be justified in the case of people from the Education Department appointed as Registrars or Sub-Registrars. However, in case of Depart-

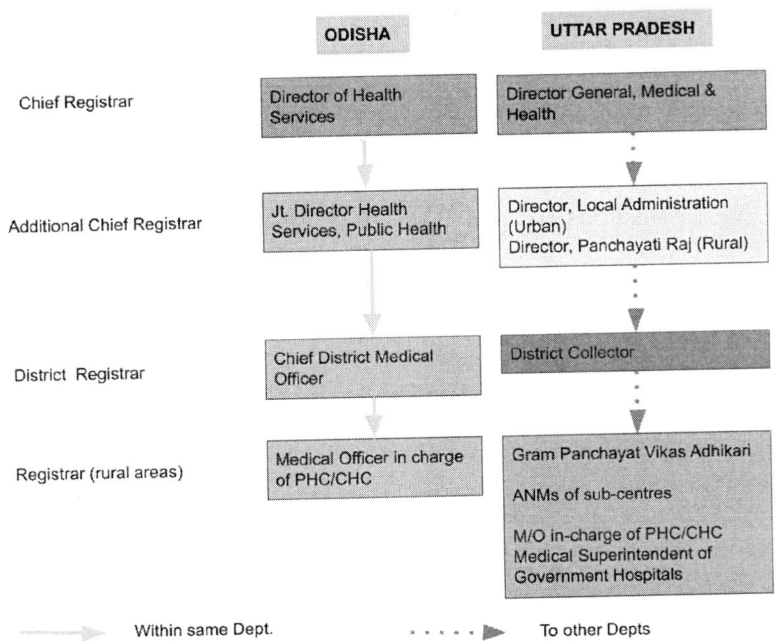

Chart 1: Registration Hierarchy in Odisha and Uttar Pradesh

ments like Revenue, Panchayats or Health such a view cannot be accepted and the Governments concerned have to take steps to ensure that these duties form part of their normal work and are supervised by people from the same Department.

Level of the Registrar: Discharging the responsibilities of the Registrar, especially ascertaining the particulars of every birth and death if they are not reported to him/her in normal course and issuing birth and death certificates, requires an official of certain stature. Unfortunately, the Registrars in many states, especially in rural areas, are not of sufficiently senior level to discharge the responsibilities assigned to them. Since death certificates have uses in claiming inheritance etc., it would be difficult for the junior level officials to withstand pressures14 if any.

In 14 states and 3 UTs Panchayat functionaries like Panchayat Secretaries are appointed as Registrars. However, there is significant variation in status and powers of the Panchayat Secretaries across the states. In Kerala where the Panchayats are largest in terms of population covered, the Panchayat Secretaries are of much higher level than in UP or Punjab where the population of a Panchayat is less than a third in size compared to that of Kerala. It may be noted that the devolution of resources and functions to local governments in Kerala are significantly higher than in any other State in India. This has also helped in enhancing the stature of the Registrars in the state.

Registration process related issues

As mentioned earlier, it is the responsibility of the Medical Superintendent or the person authorised by him to report every birth or death that occurs in the hospital to the Registrar of Births and Deaths in the forms prescribed by the State Government. In many hospitals, it has been observed that the reporting forms are given to the family for submission to the Registrar. Often, people are asked to report the event (Birth/Death) to the Registrar using the discharge slip from the hospital as proof of the event. This adversely impacts death registration more than birth registration as families not requiring a death certificate may not take pains to report the event.

In case of events occurring at home, it is the responsibility of the head of the household or an adult member to report the event. In the event of an infant/child death, it is unlikely that the family will take pains to register the event. If the child born in the household dies before its birth is reported, both the birth and death may not be reported. Similarly, the likelihood of the death of a woman being missed is high, if she did not have any life insurance or assets that need to be transferred using a death certificate.

Errors in reporting cause of death are likely when reporting is done by a family member. Even if there is a cause of death certificate, s/he may not be able to understand the medical terms used. In the absence of a medical certificate, the reported cause of death would be the one that s/he was told or s/he thinks as the likely cause.

During the current pandemic, even if a person died after having symptoms like that of Covid-19, the family member may not be aware that it is Covid-19 and may report fever, breathlessness, etc. as cause of death. It is worth noting that the WHO guidelines regarding recording of cause of death15 defines a death due to Covid as, *"A death due to COVID-19 is defined for surveillance purposes as a death resulting from a clinically compatible illness, in a probable or confirmed COVID-19 case, unless there is a clear alternative cause of death that cannot be related to COVID disease (e.g., trauma). There should be no period of complete recovery from COVID-19 between illness and death."*

Thus, it is not necessary that the cause of death is confirmed as Covid-19, but enough that it is most probably due to Covid-19 to be classified as Covid-19 death. Certainly, an ordinary person cannot be expected to classify a death as a Covid death in the absence of a medical opinion or a certificate. On the other hand, considering that the expenditure for disposing of a dead body of a Covid-19 victim according to the protocols can be prohibitive, persons may not like to show it as a Covid-19 death.

Medical Certification of Cause of Death

The state governments have specified geographical areas like Municipal Corporations/ Municipalities or certain types of hospitals under Section 10(2) for compulsory certification of cause of death. These certificates are issued in Form 4 or Form 4A depending on whether the death occurred in a hospital or outside. These forms provide for recording the Immediate cause of death (not the mode of death such as heart failure, asthenia, etc.), Antecedent cause (morbid conditions leading to the immediate cause of death) with the underlying cause of death16; other significant conditions contributing to death but not related to the cause of death and personal information like age, sex, etc. Slight revisions made in the forms by WHO are yet to be incorporated by the state governments.

These certificates are processed either along with the death reports or independently depending on the states. The tabulations prepared are based on the underlying cause of death as per the recommendations of WHO. The Death report form also has a question on cause of death. In most cases no effort is made to ensure the response therein is consistent with the medical certificate of cause of death.

One major problem in processing the data in the MCCD forms is the non availability of sufficiently trained nosologists, who can identify the underlying cause of death and code the causes of death according to the International Classification of Diseases.

The most important issue, relating to MCCD, is its coverage. In 2018, cause of death for about 1.48 million deaths were medically certified. This is about 21.1 per cent of all registered deaths. Though this percentage has been steadily increasing over the years, it is still very low.

There is substantial variation across the states in the percentage of deaths/registered deaths that are medically certified. Uttar Pradesh with only about 5% of the registered deaths being medically certified is at one end while the percentage is as high as 45% in Tamil Nadu. Moreover, the deaths covered by the MCCD scheme as the percentage of the estimated number of deaths is even lower in many states with the figure being below 5% in Bihar and Uttar Pradesh. Even in Kerala which is otherwise doing better, the figure is as low as 12.4% due to low coverage of the scheme. Table 3 provides both the percentages at state level for major states.

Table 3: Estimated number of deaths, Number of registered deaths and medically certified deaths, and medically certified deaths as percentage of total deaths and registered deaths

State	Estimated total number of deaths	Number of registered deaths	Number of medically certified deaths	Number of medically certified deaths as percentage of	
				Total deaths	Registered deaths
Andhra Pradesh	3,53,100	3,75,777	55,933	15.8	14.9
Assam	2,13,030	1,42,605	17,118	8.0	12.0
Bihar	6,18,106	2,13,989	29,112	4.7	13.6
Chhattisgarh	2,12,712	1,77,549	35,149	16.5	19.8
Gujarat	3,80,279	4,33,256	1,01,166	26.6	23.4
Haryana	1,67,460	1,85,842	37,819	22.6	20.4
Jharkhand	1,86,953	1,02,729	4,709	2.5	4.6
Karnataka	4,00,743	4,83,511	1,50,415	37.5	31.1

Kerala	2,49,263	2,58,530	30,894	12.4	11.9
Madhya Pradesh	5,38,707	4,24,257	44,467	8.3	10.5
Maharashtra	6,78,706	6,67,900	2,32,416	34.2	34.8
Odisha	3,15,652	3,28,799	36,407	11.5	11.1
Punjab	1,96,079	2,13,234	36,448	18.6	17.1
Rajasthan	4,43,721	4,43,173	58,145	13.1	13.1
Tamil Nadu	4,55,995	5,74,006	2,58,259	56.6	45.0
Telangana	2,34,420	1,36,528	51,068	21.8	37.4
Uttar Pradesh	14,91,336	9,06,653	46,310	3.1	5.1
Uttarakhand	67,766	47,894	5,318	7.8	11.1
West Bengal	5,34,061	4,90,530	63,336	11.9	12.9

Source: Table 2.4 of the 'Report on Medical Certification of Cause of Death, 2018'. Estimated number of deaths is from the report 'Vital Statistics based on Civil Registration System, 2018 and the percentage of medically certified deaths to estimated number of deaths have been calculated by the authors.

The data from MCCD is not representative of the cause profile of mortality in the country. It pertains only to people dying in the hospitals. The deaths happening outside hospitals may have a different mortality profile as they may belong to people who could not afford hospitalization due to economic situation, distance to the nearest hospital, etc. It may also have a strong urban bias as a very large percentage of hospitals are located in urban areas.

Quality of information on Cause of Death

In case of deaths occurring at home, the reported cause of death may not be correct. For example, for aged persons it is invariably recorded as 'age related ailments' without being specific. Even if a medical professional had examined the patient, s/he may not have had a complete investigation of the conditions that may point to the *underlying cause of death.* So, it is highly likely that the medical certificate is filled up just to ensure that burial/cremation can be done without any hassles. ORGI has been supporting state governments to sensitize the medical professionals on correctly filling up the form.

If the death occurred in a medical facility, a cause of death certificate is issued to the family by the hospital. However, it has been observed that only a small proportion among them indicate the underlying cause of death and in many cases the immediate cause of death or mode of death are indicated. This is true even in cases where the MCCD scheme is in operation and medical professionals have been provided instruction manuals on how to fill up the cause of death. It is seen that due to the vague nature of reporting of cause of death as much as 13% of deaths are classified as due "Symptom Signs & Abnormal Clinical Findings Not Elsewhere Classified (R00-R99)" in 2018[17]. In addition, there may be erroneous classifications due to lack of understanding of the relationships between the reported causes, faulty and careless reporting of cause of death.

Death Registration – from the citizen's point of view

The main driver for death registration in case of deaths taking place at home is the need to have a death certificate to settle inheritance and insurance claims, transfer bank accounts and other financial investments, etc. In many parts of the country the death registration form is required to be filled up at the crematoria/ burial places. Even though it is mandatory for the hospitals to report the deaths occurring therein directly to the Registrar of births and Deaths, in many places the forms are filled up only at the crematoria/burial places even in urban areas.

The forms for reporting deaths (for that matter even births) looks complicated without having enough guidance on how to fill them up. For example, it has place for addresses at three different places – that of the deceased, the place of occurrence of the death and the that of the person reporting the death. In many hospitals, instead of the authorised person, the family member is asked to sign the reporting forms, mainly because they are not clear about how it is to be filled up.

When the rules were amended in 1999-2000 bringing in new forms, it could not be visualized that computerization may catch up so fast in the country that the format designed to help off line data processing would soon become obsolete. Changes in the forms is a time-consuming process as it requires the rues framed by the state governments to be amended. Though some states have started using different forms, it does not appear that they follow the standards set by RGI.

Though the law is clear that once the information on death is given to the Registrar by the designated informant it has to be registered and a certificate issued to the informant on completion of registration, this is rarely followed.

Errors in names and ages in the registration records has been a serious problem faced by many people. In case of deaths in hospitals, this happens because of incomplete names being provided at the time of admission and errors in transcription/transliteration to the language in which records are maintained (official language of the state).

Difficulty in getting death certificates has been another serious problem. In many places where computerised certificates are being issued there is a transaction charge being levied in addition to the fees prescribed under Section 17 of the Act. Where it has not been computerised, sometimes one needs to visit the registrar's office several times and this leads to corruption.

Sample Registration System and Verbal Autopsy

The Sample Registration System (SRS) is essentially a demographic sample survey with the same sample villages being surveyed for a decade. The main objective of the survey is to provide vital rates at state level with reasonable accuracy in the absence of similar data from Civil Registration. It also collected related information so that a host of demographic indicators can be estimated. The survey does not provide estimates of number of births or deaths but only the related demographic indicators.

A survey was instituted in the late 1960s to collect data on causes of death in rural areas. This used the technique known as *Verbal Autopsy*, wherein an effort is made to identify the underlying cause of death through a series of structured questions. The arrived cause of death is then reviewed by one or more medical professionals. The sample villages used to be selected near to Primary Health Centres. However, such a selection resulted in a sample that is not representative in its character. Hence, in the late 1990s it was decided to integrate it with the SRS. However, the release of data on cause of death from this survey has not been regular. Data on maternal mortality rates only have been released in recent years with the latest bulletin giving data for the period 2016-18.

It may be mentioned here that even the data on birth and death rates from SRS for a particular year would be available only after more than a year due to the way in which the survey is structured. Hence the results from the survey cannot be used for monitoring death rates on a near to real time basis, that would be possible with the CRVS system.

Data using *Verbal autopsy* in India suffers from small sample and quality issues, though several efforts have been taken in the last two decades to improve its quality.

Health Management Information System (HMIS)

Launched in 2008, the Health Management Information System is used by the Ministry of Health and Family Welfare to track the outcome of several programmes through an online reporting system. It covers about 2 lakh hospitals and smaller health facilities including about 15000 in private sector. The deaths happening in these facilities along with the probable cause of death are reported every month through this system. The facilities are required to report only the total numbers and not information about individuals. The data are compiled and the reports are available on the website[18].

It provides the number of deaths among three groups – infants (separately for those aged 0-23 hours, 1 day to I month and 1 -12 months); children (1-5 years); and adolescents & adults. The number of maternal deaths and those due to specific causes are also reported.

The reports are released on a monthly basis with annual figures also being available. Data ae available at district and sub-district level. Since all institutions do not report through this system, it does not provide the count of all deaths in medical institutions. However, it has the potential to grow into a system for collecting the count of all deaths.

Data on deaths due to Covid-19 are collected through a different system established specifically for this purpose at the district level. Deaths occurring at designated Covid hospitals and all other peripheral health facilities both in the government and private sector are reported by the treating doctor through a Death Reporting Portal to the district headquarters. These reports are reviewed in a committee chaired by the District Medical officer each day. If the committee requires more information, they refer it back to the treating doctor. When cleared by this committee the numbers are reported to the State Government who would release the figures occurring in a 24 hour period at a fixed time on each day. HMIS does not report Covid deaths separately.

Data on Deaths and those due to Covid-19

The rules framed under the RBD Act provide a list of tables that shall be included in the Statistical report to be submitted by the Chief Registrar to the state governments and is required to be published. Very few states have been publishing data according to this mandate and no state have come out with the reports within time[19]. No state has ever gone beyond this list to produce tables that are useful to the government or data users. Many states have not been preparing reports and publishing them. It is a shame that people had to resort to RTI applications to get data on registered deaths in Uttar Pradesh[20] while publishing the data every year is a statutory responsibility of the state government. The reported observations and directions of Patna High Court to the Government of Bihar is very relevant[21].

Availability of data and the users' understanding of the same with all caveats is important for arriving at correct conclusions from the data. Apart from the fact that even the number of deaths registered are not available for most states even after a year, there are misunderstandings about the figures themselves. There are also serious misunderstandings about cause of death certification and its relation to death registration and MCCD among some data users.

The pandemic has brought the data on the number of deaths registered into focus more than ever before. Increase in the number of deaths registered for any period since the pandemic started from the corresponding period in the most recent non Covid year, i.e., excess deaths, indicates the impact of Covid-19. There have been several research papers and articles comparing the excess mortality with thc number of deaths due to Covid-19 as per government data. In a report, using CRVS data *The Hindu* estimated that excess deaths may be as high as 8 times the official death toll due to covid based on data from eight states[22]. Other studies using data from CRVS and other sources indicate that covid deaths may be as high as 4.9 million[23](See Annexure for references to several studies/ reports). The main reason for such wide difference in the estimates of excess deaths is the quality of CRS data in its coverage, timeliness and dissemination. In a forthcoming paper co-authored by Chinmay Tumbe, Prabhat Jha and others[24] three different sources of data have been used to assess the excess mortality during pandemic. Data from CRVS, HMIS and a survey have been used. It also indicates that the excess deaths are several times the official death toll from covid.

Another area that has come into focus is the medical certification of cause of death. Many researchers are not very clear about the coverage and quality of the MCCD scheme.

There seems to be some misunderstanding about the data on deaths and causes of deaths reported by the states. In an article titled 'The challenges in counting the dead', Giridhara R. Babu[25] had presented the number of deaths per 100 population due to Covid and suggested that the higher figures in some of the states are due to better registration levels. Unfortunately, this is not possible as the number of deaths due to Covid that has been registered in 2020 were not available at the time of writing that article. He probably assumed that all deaths due to Covid-19 reported by the government are taken from the registration data.

In another article Hemant Deepak Shewade & Giridara Gopal Parameswaran[26] assumed that all the reported Covid deaths are covered by the MCCD scheme. This is totally incorrect as only deaths in areas or hospitals notified by the State Government for the purpose are covered under the scheme. These indicate that the data on registered deaths as well as those from MCCD are not clearly understood by all data users. There is a need to focus better on this area so that people understand the shortcomings.

Jahnavi Reddy[27] used the number of health insurance claims to assess the number of deaths due to Covid-19. This is an example of the extent to which well-meaning researchers are running about for accurate data and are sometimes making wild assumptions in trying to get the true picture. The CRVS system has to orient itself to satisfy the need for data for all such researchers.

Future of CRVS and MCCD

In order to fully realize the advantages of the CRVS system in normal times as well as to make it responsive to the need of providing data at times of pandemics, several steps should be taken. This section discusses the most important actions required.

There are changes required in the RBD Act, 1969 as it has become outdated to some extent. However, we are not discussing it here since it is a time-consuming process and much can be achieved within the current legal provisions themselves.

One issue needs to be flagged here. There is a need to provide for changes in the procedures at short notice when required. For example, travel restrictions during Covid-19 may have resulted in late reporting of deaths. Similarly, when natural disasters like earthquakes, landslides or floods occur, sometimes dead bodies are recovered and identified several days later and by that time the period for reporting the events may have passed. Probably a provision can be made in the Act empowering the Central Government to relax the period through a notification and direct the State government to take action to ensure registration of deaths at such times. Alternatively, it can be provided that the state governments may relax the rules with the approval of the central government.

The rules framed under the RBD Act, 1969 by the state governments allow a window of 21 days for registration of births and deaths. In most of the States, the time available for reporting deaths used to be 3 days in municipal areas and cantonments and 7 days in other places till the rules were amended in late eighties. The period of 21 days is too long, especially if sudden surges in deaths in any area due to epidemics are to be identified. With more registrations taking place through computer networks, it should be possible to reduce the period to not more than five days. This can be done in a phased manner by reducing it in municipal areas in the first phase and extending it to other areas subsequently.

In many countries a burial/cremation permit is required for burial/cremation of the dead body. The Registrar of Births and Deaths of several countries are responsible for the issue of such permits with the result that all deaths are registered. In urban areas of the country, starting with the large cities, the requirement of a burial/cremation permission from the Registrar of Births and Deaths may be introduced in a phased manner. This would ensure that the deaths are registered in time. Systems for providing death registration and issue of cremation/burial permits as soon as a death takes place shall be put in place before implementing any such scheme.

Streamlined command structure

Single structure all across the country is not possible due to a variety of reasons. However, for better command and control, there is a need to streamline the systems in several States.

To the extent possible the Chief Registrar should be from the same Department from which the Registrar and District Registrars are chosen. The appointment of District Collector as the District Registrar in several states does not seem to have had any positive impact on the system as s/he has so many activities and it is rare that the subject of registration of births and deaths captures the attention of the Collector. In Rajasthan, the District Collectors have been designated as Additional Chief Registrar which appears to be a similar position. Being the administrative head of the district, a District collector can always review or take action to improve the registration related activities in the district. In view of this, the state governments may review this position.

Where the Registrars do not have enough reach due to the large area covered by them, Sub-Registrars can be appointed. They should be keeping in touch with the Registrars regularly.

The percentage of births and deaths occurring in medical institutions has been increasing over the years. They are duty bound to report births and deaths to the Registrar under Section 8 of the RBD Act. Thus, the health facilities have an important role in registering births and deaths. Thus, the Health Department in States is in a better place to exercise control over this activity than any other Department. Such a close integration of the registration related activities with the Health Department would benefit it as it is the greatest beneficiary of the data from birth and deaths registration and cause of death certification.

It appears from the foregoing that the Health Department looking after the work of Registration at all levels would be more efficient. The Odisha model shown in Chart 1 may be more efficient in the management of the system and the States may consider changing to this system with a person-in-charge at the sub-centre appointed as the Sub-Registrar in rural areas. However, this may require some strengthening of the offices of the PHCs/CHCs that are to handle the work. However, it may be pointed out that in states like Kerala with a strong and empowered Panchayat system, it is better to continue with the current system.

At all levels departments that have some stake in the process should be involved. As civil registration involves multiple agencies, an Inter-Departmental Coordination Committee that meets regularly to sort out coordination issues is very important.

Once the persons have been given responsibility under the Act, it should also be made clear that s/he is accountable not only to the Department, but also under the law. There is a need to strengthen the penalties under the law as the maximum penalty of Rs 50 provided in 1969 is of no value today.

In many places the staff at various levels handle the work of CRVS as if it is some extra work given by some other Department. This attitude has to change. The responsibilities should form part of their work and review of the work should be part of the Annual Confidential Report by whatever name it is known in various states. This can effectively happen only if the officials of the same department handles the work at all levels.

The Chief Registrar should be able to devote some time for the work on a regular basis and should be in a position to interact with the concerned officials from other Departments charged with responsibility under the Act. There was a suggestion from RGI to appoint an officer on full time basis as the Chief Registrar. This alone may not help unless the officer is of sufficiently high rank. On the other hand, there may not be enough work for such a high ranking official on a regular basis, especially once the system stabilizes. One alternative is for the state governments to take up the improvement of the CRVS system on a 'Mission Mode' and appoint some senior officer as the Chief Registrar till the system stabilizes with 100% efficiency in registering births and deaths and MCCD.

In Bihar, Anganwadi workers have been appointed as Sub-Registrars. Similarly, In West Bengal, Panchayat Pradhan, who is an elected official, has been appointed as the Sub-Registrar. The effectiveness of these appointments needs to be reviewed with regard to their contribution and the quality of their work.

Regular auditing/evaluation

In many States where it appears that all events are being registered now, it may not be the fact. As the actual number of births and deaths taking place in a state are not known, estimates are being used to assess the percentage of births/deaths that are registered. These estimates are based on sample surveys and relate to the population that is usually resident in the State. So, for States like Delhi that see a large number of people from outside Delhi using medical facilities therein, the actual number of registrations does not relate to Delhi and is not strictly comparable with the estimates.

In some states, especially in the North Eastern region, it appears that the birth/death rates from SRS are gross under estimates. The birth rates for the smaller States in the region are in the range of 12.9 in Nagaland to 22.1 per 1000 in Meghalaya while the death rates vary from 3.5 in Nagaland to 6.0 in Arunachal Pradesh. Most of these seem implausibly low. With the number of births and deaths estimated from these rates and used as the denominator for estimating the percentage of births/deaths registered, one would overestimate these percentages. The point is that one should not be complacent after seeing an estimate of 100% registration as this may not be correct.

To get a better idea of the efficiency of the system, there is a need to evaluate the activities under the CRVS system periodically by tracing births and deaths to the registration records and vice versa on a sample basis to see whether there are omissions and duplications. This should be a regular feature and built into the system. Unfortunately, this effort cannot be integrated with the SRS. Its sample areas remain the same for a decade and once it is known that these areas are being monitored, the registration staff can concentrate their work there.

Covid-related lockdown and travel restrictions may have had an adverse impact on the registration of non institutional births and deaths. However, as data for 2019 and 2020 are not available for most states we cannot confirm this possibility or its impact. Kerala recorded a fall of about 8% in the number of deaths registered in 2020 compared to 2019. It is not clear whether this is due to travel restrictions impacting people's ability to access hospitals or lockdowns affecting reporting by hospitals. However, it is seen that the deaths outside medical institutions have fallen by less than 3%. These figures also point to the need for an audit of registration of events occurring at hospitals.

Integrated approach

National ID system and Birth and Death Registration

The Citizenship Act was amended in 2004 and it mandated that the Central Government to maintain a National Register of Indian Citizens[28]. Maintenance of such a register would require that it is updated regularly for every birth and death. Instead of trying to do this periodically, it is administratively convenient to organically link CRVS with the National Register of Citizens (or the National Population Register that the Government is planning to establish as the first step towards a Citizen's Register). This is being done in several countries. The following is an illustration adapted from the World Bank publication 'Integrating unique identification numbers in civil registration'[29] that shows the linkages possible between CRVS, the National Population Register, the National ID and National Statistics as also the various practical uses to which such an integrated data system can contribute(Figure 1).

There has been a proposal for compulsory registration of marriages in the country. A bill for this purpose was passed by Rajya Sabha in 2012 that sought to amend the RBD Act, 1969 to include marriage registration also in the scope of the

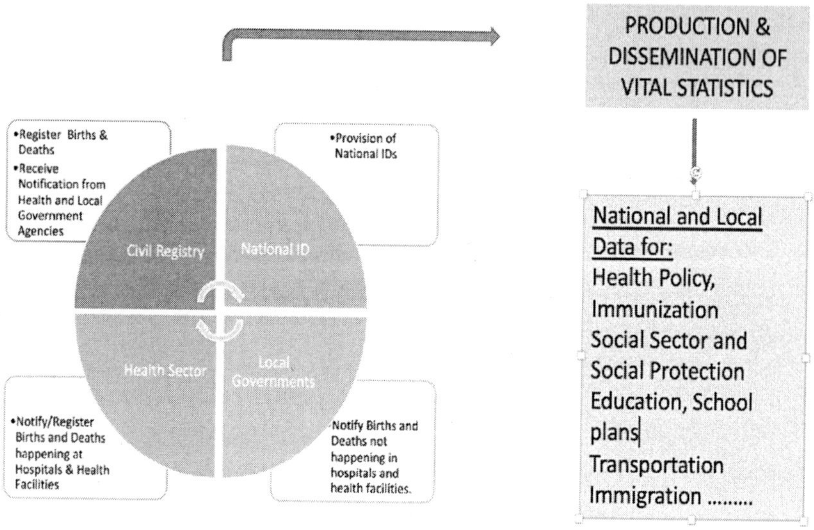

Act. The issue seems to be under consideration of the present government after the Law commission has recommended legislation for the purpose in 2017. It has nothing to do with deaths or cause of deaths. However, in case legal provisions for registration of marriages is planned to be done through integrating the activity with birth and death registration, it would be better to link it also with National ID envisaged in the Citizenship Act. We are not referring to the law on Aadhaar as the Government, in its wisdom, restricted the use of the Aadhaar number to certain specific purposes.

Births, Deaths, Medical certification and Marriage Registration shall be taken together and linked to an identity management system. Currently many of the Covid related records, including test reports mention the Aadhaar number. Whether its use for this purpose comes under the law on Aadhaar is not clear. The instruction to include Aadhaar number in the death records, issued by the RGI, has been withdrawn.

It may be worth noting here that the responsibility for registration of births and deaths is with the State Government while that of registering citizens is with Central Government and thus there are two authorities at state level - the Chief Registrar of Births and Deaths and the Director of Citizen Registration (same as the Director of Census Operations). An integrated approach may require close coordination between them and interoperable systems and software.

Better use of Technology

Currently, there is hardly any integration at the field level between death registration and MCCD. Rarely there are attempts to see that the cause of death in the death report is the same as that in the MCCD form. Now with computerization of registration and processing of MCCD form, it should be possible to ensure consistency between these forms. When more deaths are medically certified, it would be possible to generate data on them cross classifying with social and demographic parameters on which data are collected during death registration.

Wherever computerisation has been done, before final registration a print-out of the information entered into the network can be shown to an authorised family member and signature obtained in token of correctness. This would avoid errors in registration documents that may result in undue hardship to the family. This is a process now followed in many places in Kerala.

Most government run health facilities now have access to computer networks. Same is true about a large number of private medical institutions as well. The percentage of medical institutions using computer networks for patient management and related services are very high, though the software used by them may not be standard. Government may specify a minimum set of standards for such software that includes facility for collecting personal information required for various purposes at the time of admission, preparation of various reports to be submitted to HMIS and other such government systems, preparing reports on births, still births and deaths to be submitted to the Registrar of births and deaths, etc., and submitting such reports online to the concerned authorities including Registrar of Births and Deaths. This would ensure consistency between various databases and reduce redundancy in the work being handled at the hospitals. However, it should ensure that personal information about the parents in case of births and the deceased in case of deaths are not shared to unauthorised personnel.

Where registration records are available in computerised databases, it can be thrown open for search and taking out of extracts as provided for in Section 17 of the Act. The governments can notify that such extracts downloaded from the computer network is acceptable for all purposes. This would reduce the workload of the registrars and reduce corruption in issuing the certificates. This is also an initiative taken by the Government of Kerala. Provision can be made that if anyone requires signed and stamped certificates for any purpose, the same can be provided on payment of certain fee.

There have been cases of fake death registrations for the purpose of transfer of property or for getting monetary compensations in accidents, etc. Using the

Aadhaar number as part of the death registration document can help reducing such incidents. It appears that this is under consideration of the Government[30].

With digitization of CRVS systems in many parts of the country, we find the possibility of interoperability of different data systems as indicated in the illustration in the previous section. Such interoperability will require a common message structure for data exchange as well as common coding and vocabulary so that a meaningful interpretation is shared across systems. New software platforms are now available to meet the demands for real time data through interoperable systems. Use automated tools like IRIS for coding of cause of death and tools like ANACONDA for assessment of quality of mortality data are examples of such development.

Application programming interfaces (API)s are a set of concise procedures that allow different computer systems to seamlessly exchange information. Thus, software developers can create APIs to exchange information between electronic medical records or health information reporting software to a digital notification form that the registrar uses to complete registration.

As an alternative in situations where this may not be feasible at present, mobile phone applications may be used for communication of notifications for registration of births and deaths. This is functional in countries like Tanzania where the national registration agency RITA receives and stores registration information transmitted through mobile devices[31].

Software can be tuned to identify and warn about sudden increase in the number of deaths due to specific causes in any area.

Causes of Death for deaths outside medical facilities

A well organized MCCD can provide causes of death data for all deaths covered under the scheme. It is impossible to visualize that all deaths would take place in hospitals. Neither is it possible in the near future a medical professional would have attended all deceased persons before death so that the cause of death could be ascertained with some degree of certainty. To have a cause of death of persons who die outside hospitals, especially those without medical attention, it is necessary to make use of *Verbal Autopsy* techniques.

It is not feasible to implement a scheme to conduct a verbal autopsy for every death that is not medically certified. So, the best alternative is to do it on a sample of the deaths registered that did not have a medical certificate. A system needs to be developed through which a certain minimum number of deaths that occurred in every district outside the MCCD system is subjected to a VA to determine the most probable cause of death.

Data Dissemination

Currently use of data on causes of death is very low due to the drawbacks in the system and quality issues. In many states the Health Department may not be even aware of the CRVS as a source of data though reports are prepared every year and the work is done in the same Department in more than 20 states. Simultaneous with efforts to improve the system, the use of the data needs to be promoted.

While the accent till now was mostly on improving the percentage of births/deaths registered, it is time to start focusing on the quality, timeliness and dissemination of the statutory reports and more detailed data.

Chief Registrars used to report to ORGI district wise number of registrations on a monthly basis. Many states were not able to provide the data on time when the work was completely manual. However, now it is time to encourage states to release monthly data on births and deaths. These should not be restricted to the number registered, but may include the number that occurred in that particular month to residents of the district/state and distribution by cause of death.

A policy on release of individual data, devoid of any information that can be used for identification of the individual concerned, would be useful for involving more researchers in the use of the data. The National Data Dissemination Policy may not apply here as the data are with the state governments.

Ability to be proactive

In a situation like that of the almost sudden appearance of a Pandemic, the ability to take a proactive approach towards ensuring the registration of all deaths and having MCCD for maximum number of deaths is important. However, due to the decentralized nature of the operation of the CRVS system in the country it is not easy.

In the United Kingdom, some changes were made in the death registration and MCCD process in the wake of Covid-19. These included liberalization of the procedures for MCCD, application process, etc[32].

In India, most of the actual processes are in the rules framed by the State Government. Any changes in them would require amendment in the rules. It has been the experience that amendment in the rules is a time consuming process in most states. For example, the rules were amended in most states in 1999-2000, to be effective from January 2000. However, it took another three years for all states to make the corresponding changes.

Develop State wise action plans

Every state in India is different, even from their neighbours, in several aspects. This is reflected in the performance of CRVS systems also. There is no single solution that can be applied across all states to improve the system. The prevailing situation in each state needs to be assessed independently using standard tools developed for such assessments that are adapted to the specific conditions. This should lead to preparation of state specific, time bound, action plans for improving the CRVS systems and MCCD.

An innovative approach to strengthen civil registration was adopted in Africa under the Africa Programme for Accelerated Improvement of Civil Registration and Vital Statistics systems (APAI-CRVS) from 2010. Implemented in several countries, these were government led initiatives. Staff working in the agencies connected with CRVS implementation including the CRVS office, Heath, Local Government and the National Bureau of Statistics came together for a residential training programme for a week. Here they were facilitated in undertaking a "Business Process Analysis", looking at how registration processes were currently happening in the country. This was supplemented by field validation through small teams including staff from various agencies visiting different parts of the country to assess the functioning of the systems in urban, rural and remote communities. Looking at good practices from other countries and benchmarking their current practices with international standards for CRVS, the group then proceeded to identify how the system could make progress meeting required quality standards. From this came a time bound and costed Strategic Plan that the government would then take forward for implementation. A similar approach, suitably adapted to local conditions could be taken up in Indian States where the CRVS systems are currently lagging.

ANNEXURE

Selected research/news reports relating to the number of deaths due to Covid-19 in India and its under reporting.

Publication, date and author	Link and main points discussed
Nature 9th Apr 2020 Nidhi Subramanian	https://www.nature.com/articles/d41586-020-01008-1 Delays in testing, confusion over the identification of a Covid-19 death, inability of overworked systems to do proper data collection – all this could lead to less than accurate death reports across the world
The Lancet 22 Apr 2020 David Leon, Vladimir Shkolnikov et al.	https://www.thelancet.com/journals/lancet/article/PIIS0140-6736(20)30933-8/fulltext Need for monitoring weekly excess mortality, proper death certification
The Lancet, 5 Sep 2020 Patralekha Chatterjee	https://www.thelancet.com/journals/lancet/article/PIIS0140-6736(20)31857-2/fulltext Weakness in vital registration, deaths outside hospitals not being medically certified, impact of different diagnostic tests on identifying Covid-19 deaths
Imperial College, London, 10 Sept 2020 Thomas Beaney	https://journals.sagepub.com/doi/full/10.1177/0141076820956802 Why "excess mortality" could tell us more about Covid-19 deaths, variation across countries in identifying Covid-deaths, need to take country specific factors while analysing data on Covid-19 deaths

Times of India, 16 Apr 2021 News report	https://timesofindia.indiatimes.com/india/gujarat-covid-toll-higher-than-official-count/articleshow/82093975.cms Compares number of cremations with official death toll from Covid-19 in cities of Gujarat
The Hindu, 19 Apr 2021	https://www.thehindu.com/news/national/other-states/coronavirus-covid-19-deaths-in-gujarat-far-exceed-government-figures/article34352916.ece Under reporting of Covid-19 deaths in Gujarat
New York Times, 24 Apr 2021 effrey Gettleman, Sameer Yasir, Hari Kumar and Suhasini Raj	https://www.nytimes.com/2021/04/24/world/asia/india-coronavirus-deaths.html Study based on various media reports
Scroll.in 12 May 2021 Anuprova Ghose, Isha Bajpai	https://scroll.in/article/994631/explained-how-indians-states-are-able-to-misreport-the-covid-19-death-toll Flawed death reporting, poor medical certification of cause of death, possibility of beneficiaries, of Covid-19 death related support, missing out due to inaccurate recording of cause of death, need to restart verbal autopsy
The Hindu, 13th May 2021 P V Sreevidya	https://www.thehindu.com/news/national/tamil-nadu/bagged-but-not-counted-the-under-reporting-of-covid-19-deaths-in-tn/article34550432.ece Under reporting of Covid deaths in Tamil Nadu

The Wire, 14th May 2021 Based on study by Katherina Bucholz, Washington University	https://science.thewire.in/health/chart-the-global-problem-of-underreporting-covid-19-deaths/ And the study available at http://www.healthdata.org/special-analysis/estimation-excess-mortality-due-covid-19-and-scalars-reported-covid-19-deaths Examines the direct and indirect effects of Covid on mortality and concludes that the actual death count on account of Covid-19 in many states is 3-4 times the official figures and may be in the region of 2-2.5 times in Maharashtra
Divya Bhaskar 14 May 2021 News report	https://www.divyabhaskar.co.in/local/gujarat/ahmedabad/news/the-government-hiding-its-true-figures-was-exposed-by-its-own-departments-123-lakh-death-certificates-were-issued-in-71-days-but-only-4218-deaths--were-reported-from-corona-128490344.html Looking at the abnormal increase in the number of death certificates issued during comparable periods of 2020 and 2021 it concludes that there is under reporting of Covid-19 deaths in Gujarat
Economist, 15 May 2021	https://www.economist.com/films/2021/05/14/covid-19-how-many-people-have-really-died Statistical model to estimate the death count due to Covid-19

Times of India, 23 May 2021	https://timesofindia.indiatimes.com/india/explained-why-reported-deaths-from-covid-dont-match-the-official-count/articleshow/82277171.cms Records from crematoria point to under-reporting of Covid deaths in Gujarat and Madhya Pradesh. Comments on all cause mortality going up in Mumbai and Delhi compared to previous years. Also talks about the upward revision in number of deaths in several places after media reports
Deccan Herald, 21 May 2021 quotes WHO press conference	https://www.deccanherald.com/international/covid-19-death-toll-likely-a-significant-undercount-says-who-988308.html Covid deaths may be three times of the reported count. Excess mortality could give a better picture of deaths caused directly and indirectly by Covid-19
New York Times, 25 May 2021 Lazaro Gamio, James Glanz	https://www.nytimes.com/interactive/2021/05/25/world/asia/india-covid-death-estimates.html Estimates the possible death count in various scenarios ranging from 0.6 to 4.2 million deaths
Indian Express, 8 Jun 2021 Nandita Saikia and Krishnakumar	https://indianexpress.com/article/opinion/india-covid-death-toll-opinion-7348936/ Lack of an efficient death registration system at the local level – municipalities and panchayaths, non release of data from death registration in a timely manner. Exaggeration of death count in social media

The News Minute, 4 June 2021 Jahnavi Reddy	https://www.thenewsminute.com/article/least-8000-covid-19-deaths-went-unreported-telangana-insurance-claims-suggest-150077 Used a comparison of insurance claim data for hospitalization to assess hospitalization and death claims and to estimate under reporting of deaths. Points to the possibility that the Covid-19 deaths in Telengana might be much higher than reported by the government.
The Hindu, 11 Jun 2021 Amarnath Tewary	https://www.thehindu.com/news/national/other-states/covid-19-toll-in-bihar-jumps-by-72-after-recount/article34776002.ece Bihar's Covid death toll jumped by 72.84 percent after a recount of deaths in all districts
Scroll.in, 12 Jun 2021 Rukmini S	https://scroll.in/article/996772/madhya-pradesh-saw-nearly-three-times-more-deaths-than-normal-after-second-wave-of-covid-19-struck Uses all cause mortality and excess deaths to point to large number of deaths due to Covid-19 in Madhya Pradesh. There are about 1.7 lakh excess deaths in the state till May 2021
The Hindu, 14 Jun 2021	https://www.thehindu.com/news/cities/Hyderabad/excess-deaths-in-hyderabad-are-10-times-the-official-covid-19-toll-for-telangana/article34807214.ece Uses death registration statistics for Greater Hyderabad Municipal Corporation area to look at excess mortality and deaths due to Covid-19

The Hindu, 17 Jun 2021 Srinivasan Ramani, Ramya Kannan	https://www.thehindu.com/news/national/tamil-nadu/excess-deaths-in-tamil-nadu-over-four-times-official-covid-19-tally/article34834150.ece Uses Excess mortality to conclude that the number of deaths in Tamil Nadu may be over four times the official tally
News18	https://www.news18.com/news/india/covid-19-bihar-death-toll-could-be-ten-times-the-official-figure-data-suggests-3868547.html Using death registration data and excess mortality, it suggests that the death toll in Bihar could be ten times the official numbers
The Hindu, 20 Jun 2021 R Prasad	https://www.thehindu.com/sci-tech/health/coronavirus-do-excess-deaths-suggest-mortality-crossed-one-million/article34860615.ece Analyses the excess deaths using data from death registration in several states and focus on the need for transparency and timeliness in death reporting.
Article 14 (Web site) Saurav Das	https://www.article-14.com/post/untitled-60cf605395758 Death count in 24 UP districts 43 times more than official covid-19 toll. Uses data on death registration obtained under RTI Act.
Deshmukh Yashwant, Wilson Suraweera, Chinmay Tumbe, Aditi Bhowmick, Sankalp Sharma MA, Paul Novosad, Sze Hang Fu, Leslie Newcombe, Hellen Gelband, Patrick Brown, Prabhat Jha (forthcoming)	https://www.medrxiv.org/content/10.1101/2021.07.20.21260872v1 Excess mortality in India from June 2020 to June 2021 during the COVID pandemic: death registration, health facility deaths, and survey data

ENDNOTES

1. The authors would like to place on record the appreciation for the excellent research support provided by K P Rajesh with the support of Azim Premji University. We also acknowledge the valuable comments received from Joy Oommen.

2. Office of the Registrar General India (2020) - Vital Statistics of India Based on the Civil Registration System 2018

3. Office of The Registrar General, India (2020): Special Bulletin on Maternal Mortality In India 2016-18

4. National Population Commission (2000): National Population Policy 2000, Planning Commission

5. https://www.who.int/news-room/fact-sheets/detail/the-top-10-causes-of-death#:~:text=The%20top%20global%20causes%20of,birth%20asphyxia%20and%20birth%20trauma%2C accessed on 04 July 2021

6. The World Bank (2017): Civil Registration And Vital Statistics (CRVS) For Monitoring The Sustainable Development Goals (SDGs)

7. United Nations, Department of Economic and Social Affairs (2014): Principles and Recommendations for a Vital Statistics System - Revision 3 - ST/ESA/STAT/SER.M/19/Rev.3 United Nations publication Sales No. E.13.XVII.10

8. Section 3(3): The Registrar General may issue general directions regarding registration of births and deaths in the territories to which this Act extends, and shall take steps to coordinate and unify the activities of Chief Registrars in the matter of registration of births and deaths and submit to the Central Government an annual report on the working of this Act in the said territories.

9. Section 7(2): Every Registrar shall, without fee or reward, enter in the register maintained for the purpose all information given to him under section 8 or section 9 and shall also take steps to inform himself carefully of every birth and of every death which takes place in his jurisdiction and to ascertain and register the particulars required to be registered.

10. Section 8. Persons required to register births and deaths—(1) It shall be the duty of the persons specified below to give or cause to be given, either orally or in writing, according to the best of their knowledge and belief, within such time as may be prescribed, information to the Registrar of the several particulars required to be entered in the forms prescribed by the State Government under sub-section (1) of section 16,--

a. in respect of births and deaths in a house, whether residential or non-residential, not being any place referred to in clauses (b) to (e), the head of the house or, in case more than one household live in the house, the head of the household, the head being the person, who is so recognized by the house or the household, and if he is not present in the house at any time during the period within which the birth or death has to be reported, the nearest relative of the head present in the house, and in the absence of any such person, the oldest adult male person present therein during the said period;

b. in respect of births and deaths in a hospital, health center, maternity or nursing home or other like institution, the medical officer in charge or any person authorized by him in this behalf;

c. in respect of births and deaths in a jail, the jailor in charge;

d. in respect of births and deaths in a choultry, chattram, hostel, dharmasala, boarding house, lodging house, tavern, barrack, toddy shop or place of public resort, the person in charge thereof ;

e. in respect of any new-born child or dead body found deserted in a public place, the headman or other corresponding officer of the village in the case of a village and officer in charge of the local police station elsewhere :

   Provided that any person who finds such child or dead body, or in whose charge such child or dead body may be placed, shall notify such fact to the headman or officer aforesaid ;

f. in any other place, such person as may be prescribed

11. Section 10 (2) In any area, the State Government, having regard to the facilities available therein in this behalf, may require that a certificate as to the cause of death shall be obtained by the Registrar from such person and in such form as may be prescribed.

(3) Where the State Government has required under sub-section (2) that a certificate as to the cause of death shall be obtained, in the event of the death of any person who, during his last illness was attended by a medical practitioner, the medical practitioner shall, after the death of that person, forthwith, issue without charging any fee, to the person required under this Act to give information concerning the death, a certificate in the prescribed form stating to the best of his knowledge and belief the cause of death; and the certificate shall be received and delivered by such person to the Registrar at the time of giving information concerning the death as required by this Act

12. Registrar General India (2020) - Vital Statistics of India Based on the Civil Registration System 2018

13. In Rajasthan all District Collectors have been designated as Additional Chief Registrars. This does not appear to have any impact on the functioning of the system.

14. In many places people have been approaching the Registrars to change the name of the child, make a second registration with a different date of birth that may have some advantages, etc. There have been cases of fake death registrations, some of which may have been done under pressure.

15. WHO (2020) - International Guidelines for Certification and Classification (Coding) of Covid-19 as cause of Death

16. Underlying cause of death is defined as "(a) the disease or injury which initiated the train of morbid events leading directly to death or (b) the circumstances of the accident or violence which produced the fatal injury. (WHO (1979) - Medical Certification of Cause of Death - Instructions for Physicians on the use of International form of Medical certificate of cause of death)

17. Registrar General India (2020) - Report on Medical Certification of Cause Of Death 2018

18. https://hmis.nhp.gov.in/#!/

19. According to the rules the reports are required to be submitted to the state governments by 30th June of the succeeding year and published within five months thereafter.

20. Sourav Das(2021): 'Death Count In 24 UP Districts 43 Times More Than Official Covid-19 Toll' https://www.article-14.com/post/untitled-60cf605395758

21. https://www.thehindu.com/news/national/other-states/covid-19-people-deserve-to-know-death-toll-patna-hc-to-bihar-govt/article34864132.ece

22. The Hindu Data Team (2021): Data | India's excess deaths could be highest among nations with the most recorded COVID-19 fatalities, The Hindu, dated 30 July 2021

23. Abhishek Anand, Justin Sandefur, and Arvind Subramanian (2021): Three New Estimates of India's AllCause Excess Mortality during the COVID-19 Pandemic - CGD Working Paper 589. Washington, DC: Center for Global Development

24. Deshmukh Yashwant, Wilson Suraweera, Chinmay Tumbe, Aditi Bhow-

mick, Sankalp Sharma MA, Paul Novosad, Sze Hang Fu, Leslie Newcombe, Hellen Gelband, Patrick Brown, Prabhat Jha (forthcoming) Excess mortality in India from June 2020 to June 2021 during the COVID pandemic: death registration, health facility deaths, and survey data, https://www.medrxiv.org/content/10.1101/2021.07.20.21260872v1

25. Babu, Giridhr R (2020) - The challenges in counting the dead, published in The Hindu 14 Aug 2020

26. Shewade,Hemant Deepak & Giridara Gopal Parameswaran (2020) - 'COVID-19 deaths may be higher than reported' published in The Hindu dated 20 Aug 2020

27. Jahnavi Reddy (2020) "At least 8000 COVID-19 deaths went unreported in Telangana, insurance claims suggest", The News Minute 4 June 2021

28. A new Section 14A has been added. Subsection (2) of this section says, "The Central Government may maintain a National Register of Indian Citizens and for that purpose establish a National Registration Authority." Under sub-section (3), the Registrar General, India appointed under the Registration of Births and Deaths Act will be the National Registrar of Indian Citizens.

29. World Bank (2018): Integrating Unique Identification Numbers In Civil Registration (Available for download at https://documents1.worldbank.org/curated/en/674401531758210363/pdf/27385-Integrating-Unique-Identification-102518-v6.pdf)

30. Reply to Lok Sabha question number 2542answered on 04.08.2021

31. UNICEF Review of Civil registration and Vital Statistics innovations in Eastern and Southern Africa, digitization, processes and strategies, 2020

32. https://www.local.gov.uk/sites/default/files/documents/50.14%20Flow%20chart%20for%20death%20registration%20process%20WEB.pdf

2

THE COVID-19 PANDEMIC AND THE HEALTH SECTOR: WHAT HAVE WE LEARNED?

Shreelata Rao Seshadri

***Abstract*:** *This paper examines some of the issues that emerged from India's handling of the Covid-19 pandemic, the context in which they emerged, and lessons for the future. What follows is a brief look at why it is critical to ensure that India's health system is strong and resilient. For most individuals and institutions (public and private), the importance of good health had perhaps never before been as salient as in 2020-21. The disruption caused by the pandemic starkly highlighted the link between physical and economic survival, as well as the continuity of society as we know it. This was true even before, as the data show, yet it has only now become a wider concern. Thus, policymaking has to bring together multi-disciplinary teams who can bring together science, statistics and society to develop genuine safety nets during times of crisis. Importantly, we need to treat this as a public health challenge and not one of law and order. Policy needs to be inclusive and bring people together, with a sense of purpose and urgency to overcome the virus.*

Key Words: Health system, multidisciplinary teams, public health, pandemic.

Introduction

As on January 8, 2022, the Ministry of Health and Family Welfare (MOHFW), Government of India website recorded a total of about 35.2 million cases and about 483,000 deaths due to Covid-19 since the diagnosis of the first case in January 2020. As the numbers of cases and deaths due to the Covid pandemic rose across the country, particularly during the so-called 'second wave' in March-June, 2021, there was rising anxiety on various fronts. Primary among these was the anxiety over whether the health system had the capacity to cope with a health crisis of this dimension. The messages from the Government have been mixed: initially, there were attempts to soften the blow by comparing, for example, cases and deaths per million population – which showed India as being substantially lower than countries such as Spain, the United Kingdom and the United States, largely an artefact of population size.

However, this has been cold comfort for the public experiencing the daily reality and dread of contracting the virus through some chance encounter. Apart from the periodic lockdowns, measures such as wearing masks, washing hands, avoiding crowds and remaining sequestered within the home as far as possible, are being forcefully promoted as the best protection against infection. Yet these are all actions that are to be taken by individuals and households. It begs the question: How well prepared was the country for a pandemic like we are living through today?

Pandemics Old and New: The current Covid-19 pandemic is not the first one faced by India. Going back more than a century, we can recall the Great Plague which hit the port city of Bombay around 1855, and then spread to Pune, Kolkata, Madras, Karachi and eventually most of India. Over the next three decades or so, it is estimated to have killed about 13 million people in India alone. The country was next ravaged by the Spanish Flu between 1918 and 1920. Again, about 13-17 million Indians are estimated to have died, globally the heaviest toll paid by any country. I mention these two instances for a particular reason which I will come back to later.

More recently, two notable pandemics that have impacted India are the HIV/AIDS pandemic beginning in 1986, and the SARS pandemic of 2002. Adult prevalence of HIV reduced from 0.36% in 2005 to 0.22% in 2019, and annual AIDS deaths peaked at 24.34 per 100,000 population in 2005, declining to 2.37 per 100,000 population in 2020 (NACO 2021).1 The SARS pandemic did not take much of a toll in India, with only a handful of cases and deaths reported.

The Phases of the Covid-19 Pandemic in India: The pandemic has played out in three distinct phases in India. It is worth examining each phase, since they have several unique features which have a bearing on lessons for the future.

Phase I extended from the inception in January 2020 to approximately October 2020. While cases were detected in January and February 2020, the seriousness of the situation only started being acknowledged both globally and in India around March 2020. Despite a very low case load and deaths in the single digits, India took some early actions which arguably slowed the initial spread of the virus. An analysis by the Brookings Institution pointed out that India instituted a series of early actions, including travel advisories and restrictions, and efforts to repatriate and quarantine Indian nationals arriving from abroad (Brookings Institution July 2020).2 Other positives actions taken were:

i. Participation in global coalitions such as CEPI and GAVI, which allowed for a coordinated approach on vaccines including stockpiling, rapid development and manufacture, knowledge sharing, trials etc;

ii. Leveraging India's world class vaccine production network, supported by the TRIPS agreement at Davos, putting in place a provision of generics of even vaccines on patent during pandemics. This made it possible to make available low cost or even free vaccines as appropriate; and

iii. Developing modern digital systems to test, trace and track cases, which allowed for the generation of vital data for modeling the progression of the epidemic and resource planning.

However, there were some serious issues during this phase as well:

i. It took a while for testing capacity to ramp up. Experts both at the global and national levels were repeatedly emphasizing that widespread testing to identify as many cases as possible, tracing of their contacts and isolation/quarantine of both cases and contacts were the core of a successful strategy to contain the virus. While the number of laboratories capable of testing increased over time, and tests per day also increased gradually, the tests per million in India trailed well behind the global average (there was significant variation between the different states). As late into the pandemic as October 2020, India's testing rate was @62 per 1,000 population, compared to (for example) Denmark at @745 per 1,000, the USA at 395 per 1,000 or Canada at 250 per 1,000 population (https://ourworldindata.org/grapher/full-list-cumulative-total-tests-per-thousand);

ii. The fragility of health infrastructure was starkly revealed, especially for migrants and the poor who could not afford to avail of private services. The crumbling health system failed them even in normal times, but in this time of crisis the problem was exacerbated many times over. Not only Covid-related services, but even normal health services also collapsed. The Brookings report estimated that between 100,000 and 200,000 children missed their vaccinations during February and March, 2021. TB patients did not receive treatment. A modeling exercise by the Stop TB Partnership estimated an excess mortality of @6-20% depending on the period of lockdown. Normal ante-natal and delivery care also suffered. The long-term impact of this will be staggering, and perhaps end up causing more deaths than Covid.

iii. PM-JAY data showed that claims for hospitalization for conditions covered by the insurance scheme were down by 50% during this phase. There is no data on the clinical outcome of those patients who had to forego treatment – again, they largely belong to the poorest economic groups.

Phase 2 was the so-called 'second wave', which began in early March 2021 and continued until mid-June, 2021. At its worst, India recorded more than 400,000 cases per day; and media reports highlighted the fact that more than half of all COVID-19 deaths occurred in April-May 2021 (*Hindustan Times*, July 25, 2021). The wave was preceded by complacency on the part of the government and the public at large: at the World Economic Forum, the Prime Minister stated that India had defied dire predictions and beaten all odds to successfully contain the pandemic, and predicted that the nascent vaccination programme at the time would be equally successful (Mint, January 28, 2021); events such as the *Kumbh Mela* were celebrated with fervour, with more than 9 million pilgrims thronging the venue between January and April 2021 despite evidence that infections were beginning to surge (*Hindustan Times*, April 30, 2021). This also resulted in the infection spreading to rural areas – a marked change from the previous phase which had been largely urban – after which the government's strategy of test-track-treat became much harder to implement, given the state of rural health infrastructure.

Alarming scenes of overcrowded hospitals, shortage of vital oxygen, medicines and hospital beds, and the emergence of new symptoms were a constant reminder of the dire situation that the country was in. Several hypotheses have been put forward for the chaos that reigned during the second wave (Menon et al 2021; Kar et al 2021).3,4 Unlike during 2020, the sense of the government taking charge and putting together a coordinated response was noticeably missing: instead, there was chaos. Kar et al (2021) suggest there could be three reasons for this:

i. Health being a State subject under the Indian Constitution, the response was left to the states, and could therefore not be coordinated. Yet, during the first wave, the Central government had set this provision aside and imposed a nationwide lockdown;

ii. Health infrastructure in most States is weak and was unable to cope with the onslaught of cases, particularly without Central backing; and

iii. Apex scientific bodies such as the Indian Council of Medical Research and the National Health Systems Resource Center were reduced to an advisory role, limiting their ability to respond to the crisis.

Asrani et al (2021) have suggested that the mutant strain of the virus encountered in the second wave behaved very differently from the previous version, contributing to the high levels of infectivity and mortality.[5] There were also many more cases and deaths among younger age groups; and certain manifestations of the disease such as a sudden drop in oxygenation among patients who appeared to be recovering were hard to explain. In short, the second wave was qualitatively different from the first and the country was not sufficiently prepared for the challenge. The reasons for this are yet to be systematically studied and the literature is currently thin.

Phase 3 (partly overlapping with Phase 2) is the vaccination drive which was rolled out in January 2021 with the vaccination of frontline workers with the Astra Zeneca vaccine (Covishield) or the Bharat Biotech vaccine (Covaxin); this was later expanded in March to those over 60 years of age and those over 45 with one co-morbidity; this was extended unconditionally to all over 45 years of age in April, and eventually expanded by May to all adults over age 18. After several initial hiccups with the CoWin app which was launched for registration, scheduling and certification of those who had been vaccinated, the rollout proceeded as planned.

However, progress was slower than expected and the subject of much analysis and criticism (BBC News, July 16, 2021). There were shortages in vaccine supply, relating initially to India having donated significant numbers of vaccines to other countries without ensuring internal vaccine sufficiency; early centralization of all vaccine supplies, and when that failed, passing on the responsibility to the States without proper prior preparation; changing protocols on pricing both in the public and private sectors, leading to a lot of confusion and delays in people registering themselves; mixed messaging on how the private sector would access the vaccine: whether through government sources or independently. Added to this were media reports of some cases of adverse reaction, plus unfounded fears in certain pockets of long-term harm caused by the vaccine, which led to vaccine hesitancy. Approval of additional vaccine such as Moderna, Pfizer and Sputnik, which would have eased vaccine shortages, also took time; as didthe indigenous development of candidate vaccines, several of which are in different stages of trial and testing.

However, by July, the vaccination programme did pick up and as of mid-July 2021, about 450 million doses of vaccine were administered, with 350 million eligible residents having received at least one dose. The government announced that by August 2021, 180 million additional vaccine doses would be available (*The Times of India*, July 28, 2021). Major challenges remained in the effort to reach 100% coverage, including the limitations of the existing cold chain and how much of its capacity will be available for COVID vaccination, given that there is an ongoing immunization programme that needed the same storage and distribution facilities; availability of adequate trained human resources to administer the vaccine safely; and availability of other logistics such as IT and management support (Kumar et al 2021).[6]

The need to strengthen our health system

Given this scenario, this paper examines some of the issues that emerged from India's handling of the pandemic, the context in which they emerged, and lessons for the future. What follows is a brief look at why it is critical to ensure that our health system is strong and resilient. For most individuals and institutions (public and private), the importance of good health had perhaps never before been as salient as in 2020-21. The disruption caused by the pandemic starkly highlighted the link between physical and economic survival, as well as the continuity of society as we know it. This was true even before, as the data show, yet it has only now become a wider concern.

Over time, basic health indicators in India have been improving yet there is a way to go. The Infant Mortality Rate (IMR) is 32 per 1,000 live births,7 and the United Nations Inter-Agency Group for Child Mortality Estimation calculate that 3 infants die every two minutes in India, the highest level in the world.8 The most recent estimate of the Maternal Mortality Ratio (MMR) is 113 per 100,000 live births (2016-18).9 This translates to about 26,500 women dying annually due to pregnancy complications; with girls between the ages of 15 and 19 at the highest risk.10 A third important indicator of the health system performance is Life Expectancy at Birth (LEB) which has been estimated by the World Bank (2019) at 70 years for women, 68.5 years for men.11 Our neighbours such as Sri Lanka are doing much better, with an MMR of 36 per 100,000 live births and an IMR of 6.1 per 1,000 live births (2017); as is the other Asian giant China, with an MMR of 18.3 per 100,000 live births (2018), and an IMR of 9 per 1,000 live births (2020).

The economic cost of ill-health is staggering. Apart from the short term financial impact of episodes of ill-health on individuals and households (discussed below), there are long-term macro-economic implications of ill health as well: the Institute of Health Metrics and Evaluation has estimated that Indians work only 6.5 years at peak productivity, as compared to 20 years in China, 16 in Brazil and 13 in Sri Lanka. India ranks 158th out of 195 countries on the global Human Capital Index (2018).[12] Poor sanitation, for example – a key cause of avertable morbidity and mortality – was estimated to cost the Indian economy INR2.44 trillion in 2006.13.Indoor and outdoor air pollution, both problems that have been allowed to run rampant in India, are estimated to cause 8 million deaths globally, of which one in five is in India. The price paid in terms of lost productivity and healthcare costs is estimated at around 7% of GDP (*The Financial Express*, November[13], 2020). Similarly, the WHO estimates that poor mental health will cost India $1.03 trillion in economic losses between 2012 and 2030. The costs of micronutrient deficiency has been estimated at 0.8-2.5% of GDP or $15-46 billion a year (2016). Malnourished children go on to earn 20% less than their well-nourished peers.[14] Non-communicable diseases (heart disease, diabetes, stroke and cancer) and mental illness will cost the economy $3.58 trillion between 2012-2030 due to lowered productivity of the workforce.[15]

Issues and Challenges in the Health Sector

a. Weak health service provision

While the public sector continues to provide the bulk of preventive care, including ante-natal care and safe delivery, child immunization, safe water and sanitation; as well as limited curative care through the network of public hospitals, evidence from the National Sample Survey indicate that utilization of public health services, for both ambulatory and in-patient care, is declining.[16] Bagchi et al (2020) looked at the reasons for this decline, by asking women members of the household aged between 15 and 49 years why public hospitals were not being used even when sick.[17] The responses pointed to a combination of poor access ('no hospital nearby') and poor perceived quality of care ('doctor is not there', 'waiting time is too long').

Access to services is a serious issue: both in terms of number of facilities and availability of health workers, there are significant shortages across the country. There is substantial variation between states: Rural Health Statistics (2019) show that Bihar, for example, has a shortfall of 53% of Sub-Centres, 46% of Primary Health Centres (PHCs) and 83% in Community Health Centres (CHCs) as compared to the requirement indicated according to population-based norms (https://main.mohfw.gov.in/sites/default/files/Final%20RHS%202018-19_0.pdf; pg. 143).[18] In Maharashtra, the shortfall is much lower, at 24%, 20% and 37% at Sub-Cs, PHCs and CHCs, respectively. States like Andhra Pradesh and Karnataka have no shortfalls in Sub-Cs and PHCs, but some shortfall in availability of CHCs; while Tamil Nadu and Kerala have no shortfall in any category.

Data for urban areas, which were the worst hit particularly during the first wave of the pandemic, show a similar variation across States, with the situation being quite dire in some States (one of them being Kerala) (*ibid.*, pg. 188). And within urban areas, the most vulnerable are the least served: a study from Ahmedabad showed that health facilities were the farthest away in urban slums.[19]

It is therefore not surprising that the National Sample Survey 75th Round (2017-18) reported that 42% of hospitalizations took place in government hospitals (46% rural, 35% urban), while 55% were in private hospitals (52% rural, 61% urban). 33% and 26% of outpatient care was availed at public facilities in rural and urban areas respectively; and the remaining in both rural and urban areas were treated by private hospitals, private doctors/clinics, and informal health care providers (5.2%). Only 14% of the rural population and 19% of the urban were found to have any kind of insurance coverage.[20]

Muraleedharan et al (2020) examined two rounds of the National Sample Survey (71st Round 2014 and 75th Round 2017-18) and concluded that there had been an increase between the two Rounds in utilization of public health facilities for both in-patient and out-patient care; and that this increase was across EAG and non-EAG States studied. This was particularly true of the poor, and hence represented a net decrease in out-of-pocket expenditure. They strongly recom-

Map 1: State-wise shortfall in Primary Health Centres and Health and Well-ness Centres in Urban Areas of India (2019)

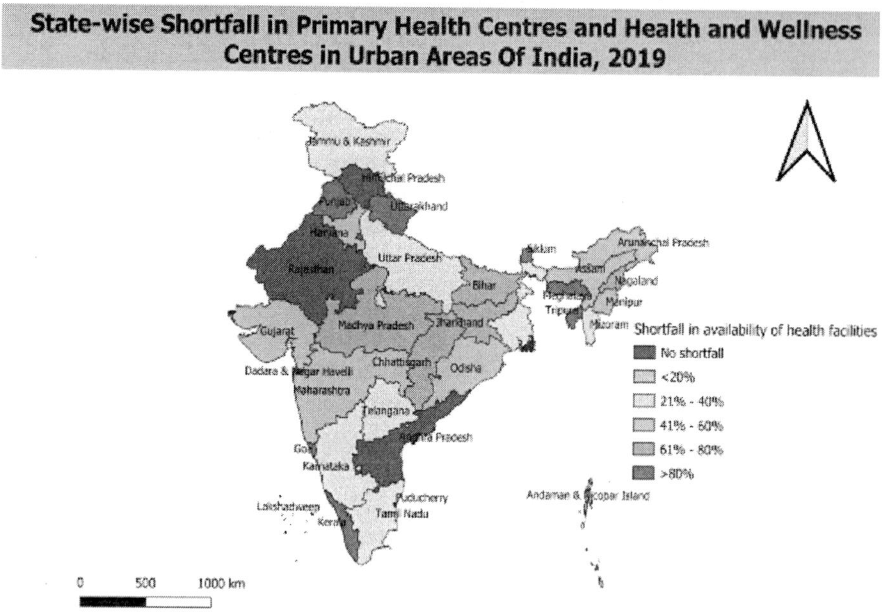

Source: Ministry of Health and Family Welfare, Govt. of India. (ON2268).

mend increasing investment in public health facilities.[21] During the pandemic, the public health system played a key role in doing the essential public health work of testing, contact tracing, facilitating quarantining of positive cases and treatment for those who needed it. Yet, the shortages in basic infrastructure were starkly revealed: on average, India has only 0.55 beds per 1,000 population (National Health Profile 2019). The WHO standard is 2 beds per 1,000. States such as Bihar, Jharkhand, Gujarat, Uttar Pradesh, Andhra Pradesh, Chhattisgarh, Madhya Pradesh, Haryana, Maharashtra, Odisha, Assam and Manipur have fewer than that, and they are home to more than 70% of the population. Delhi, Tamil Nadu and Kerala have more than 1 bed per 1,000 and West Bengal does well with 2.38 beds. The situation of beds for the elderly (>60) is better with an average of 5.18 beds per 1,000.[22] In a crisis which entailed high levels of hospitalization to prevent mortality, a shortage in something as critical as hospital beds contributed significantly to the final tally of deaths. In rural areas, the lack of testing facilities, weak surveillance and poor medical infrastructure posed even greater challenges.[23]

Low financing of health

Apart from uneven access, quality of care in the public health systems in India is poor, and it was never more obvious than during the pandemic. Lack of personnel, lack of beds, lack of oxygen became the topic of daily debate. thanks to persistent under-investment despite impressive economic growth. National Health Accounts estimates generated by the National Health Systems Resource Center show that in 2016-17, public financing of healthcare in India amounted to 1.2% of GDP.24 The target set for government health expenditures in the National Health Policy 2017 is 2.5% of GDP – double the levels at which it has stagnated in recent years. Government health expenditure as a share of total health expenditure is a mere 29% - the global average is 51%. The remaining is made up largely by households from their personal funds, since insurance coverage is low.

Despite having established a wide network of publicly funded health facilities across the country, out-of-pocket expenditures (OOPE) for healthcare remain high, with high inter-state variation: the burden of OOPE for the poor in the poorer states of India are significantly higher.25 Out of pocket expenditure as a percentage of total health expenditure is 62.6% in India (global average: 35%). Keane and Thakur (2018) estimate that 4.1% of the population or about 50 million people are in a state of 'hidden poverty' due to OOPE; and while overall there has been a decline in poverty between 1999/00 and 2011/12, the fraction contributed by medical expenditures has risen. In fact, economic growth can be seen as much less 'pro-poor' if medical expenditures are factored in.[26,27] High OOPE is largely due to low public health expenditures, lack of adequate social safety nets (such as health insurance) and poor access to essential public services of adequate quality.[28] Studies have found that a higher share of OOPE in household expenditure means that families cut back on other essential expenditures; and while food expenditures are largely protected, other expenses, particularly on education, are severely impacted.[29] Other ways of 'smoothing' household expenditure include borrowing from family, friends and moneylenders, all of which have their own negative consequences.[30] OOPE impact poor rural households the most, with 10.1% of rural vs. 6.2% of urban households becoming poor or poorer as a consequence of healthcare expenditures in 2012.[31] Evidence shows OOPE soared during the pandemic: the multiple tests, costs of hospitalization, medicines and aftercare all added up to mountains of bills that most people struggled to cope with (India Today, June 21, 2021). All the more reason to control OOPE to within 'tolerable levels' through better health coverage, particularly for the poorest households, as one of the most effective poverty reduction measures.[32]

Poor human resource and skilling

One of the most critical issues facing the health system today is the shortage in personnel at all levels. Those who are available have not been adequately trained for their roles. Karan et al (2021) examined the National Health Workforce Accounts (2018) and the Periodic Labour Force Survey (2017-18) and found that:[33]

The study estimated (from NHWA 2018) a total stock of 5.76 million health workers which included allopathic doctors (1.16 million), nurses/midwives (2.34 million), pharmacist (1.20 million), dentists (0.27 million), and traditional medical practitioner (AYUSH 0.79 million). However, the active health workforce size estimated (NSSO 2017–2018) is much lower (3.12 million) with allopathic doctors and nurses/midwives estimated as 0.80 million and 1.40 million, respectively. Stock density of doctor and nurses/midwives are 8.8 and 17.7, respectively, per 10,000 persons as per NHWA. However, active health workers' density (estimated from NSSO) of doctor and nurses/midwives are estimated to be 6.1 and 10.6, respectively. The numbers further drop to 5.0 and 6.0, respectively, after accounting for the adequate qualifications. All these estimates are well below the WHO threshold of 44.5 doctor, nurses and midwives per 10,000 population. The results reflected highly skewed distribution of health workforce across states, rural–urban and public–private sectors. A substantial proportion of active health worker were found not adequately qualified on the one hand and on the other more than 20% of qualified health professionals are not active in labor markets (Karan et al, 20201; pg 1).

Table 1: Structure of Public Health System			
Primary Level	Sub-Center (1 per 1,000 population)	ASHA ANM Male Health Worker (MHW)	17% ANM, 50% MHW posts vacant
	Primary Health Center (1 per 30,000 population)	4-6 beds; 3 Medical Officers, 3 Staff Nurses, Pharmacist, lab technician, office staff	10% doctors, 16% lab technician, 20% pharmacists vacant
Secondary Level	Community Health Center/ Taluk Hospital (1 per block/ taluk)	30-50 beds; 4 specialists (physician, surgeon, gynecologist, pediatrician) 21 support staff	90% of CHCs lack the full complement of specialists
	District Hospital (1 per district)	100-500 beds; >20 specialists and 100 or more support staff	31% specialist posts vacant

Tertiary Level	Teaching Hospitals (No population-based norm)	No standard pattern – can also be specialty based (cardiac care, mental health, cancer etc).

Source: Rural Health Statistics 2019.

This was perhaps the most critical gap experienced during the pandemic. With the increasing case count came the two-pronged challenge of managing both hospital-based cases as well as essential community outreach and prevention activity. As Table 1 shows, there are critical shortages in all cadres, and the available staff resources were unfortunately victims of the disease themselves in fairly large numbers. State governments scrambled to fill posts that had been left vacant for ages, with mixed success.[34] As the pandemic extended month after month, with increasing ferocity, health workers began to face both violence from the community they served as well as their own fears of constant exposure and its consequences.[35]

Changing burden of disease

It is now commonly acknowledged that India faces a double burden of disease.[36,37] Infectious diseases such as tuberculosis continue to kill over half a million people every year (highest in the world). At the same time, there is a rising tide of non-communicable diseases (NCDs) – India is the diabetes capital of the world with about 72 million cases of diabetes. Cardiovascular disease sets in earlier, accelerates faster and has a higher case fatality rate in India.[38] An underlying cause of all disease – malnutrition – is rampant. 38% of children <5 are stunted, 36% are underweight – worse than sub-Saharan Africa (National Family Heath Survey 2015-16).[39]

Clearly, there is a shift in the last few decades in the kinds of diseases that are making us sick or killing us. In the 1990s, the top five causes of the disease burden in the country were communicable diseases: diarrheal diseases, lower respiratory infections, neonatal preterm birth, tuberculosis, and measles. By 2016, three of the top five were NCDs: ischemic heart disease, chronic obstructive pulmonary diseases, cerebrovascular disease (Mohan et al 2020). However, there are important differences based on age, geographic distribution and socio-economic status; and this means that the health system has to be able to handle the significant unfinished agenda of communicable disease in many pockets around the country while at the same time gearing up for rising morbidity and mortality due to NCDs. A further layer has now been added by the COVID-19 pandemic: gearing up for the sudden and devastating onslaught of new and deadly viruses and bacteria for which no known or readily available treatments exist.

Persistent Health Inequalities

Health inequalities based on caste, class, gender and residence are growing rather than shrinking. It has been argued that this is due to the impact of globalization and liberalization of the Indian economy, which has exacerbated all types of inequities, including in health.[40] In addition it has been argued that health inequities fall largely into three buckets: historical inequities, rooted in colonial policies and practices; inequities based on social categories of caste, class and gender; and inequities based on access to and affordability of health services.[41] While this impacts the sector as a whole, variations within the country are stark. 'It is well known that health inequities in India are shaped by region, by socio-economic development, by class, religion, caste, gender and sexuality. In general, states of the south are doing better in terms of human development indicators than states in the North. But there are also sharp differences by regions within states.' (Ravindran and Rao n.d.; pg 1).[42] For example, a baby girl in rural Uttar Pradesh is at four times greater risk of dying before the age of one than a baby girl in Kerala. Poor children are 3 times more likely to be malnourished than economically better-off children. Certain groups, such as *adivasis*, are particularly vulnerable: studies have shown that they have higher rates of morbidity and mortality caused by communicable diseases and higher rates of malnutrition among children as compared to the general population.[43]

All the existing health inequities were severely exacerbated during the pandemic. Pandey et al (2021) found that higher concentrations of COVID-19 infections coincided with areas with lower scores on the social determinants of health. 'The better health infrastructure could manage the COVID-19 cases and prevent the death, but it cannot stop the outbreak of infection. It is dependent on other social determinants such as population density and availability of basic amenities such as drinking water and sanitation in households along with demographic factors such as migrant population, elderly population and people with comorbidities (Pandey et al 2021; pg.12).[44] Historically, as well, pandemics have been disproportionately devastating for the poorest and most marginalized: they suffer greater rates of morbidity and mortality due to a host of factors such as poorer nutrition, untreated comorbidities, poor living conditions and the like. However, in addition, measures such as the lockdown during the COVID-19 pandemic have added to the misery with loss of livelihood, displacement and economic barriers to seeking healthcare, as well as increased vulnerability to stigma, mental illness and gender-based violence.[45] Addressing the root causes of such inequalities is essential; and health policies and systems must take this into account when formulating a response.[46]

The Policy Framework for Pandemic Response

What has been the policy response to the pandemic? Much of the discourse around the role of the State in responding to an epidemic arises from the idea of contagion – of disease spreading from person to person through human agency. This was very much at the heart of the understanding of the etiology of the plague more than a hundred years ago. Kidambi (2004) describes the public health principles that rose out of this 'contagionist' understanding of the plague:47 breaking the chain of transmission, cordoning, quarantine and sequestration, resulting in what was, in retrospect, nothing short of an 'unprecedented assault on the body of the colonized' (Arnold, 1993).[48]

If all of this sounds familiar, it is. The response to the current Covid-19 pandemic eerily evokes the memory of the great plague, and its aftermath. Interestingly, the legal framework invoked in India to set in motion the State's response is the same – the Epidemic Diseases Act, 1897. It is important to recall that the Act was originally promulgated when India was a British colony – presumably with a very different relationship between the State and its citizens. The Act itself is very short, consisting of four sections: the first section mentions the title and extent of the Act; the second outlines the powers of the government to take special measures and prescribe regulations (including inspection of persons and premises at will); the third spells out penalties as prescribed under section 188 of the Indian Penal Code; and the fourth prohibits any action, including legal, against those enforcing the Act.[49] Given its antiquity, the Act stops short at quarantine and sequestration (practices in force even during the Black Death in the mid-13th century) and makes no reference to modern public health methods of testing, contact tracing, surveillance, immunization and the like. Notably lacking is also any mention of the rights of citizens.

Another legal provision that has shaped the current Covid response is the National Disaster Management Act (2005). Intended to 'provide for the effective management of disasters', the NDMA led to the formulation of the National Disaster Management Plan (2019) which includes biological disasters and health emergencies. This is an extremely detailed document, and broadly focuses on (i) surveillance, (ii) data-related issues such as risk assessment, data management, research and knowledge generation, (iii) information dissemination, IEC, (iv) training and capacity building, including development of guidelines and SOPs, (v) hospital preparedness including stockpiling, supply chains of essential medicines and consumables and so on, and (vi) community engagement – as an afterthought.

It is under these two legal provisions that the lockdowns, quarantining/sequestration, house-to-house investigations, police involvement for enforcement of all these measures, including more recently the mandatory use of masks, have been instituted. As we can see, neither of these is a health policy.

Let us, then, turn to health policies and their approach to dealing with pandemics. The WHO's Pandemic Influenza Preparedness (PIP) Framework specifies the following aspects that need to be addressed by health policies to genuinely gear up for a pandemic:

- early warning systems;
- good epidemiological surveillance;
- a strong laboratory network;
- functioning health systems with well-trained people able to recognize and manage potential pandemic influenza as it emerges;
- an emergency response system, regularly tested, supported and supplied to respond rapidly and effectively; and
- good risk communications to explain the nature of the threat and engage communities in behaviors needed to overcome the threat.

Ironically, a meeting was convened on December 16-17, 2019 in New Delhi, hosted by the Ministry of Health and Family Welfare and the WHO and bringing together lead experts from the fields of public health, virology, epidemiology, surveillance, clinical medicine, one health, disaster management, behavioral science, risk communication and defense sector to identify and address challenges that India would face during an influenza pandemic. They would have had no idea of how extremely urgent and critical their efforts would very soon become. Unfortunately, Covid-19 struck us before the Pandemic Preparedness Plan[50] could be formulated.

The most recent policy formulation in India, the National Health Policy 2017,51 contains a short section of emergency preparedness and disaster management. It recommends support for:

- dispersed and effective capacity for emergency management;
- an army of community members trained as first responder for accidents and disasters;
- close collaboration with the local self-government and community-based organizations;
- development of mass casualty management protocols for CHC and higher facilities and emergency response protocols at all levels;
- a public healthcare system needs to be adequately skilled and equipped at defined levels, so as to respond effectively during emergencies;

- a unified emergency response system, linked to a dedicated universal access number, with network of emergency care that has an assured provision of life support ambulances, trauma management centers.

The framing of the policy appears better geared towards road/rail accidents, earthquakes, tsunamis and the like, but not for a pandemic caused by a biological agent. Some of the basic requirements spelled out in the WHO PIP Framework are missing: effective surveillance, laboratory networks, risk communication.

Another issue that is critical but has barely been mentioned is the issue of mental health. More and more, the lockdown, the economic crisis and dread of illness are contributing to spikes in domestic violence, suicide and mental illness. There is no policy framework that covers outreach and care of those who are coping with the associated trauma of isolation, alienation and despair.

What has the pandemic taught us?

India's response is consistent with its 2019 scores on the Global Health Security Index. In terms of health security—pandemic preparedness and capacity — India is ranked 57th out of 195 countries. Its score of 46.5 was above the global average of 40.2, but much lower than Asian middle-income peers such as Indonesia and Thailand that had scores of 56.6 and 73.2, respectively. India scores high on communications with health care workers during a public health emergency, trade and travel restrictions, laboratory systems, immunization, and socioeconomic resilience. But it does less well in zoonotic disease prevention, emergency preparedness and response planning, capacity of health facilities, health care access, and medical countermeasures and personnel deployment. The elements that it does poorly on are precisely those that were required for a sustained effective response against Covid.

The problems we are now facing should not come as a surprise. They are the result of systematic neglect and under-resourcing of the health system. The experience of 2020-21 has highlighted some basic gaps that need to be urgently addressed:

First, we must recognize that there is no alternative to a strong primary healthcare system.[52] This means supporting our frontline workers with necessary resources – the ASHAs, ANMs and AWWS – to be our eyes and ears on the ground, and do the basic surveillance, testing and tracing that are essential in containing disease spread. Panchayats and Village Health Sanitation and Nutrition Committees (VHSNC) are responsible for the health and well-being of their communities. They should be given necessary resources to respond quickly and appropriately, taking local action. This has been done in Kerala and, in the early stages, even in Karnataka with good results.

Second, the health system should be ready and equipped to apply the science. For example, the capacity to conduct the number of tests necessary to track and contain the infection ramped up very slowly across the country. Tests per million lagged well behind the global average; and even when tests were conducted, they often could not be returned expeditiously because of a paucity of laboratory facilities.

Third, health sector allocation must go up to meet at least the NHP goal of 2.5% of GDP. This would allow far more resources – money, doctors and paramedics, beds, ventilators, laboratories – to our hospitals. Not only would this result in a stronger and better coordinated response during a crisis, it would also avert the other problem faced during the pandemic: people have faced major challenges in accessing routine medical care. A report by the Brookings Institution estimates that between 100,000 and 200,000 children missed their vaccinations during February and March. TB patients have not received treatment, which may result in an excess mortality of around 6-20%. Normal ante-natal and delivery care have suffered. This is for two reasons: (i) they have not been able to visit a healthcare facility due to lockdown, and this has impacted access to timely care; (ii) the health system has been stretched paper thin with the demand for beds, equipment and mainly doctors and nurses, because of which hospitals are driving away all other patients. The long-term impact of this will be staggering, and perhaps cause more deaths than Covid eventually. Overall health system strengthening is absolutely essential, particularly for communicable diseases which are still widely prevalent and disproportionately affect the poor, if we are to avoid a total collapse of healthcare services.

Fourth, there needs to be a regulatory framework in place that ensures that the private sector steps up and supports the government not only during times of crisis, but also in actions of public health importance. The case of Karnataka, which was able to mandate the cost of testing and certain other services in the private sector during the pandemic, as well as commandeer private beds for COVID patients is worth studying. If such actions are possible to implement in times of crisis, there is no reason why reasonable reporting requirement (for notifiable diseases such as TB, for example) or treatment protocols (again, for TB) should not be enforced even during times of relative 'peace'. Government can and should assert its regulatory role much more strongly.

Fifth, policies that privilege high-end curative procedures through programs such as Ayushman Bharat are further skewing our priorities away from comprehensive primary care. Strengthening the public health system with better financing, more skilled human resources and free medicines will strengthen primary preventive care, which is always more cost-effective than secondary or tertiary level hospital-based curative care.[53] A big gap in current public health insurance policies is the complete neglect of out-patient and preventive care. At the very least, these should be added to the package. For example, screening for people between the ages of 30-69 years for hypertension, and putting those with elevated blood pressure on a 'polypill' for hypertension control has been shown to be extremely cost-effective and significantly avert mortality. This would cost Rs. 4,000 per year per person. Without this, untreated hypertension could lead to that same person requiring a stent (Rs. 50,000-1 lakh) or bypass surgery (Rs. 1.1-2.25 lakhs) a few years down the line.[54]

Sixth, information must be disseminated transparently so that citizens know when to seek care, who to contact, where to go and wat to expect. This is currently one of the weakest links in the system: there is confusion about where to get tested, how much it will cost, where to quarantine, whether beds are available and on and on. This leaves people fearful, mistrustful and stigmatized. However, the government has been quick to impose fines for not wearing a mask! This is not a law-and-order problem, it is a public health and humanitarian disaster. It needs a humane response that is inclusive and reassuring.

There is a need for a policy framework that goes beyond only the health sector to deal with disease outbreaks as serious and complex as what we are facing today. As we have experienced, public health concerns are no doubt of paramount concern – how to apply basic public health principles of prevent, test, trace and treat in a comprehensive and effective manner. But apart from the public health crisis, there is a humanitarian crisis which will also have long-term health impacts – for example, the effects of malnutrition during this period, or mental stress, will stay with us even after the pandemic has passed. In order to address this, there is a need to look at livelihoods, migration, agricultural support – the complexity of a pandemic calls for a multi-sectoral, multi-agency response that requires a policy framework of vision and imagination.

Finally, the evidence base for policy has to be strengthened. Reliable data, data analytics, epidemiology are all essential and need to be built up. Capacity to run well-designed trials to understand the behavior of the virus and develop new treatment protocols is also essential. In the wake of the SARS scare of 2002, the Government, with funding from the World Bank, launched the Integrated Disease Surveillance Program (IDSP 2004), with the objective of strengthening decentralized laboratory based IT enabled disease surveillance system for epidemic prone diseases to monitor disease trends and to detect and respond to outbreaks in early rising phase through trained Rapid Response Team (RRTs). The program consisted of (i) Integration and decentralization of surveillance activities through establishment of surveillance units at Centre, State and District level; (ii) Human Resource Development – Training of State Surveillance Officers, District Surveillance Officers, Rapid Response Team and other Medical and Paramedical staff on principles of disease surveillance; (iii) Use of Information Communication Technology for collection, collation, compilation, analysis and dissemination of data; (iv) Strengthening of public health laboratories; and (v) Inter sectoral Co-ordination for zoonotic diseases. It is, however, interesting to note that during the COVID pandemic, the IDSP has been set aside, even though it was set up to address precisely this type of situation, and the lead role has been taken up by the ICMR.

Conclusion

Our fragile health infrastructure is failing not only those requiring care for COVID-19, but even normal services have collapsed.

The health system needs to be strengthened urgently. This must be an ongoing priority, not just scrambling to plug the holes because there is an emergency like the current pandemic. If this pandemic has taught us anything, it is that a strong health system is not optional; it is critical to our physical, mental and economic well-being. To avoid, in future, the economic, social and humanitarian disaster we are facing today, we had better Invest in Health!

If this pandemic has taught us anything, it is that health is critical to our physical, mental and economic well-being. If we want, in future, to avoid the economic, social and humanitarian disaster that we are facing today, we need to put more money into strengthening the public health system: it will improve quality of services and faith in the system. It will provide vital preventive and promotive care that will avert both death and serious disease down the road. Policymaking has to bring together multi-disciplinary teams who can bring together science, statistics and society to develop genuine safety nets during times of crisis. Importantly, we need to treat this as a public health challenge and not one of law and order. Policy needs to be inclusive and bring people together, with the same sense of purpose and urgency to overcome the virus.

ENDNOTES

1. National AIDS Control Organisation & ICMR-National Institute of Medical Statistics (2021). India HIV Estimates 2020: Technical Brief. New Delhi: NACO, Ministry of Health and Family Welfare, Government of India..
2. https://www.brookings.edu/blog/future-development/2020/07/13/the-impact-of-covid-19-and-the-policy-response-in-india/
3. Menon V., Kar S.K., Ransing R., Arafat S.M.Y. Impending second wave of COVID-19 infections: what india needs to do?. *Asia Pac J Public Health.* 2021; 1010539521998862.
4. Kar S.K., Ransing R., Yasir Arafat S.M., Menon V. Second wave of COVID-19 pandemic in India: Barriers to effective governmental response. Open Access: Published:May 29, 2021DOI:https://doi.org/10.1016/j.eclinm.2021.10091[5]
5. Asrani P., Eapen M.s., Hassan M. I., Sohal S.S. Implications of the second wave of COVID-19 in India. Published:June 30, 2021DOI:https://doi.org/10.1016/S2213-2600(21)00312-X
6. Kumar, V.M., Pandi-Perumal, S.R., Trakht, I. *et al.* Strategy for COVID-19 vaccination in India: the country with the second highest population and number of cases. *npj Vaccines* [6], 60 (2021). https://doi.org/10.1038/s41541-021-00327-2.
7. https://censusindia.gov.in/vital_statistics/SRS_Bulletins/SRS%20Bulletin_2018.pdf.
8. https://www.unicef.org/media/79371/file/UN-IGME-child-mortality-report-2020.pdf.pdf.
9. https://censusindia.gov.in/vital_statistics/SRS_Bulletins/MMR%20Bulletin%202016-18.pdf.
10. https://www.unicef.org/india/what-we-do/maternal-health.
11. https://data.worldbank.org/indicator/SP.DYN.LE00.MA.IN?locations=IN.
12. Stephen S Lim, Rachel L Updike, Alexander S Kaldjian, Ryan M Barber, Krycia Cowling, Hunter York, Joseph Friedman, R Xu, Joanna L Whisnant, Heather J Taylor, Andrew T Leever, Yesenia Roman, Miranda F Bryant, Joseph Dieleman, Emmanuela Gakidou, Christopher J L Murray. Measuring human capital: a systematic analysis of 195 countries and territories, 1990–2016. www.thelancet.com Vol 392 October 6, 2018.

13. https://www.wsp.org/sites/wsp/files/publications/wsp-esi-india.pdf.

14. https://www.savethechildren.org/content/dam/global/reports/education-and-child-protection/food-for-thought.pdf.

15. Bloom, D.E., Cafiero-Fonseca, E.T., Candeias, V., Adashi, E., Bloom, L., Gurfein, L., Jané-Llopis, E., Lubet, A., Mitgang, E., Carroll O'Brien, J., Saxena, A. (2014). Economics of Non-Communicable Diseases in India: The Costs and Returns on Investment of Interventions to Promote Healthy Living and Prevent, Treat and Manage NCDs. World Economic Forum, Harvard School of Public Health, 2014.

16. Sarit Kumar Rout, Kirti Sundar Sahu & Sandeep Mahapatra (2021) Utilization of health care services in public and private healthcare in India: Causes and determinants, International Journal of Healthcare Management, 14:2, 509-516, DOI: 10.1080/20479700.2019.1665882.

17. Bagchi, T., Das, A., Dawad, S. *et al.* Non-utilization of public healthcare facilities during sickness: a national study in India. *J Public Health (Berl.)* (2020). https://doi.org/10.1007/s10389-020-01363-3.

18. According to Ministry of Health and Family Welfare norms, there needs to be a provision of 1 Sub-bentre for 5,000 population, 1 PHC for 25,000 population and 1 CHC for 50,000 population.

19. Ramani, K.V., and Mavalankar, Dileep. 2005. Health System in India: Opportunities and Challenges for Improvements. Working Paper No. 2005-07-03, IIM Ahmedabad.

20. http://mospi.nic.in/sites/default/files/announcements/Summary%20Analysis_Report_586_Health.pdf.

21. Muraleedharan et al. https://www.epw.in/journal/2020/37/special-articles/invest-more-public-healthcare-facilities.html.

22. Singh P, Ravi S, Chakraborty S. **COVID-19: Is India's health infrastructure equipped to handle an epidemic? Brookings.** https://www.brookings.edu/blog/up-front/2020/03/24/is-indias-health-infrastructure-equipped-to-handle-an-epidemic/. Date: March 24, 2020.

23. Anant Kumar, K. Rajasekharan Nayar, Shaffi Fazaludeen Koya, COVID-19: Challenges and its consequences for rural health care in India, Public Health in Practice, Volume 1, 2020, 100009, ISSN 2666-5352, https://doi.org/10.1016/j.puhip.2020.100009.

24. National Health Systems Resource Centre (2019). National Health Accounts Estimates for India (2016-17). New Delhi: Ministry of Health and Family Welfare, Government of India.

25. Dash, A., Mohanty, S.K. Do poor people in the poorer states pay more for healthcare in India?. *BMC Public Health* **19**, 1020 (2019). https://doi.org/10.1186/s12889-019-7342-8.

26. Michael Keane, Ramna Thakur, Health care spending and hidden poverty in India, Research in Economics, Volume 72, Issue 4, 2018, Pages 435-451, ISSN 1090-9443, https://doi.org/10.1016/j.rie.2018.08.002.

27. Bowser, D., Patenaude, B., Bhawalkar, M. *et al.* Benefit incidence analysis in public health facilities in India: utilization and benefits at the national and state levels. *Int J Equity Health* **18**, 13 (2019). https://doi.org/10.1186/s12939-019-0921-6.

28. Balarajan Y, Selvaraj S, Subramanian SV. Health care and equity in India. *Lancet*. 2011;377(9764):505-515. doi:10.1016/S0140-6736(10)61894-6.

29. Panikkassery AS. Impact of Out of Pocket Health Expenditure on Consumption Pattern of Below Poverty Line Households in India. *Millennial Asia*. 2020;11(1):27-53. doi:10.1177/0976399619900608.

30. Quintussi, M., Van de Poel, E., Panda, P. *et al.* Economic consequences of ill-health for households in northern rural India. *BMC Health Serv Res* **15**, 179 (2015). https://doi.org/10.1186/s12913-015-0833-0.

31. .Ladusingh L, Pandey A. Health Expenditure and Impoverishment in India. *Journal of Health Management*. 2013;15(1):57-74. doi:10.1177/0972063413486031.

32. Sirag, A.; Mohamed Nor, N. Out-of-Pocket Health Expenditure and Poverty: Evidence from a Dynamic Panel Threshold Analysis. Healthcare **2021**, 9, 536. https://doi.org/10.3390/healthcare9050536.

33. Karan, A., Negandhi, H., Hussain, S. *et al.* Size, composition and distribution of health workforce in India: why, and where to invest?. *Hum Resour Health* **19**, 39 (2021). https://doi.org/10.1186/s12960-021-00575-2.

34. Dcvcx, September 17, 2020. https://www.devex.com/news/shortage-of-health-care-workers-plagues-india-s-fight-against-covid-19-98108.

35. https://www.business-standard.com/article/current-affairs/burnout-depression-soars-among-indian-healthcare-workers-in-covid-crisis-121052600110_1.html.

36. India State-Level Disease Burden Initiative Collaborators. Nations within a nation: variations in epidemiological transition across the states of India, 1990–2016 in the global burden of disease study. *Lancet.* 2017; 390: 2437-2460.

37. Mohan P, Mohan SB, Dutta M. Communicable or noncommunicable diseases? Building strong primary health care systems to address double burden of disease in India. *J Family Med Prim Care*. 2019;8(2):326-329. doi:10.4103/jfmpc.jfmpc_67_19.

38. Sreeniwas Kumar A, Sinha N. Cardiovascular disease in India: A 360 degree overview. *Med J Armed Forces India*. 2020;76(1):1-3. doi:10.1016/j.mjafi.2019.12.005.

39. International Institute for Population Sciences (IIPS) and ICF. 2017. National Family Health Survey (NFHS-4), 2015-16: India.

40. Baru, R.V., Mohan, M. Globalisation and neoliberalism as structural drivers of health inequities. *Health Res Policy Sys* **16**, 91 (2018). https://doi.org/10.1186/s12961-018-0365-2.

41. BARU, RAMA, et al. "Inequities in Access to Health Services in India: Caste, Class and Region." *Economic and Political Weekly*, vol. 45, no. 38, 2010, pp. 49–58. *JSTOR*, www.jstor.org/stable/25742094. Accessed 4 Aug. 2021.

42. http://www.esocialsciences.org/eSSH_Journal/Repository/1_Health%20Inequities%20in%20India%20_Sundari%20Ravindran%20&%20Mohan%20Rao.pdf.

43. Expert Committee on Tribal Health in India: Report of the Expert Committee on Tribal Health in India: Bridging the Gap and Roadmap for the Future. New Dehli.2018.

44. Pandey, A., Prakash, A., Agur, R. *et al.* Determinants of COVID-19 pandemic in India: an exploratory study of Indian states and districts. *J. Soc. Econ. Dev.* (2021). https://doi.org/10.1007/s40847-021-00154-0.

45. Bambra C, Riordan R, Ford J and Mathews F. The COVID-19 pandemic and health inequalities. J Epidemiol Community Health. 2020 Nov; 74(11): 964–968. Published online 2020 Nov 1. doi: 10.1136/jech-2020-214401.

46. Karmakar M, Lantz PM, Tipirneni R. Association of Social and Demographic Factors With COVID-19 Incidence and Death Rates in the US. JAMA Netw Open. 2021;4(1):e2036462. doi:10.1001/jamanetworkopen.2020.36462.

47. Kidambi P.. (2004). 'An infection of locality': Plague, pythogenesis and the poor in Bombay, c. 1896-1905. Urban History. 31. 249-267. 10.1017/S0963926804002135.

48. Arnold D. (1993). Colonizing the Body: State Medicine and Epidemic Disease in Nineteenth-Century India. Berkeley and Los Angeles: University of California Press. 1993.

49. The Epidemic Disease Act of 1897. Act No 3 of 1897 [Accessed April 18, 2020]. Available from: http://mohfw.nic.in/showfile.php?lid=1835.

50. https://www.who.int/csr/resources/publications/influenza/WHO_CDS_CSR_GIP_2005_5.pdf.

51. https://www.nhp.gov.in/nhpfiles/national_health_policy_2017.pdf.

52. Gauttam, P.; Patel, N.; Singh, B.; Kaur, J.; Chattu, V.K.; Jakovljevic, M. Public Health Policy of India and COVID-19: Diagnosis and Prognosis of the Combating Response. Sustainability 2021, 13, 3415. https://doi.org/10.3390/ su13063415.

53. Garg S, Bhatnagar N, Singh MM, et al. Strengthening public healthcare systems in India; Learning lessons in COVID-19 pandemic. *J Family Med Prim Care*. 2020;9(12):5853-5857. Published 2020 Dec 31. doi:10.4103/jfmpc.jfmpc_1187_20.

54. https://www.copenhagenconsensus.com/rajasthan-priorities/news/diabetes-and-heart-disease-should-be-top-health-priorities.

3

SCHOOL EDUCATION IN THE POST-COVID WORLD

C K Mathew

Abstract: Among all affected sectors, the most disastrous long-term impacts of COVID-19 can be observed in the education sector, and especially in schools. It has been estimated that the pandemic has disrupted the education of more than 1.6 billion school children across the globe. In India, more than 25 crore children face the same issues. Its aftermath may affect the cognitive skills of the children as well as their future in the job market. This article looks at the literature available amongst international organizations such as the World Bank, UNESCO and UNICEF and the recommendations made by them. The virus has led to children being almost completely dependent on the digital mode of education, thus creating further disparities in a sector which was already facing discrimination in many categories and classes of students. The author thereafter prescribes a course of action that can be adopted for school education in the country with the expectation that it is brought back on its course at the earliest.

Key Words: Learning deficit, digital mode, hybrid learning, NEP, cognitive skills, education disruption.

Education has always been at the forefront of the activities of any government which places high importance on long term and sustainable economic and social development. While the estimation of GDP has been, and still is, the most prevalent measurement tool to determine the level of economic development of a country, in the past couple of decades its inadequacy to measure critical aspects of social and human welfare has been increasingly acknowledged. Economists such as Amartya Sen and Jean Dreze in their significant book 'A Uncertain Glory: India and its Contradictions'[1] have argued that it is not merely economic growth, but the attention paid by governments to the sectors of education and health, and the investment made therein, that ultimately decides the sustainable long-term development of human resources.

In a country as large as India, now with 28 states and eight union territories, this means that the potential for variations between states in the policies, plans, programs and initiatives for elementary education is vast. Periodically, national policy frameworks are created to guide states in their formulation of state-level programs and policies. State governments and local government bodies manage the majority of primary and upper primary schools. The number of government-managed elementary schools is growing. Simultaneously, as we have noted, the number and proportion of schools managed by private institutions is also growing. Poorly resourced public schools which suffer from high rates of teacher absenteeism may have encouraged the rapid growth of private (unaided) schooling in India, both in urban and rural areas. Some studies show that teacher absenteeism in government is only because of deputation of teachers for non-scholastic duties and not deliberate absenteeism.[2] Be that as it may, the growth of the private school sector is primarily due to the perception that gove3rnment schools are poorly resourced as well as the aspirations of parents that student performance turns out better in a private school. Undoubtedly, the fact that the number of private schools are increasing indicates a certain sense of frustration about the public education system run by the government or local bodies. This also means that those families unable to pay the higher fees of private schools, have to necessarily make do with the poorer infrastructure of government schools and the quality of instruction provided there.

Private schools are highly regulated in terms of what they can teach, in what form they can operate and in all the other aspects of operation. Under the provisions of the Right to Education Act, 2009, they are bound by law to provide admission to children belonging to weaker economic sections of society to the extent of 25% of the total number of seats. For them the government is expected to provide subsidies.

There is a perception that education in private schools offer better quality. Yet, certain studies have discovered that the quality of instruction in public schools is not necessarily lower than that provided in the private schools. For sensible education policy making, it is vital to take account of the changing trends in the size and quality of the private and public schooling sectors in India. Ignoring these trends involves the risk of poor policies/legislation, with attendant adverse consequences for children's future. A study in this regard4 analyses the manner in which choice of school is made by the parents: wrong perception of English-medium schools and the mistaken notion that private schools necessarily provide quality education, etc. contribute to the myth of a public school being inferior to a private school.

There have been major policy initiatives in Indian education right from the early days of Independence. The Kothari Commission 1964-1966 made broad recommendations in this area for the first time. National Education Policies have been articulated in 1968, 1986, (with some modifications in the Plan of Action of 1992), and very recently in 2020. Up until 1976, education policies and implementation were determined legally by each of India's constitutional states. The 42nd amendment to the Constitution in 1976 made education a 'concurrent subject'. Later, under specific articles of the Indian Constitution, The Right To Education Act (RTE) was promulgated in 2009 to provide for free and compulsory education as a fundamental right to children in the age group 6-14. A brief overview of the Indian School system today reveals statistics that are, by their size and scope, humungous in nature. Education in India is provided in the main by public schools, controlled and funded by the government at three levels: central, state and through local agencies of local administration both in rural and urban India. Despite the massive and comprehensive net-work of government schools across the country in urban and rural areas, it is yet ironic that almost half the students of the country are in private schools, predominantly in urban areas.

In the 2011 Census, about 73% of the population was literate, with 81% for males and 65% for females. In 2017-18, the National Sample Survey measured literacy to be 77.7% (84.7% for male and 70.3% for female). India's improved education system is often cited as one of the main contributors to its development. There has been much made of the demographic dividend that India enjoys in view of its young population: about 50% of the India's population is below the age of 25. However, if this young population is burdened with adverse parameters in both health and education, then it can only affect the prospects of the development curve of the country. There are many studies and reports with cogent arguments which establish that the quality of learning in India, especially rural India, is poor. It is this single factor, along with poor health indicators, that prevents the nation from achieving its true potential. The absence of robust health and education systems is likely to impact the prospects of our country's youth and damage our economic prospects. With this in mind, it may be argued that the high percentage of a young population, not empowered by good education and health, will only act as a weight to slow down the economic progress of the country.

The size of the elephant as far as India is concerned is indeed gigantic. We may appreciate the expanse of the school systems by examining the statistics below provided by Department of School Education and Literacy in 20185: It may be kept in mind that children in the age group 6-17 (approximating to classes I to XII) number 29.59 crores. Of them the Scheduled Castes number 5.21 crores and Scheduled Tribes 3.17 crores.

The break-up is as follows:

Table 1: Estimated population of India by Age Group of Educational At-tainment 2015 and 2016 (in crores)				
Age group	Classes	All children	SC	ST
6-10	Primary I-V	13.01	2.32	1.28
11-13	Upper Primary VI-VIII	7.28	1.28	0.68
14-15	Secondary IX-X	4.89	0.85	0.44
16-17	Senior Secondary XI-XII	4.40	0.75	0.75
Total	All classes I-XII	9	5.21	3.17

Source: Education Statistics at a Glance: Ministry of Human Resource Development, Department of School Education & Literacy, Statistics Division, New Delhi

Gross Enrollment Ratios (GER) have improved in the recent past; but in the higher classes, there are reasons to be worried. All figures are in percentages

Table 2: Gross Enrolment Ratio: All Categories of Student									
	All			SC			ST		
	Male	Female	Total	Male	Female	Total	Male	Female	Total
Primary	97.9	100.7	99.2	109.5	112.4	110.9	107.8	105.7	106.7
Upper Primary	88.7	97.6	92.8	97.8	107.7	102.4	95.4	98.2	96.7
Secondary	79.2	81.0	80.0	83.9	86.9	85.3	73.7	75.4	74.5
Sr Secondary	25.4	23.5	24.5	20.8	19.0	19.9	15.6	12.9	14.2

Source: Education Statistics at a Glance: Ministry of Human Resource Development, Department of School Education & Literacy, Statistics Division, New Delhi

These figures reveal differentiation in GER when both SC and ST are compared with the overall general figures. In fact, if we examine only non-SC and non-ST figures as against the population of the general communities, the differences become even more pronounced.

To consider that in the first two decades of the 21st century, only about 56 % of the eligible children enrolled in primary classes get to the senior secondary level should be a worrying indicator of the lack of universalization of school education. In other words, the number of children dropping out at each of the levels in school education does not bode well for us. It has long been argued that as a nation we are far from the norms advocated by the Kothari Commission about allocation of 6% of the GDP for Education. The last available figures indicate that in 2014-15, such expenditure on all education as budgeted (including higher education) was only 4.04 %.6

In the Indian context, the records show that 1.5 million schools across the country were closed due to the pandemic. Considering the level of digitization of schools in the country, it may not be possible to switch to a system of large-scale digital education at this stage. Only 24 % households have access to the Internet, according to a government survey in 2019. In rural India, these numbers are lower with only 4% having such access. Sadly, the Education Ministry's budget for digital e-learning was slashed from Rs 604 crores in the previous year to Rs 469 crores in 2020-221.7 Yet there are studies to indicate that online learning is not so much dependent on creation of digital infrastructure, (even if that were possible in such a vast country as ours) but on the conditions of such learning in the schools as well as the households, such as availability of access, conducive environment, presence of an elder, etc. Hence, a shift from classroom to online education is not likely to compensate for the closure of school and its attendant shortfall in actual real time learning.

According to data released by the Ministry of Education at the beginning of July 2021, among government schools only 12% had internet facilities (in 2019-20) while less than 30% had functional computer facilities. These were the findings of the Unified District Information System for Education Plus (UDISE+)8 which collates data from about 15 lakhs schools across the country. Since the vast majority of the 26 crores affected school children have not stepped into a school for about two years now, the adverse impact of the pandemic on the cognitive abilities of the children can only be termed as disastrous. In some states such as Kerala, more than 90% of the schools, government and private, had access to working computers. On the other hand, across all schools in states such as Assam (13%), MP (13%), West Bengal (14%) and UP (18%), less than one on five schools had working computers. In UP, less than 5% of government schools had computer facilities. Except for Kerala, Gujarat and Delhi, no state could claim connectivity in more than 50% of the schools. It would be well-nigh impossible for schools to evolve any form of hybrid learning, as they try to reopen with staggered timings after the pandemic. The rate of dropouts, already 17 % at secondary level before the pandemic, is only likely to rise even further in the days ahead.

As per the Annual Status of Education Report (ASER) published each year, while we have reached almost universal enrolment in primary school level, the enrolment levels fall when we examine statistics at upper primary, secondary and senior secondary levels. The issues regarding girl-child education are serious, as it has been noticed that in the higher levels of school education, the sex ratio plummets. So too does it fall when looked at from the perspective of the disadvantaged sections of society, namely, the Scheduled Castes (SCs) and the

Scheduled Tribes (STs) as also the Other Backward Classes (OBCs). Further, the survey establishes that even the children studying in primary classes do not have the expected levels of cognitive abilities and often lack the basic learning characteristics that is expected from a child at that age.

India's performance report in the matter of Goal 2 of the Millennium Development Goals (MDG 2000-2015) for achieving universal primary education was published by the Government of India in 2017.9 The goal sought to be achieved was stated as follows:

Ensure that by 2015, children everywhere, boys and girls alike, will be able to complete a full course of primary education.

Three indicators had been specified and the country's achievement on each of them are as follows:

- Indicator 6:Net Enrolment ratio in primary education (Grade I-V): 87.41%
- Indicator 7: Proportion of pupils starting Grade I who reach Grade 5: 84.21%
- Indicator 8 Literacy rate of 15-24 year olds: 86.1%

When expected results were not achieved, the UNDP issued in 2015, the Sustainable Development Goals (SDG 2015-2030). Goal No 4 refers to quality education and the sub-objectives under this goal are primarily free primary and secondary education: This includes

- achieving proficiency in reading and mathematics,
- equal access to quality pre-primary education,
- ensuring children are developmentally on track,
- participation in pre-primary education, equal access to affordable technical, vocational and higher education,
- increasing the number of people with relevant skills for financial success,
- eliminating all disparities in educational access,
- universal literacy and numeracy, education for sustainable development and global citizenship,
- build and upgrade inclusive and safe school,
- expanding higher education scholarships for developing countries, and
- increase the supply of qualified teachers

In the wake of COVID-19, serious concerns have been expressed by most international organisations about the severe challenges that the nations of the world face in the achievement of these goals. In an effort to foster international collaboration and ensure that education never stops, UNESCO is mounting a response with a set of initiatives that include the global monitoring of national and localised school closure. To protect the wellbeing of children and ensure they have access to continued learning, UNESCO in March 2020 launched the COVID-19 Global Education Coalition, a multi-sector partnership between the UN family, civil society organizations, media and IT partners to design and deploy innovative solutions. Together they help countries tackle content and connectivity gaps, and facilitate inclusive learning opportunities for children and youth during this period of sudden and unprecedented educational disruption.

Specifically, the Global Education Coalition aims to:

- Help countries in mobilizing resources and implementing innovative and context-appropriate solutions to provide education remotely, leveraging hi-tech, low-tech and no-tech approaches;
- Seek equitable solutions and universal access;
- Ensure coordinated responses and avoid overlapping efforts; and
- Facilitate the return of students to school when they reopen to avoid an upsurge in dropout rates.

UNICEF also scaled up its work in 145 low- and middle-income countries to support governments and education partners in developing plans for a rapid, system-wide response including alternative learning programmes and mental health support. 10

The World Economic Forum has recently brought out a paper in this regard. The paper has concluded that an additional financing of 1.7 percentage points of GDP will be required if we hope to achieve the goals prescribed under SDG.11

When the COVID-19 pandemic exploded across the world from December 2019 onwards taking a deadly toll of the human population, its direct and inevitable impact on school education immediately become all too perceptible. In response to the crisis, the immediate reaction of governments across the countries of the world was to resort to lockdowns with the intention of flattening the pandemic curve. It has been estimated that across the world, about 1.6 billion children have been adversely affected. This unprecedented crisis affects both students and educators and highlights significant issues of continuation of educational services, issues regarding learning capabilities of children, conducting assessments and examinations, and catering to the needs of special education and vocational rehabilitation.[12] The impact of the second wave on the general population and especially for the education sector has been disastrous. As early as March 2020, the UNICEF had warned about the impending calamity: "Children are not the face of this pandemic. But they risk being among its biggest victims, as children's lives are nonetheless being changed in profound ways. All children, of all ages, and in all countries, are being affected, in particular by the socio-economic impacts and, in some cases, by mitigation measures that may inadvertently do more harm than good."[13]

UNESCO in its report 'Education: From disruption to recovery' noted: One year into the COVID-19 pandemic, close to half the world's students are still affected by partial or full school closures, and over 100 million additional children will fall below the minimum proficiency level in reading as a result of the health crisis. Prioritizing education recovery is crucial to avoid a generational catastrophe in the area of children's education. [14]

World Bank too drew attention to this pending disaster when Global Director for Education Jaime Saavedra emphasized the disastrous impact of the 'learning poverty rate' at a global level. This indicator measures the proportion of 10-year olds unable to read a short, age-appropriate text. Though this rate was 53 % in low-and middle-income countries even prior to the pandemic, it is likely to rise to as much as 63% as a direct result of closure of schools in the wake of the pandemic. [15]

A second UNICEF report a year later in March 2021 reported that in India "closure of 1.5 million schools due to the pandemic and resultant lockdowns has impacted 247 million children, in elementary and secondary schools in India. In addition, there are over six million girls and boys who were already out of school even before the COVID-19 crisis began. The UNICEF India representative, Dr. Yasmin Ali Haque added that "the longer children stay out of school, the more vulnerable they become, with less chances of returning to school." The report also categorically states that online education is not an option for all as only one in four children has access to digital devices and Internet connectivity. The deeply worrying factor is that only one in four children in India has access to digital services and internet connectivity. Unfortunately most of them are in urban areas. When schools finally open in some staggered manner, it would be the responsibility of governments and civil societies to strive to support them in catching up on the learning they have missed.

Another significant issue to be considered is the harmful effects on the nutritional levels of children in Classes I-VIII in public schools across the country in the absence of the Mid-Day Meals (MDM) programme. The programme provides a nutritional meal to about 10.2 crores children in more than 11 lakhs schools across the country. It is the largest school feeding programme in the world. The entire food grains used in the programme is allotted by the Central Government, along with transportation costs. The central government's share in the cost of conversion of grains to food is about 10%, and the remaining 90% is provided by the respective states. The honorarium provided to the cooks is also shared in the same ratio of 10:90. The objectives of the programme are both educational and health in nature: to improve the nutritional status of the child as well as to improve school attendance and enrolment. The meal provides roughly 450-500 kilocalories and 20-30 gm protein per child. The central budget for 2020-21 for the programme was initially Rs 11,000 crores but in view of the pandemic it was raised to Rs.13,400. The National Food Security Act (2013)provides that where food cannot be given for whatever reason, (for example the summer vacation months) a food security allowance (FSA) is to be paid. In view of the pandemic and the closure of the schools, an additional Rs 1,600 crores has been allocated.[16]

With the closure of schools, this element of nutrition through MDM has been disrupted. The importance of the programme for the children of India cannot be ignored. Students and families relying on these programmes are further being pushed to hunger and poverty. Food programmes should be thus more flexible keeping in mind the rules and regulations of encouraging social distancing and other hygiene practices. In India, the situation is more critical. With time, the COVID-19 spread from highly urbanised centres to tier two and tier three cities and further on to rural areas. Since March 2020, schools have been closed in India following the safety protocols. About 100 million Children between the age groups of 6-14 years are no longer getting free lunch meals in schools. The actual impact of the absence of hot cooked meals, and the efficacy of its replacement by Food Security Allowance, has not been studied in detail so far although we have a study carried out by the Global Child Nutrition Foundation in 202017. The report finds that the prolonged school closure has not only disrupted learning, and halted the delivery of cooked meals for children in schools, some states have responded with innovative measures to ensure nutritious meals or a cash equivalent. However, in most states such allowances are not being given. Undoubtedly, this will have an adverse effect on the nutrition levels of children, especially those belonging to economically weaker sections of society. Another area not adequately surveyed is the impact of absence of supplementary nutrition provided to children in the age group 0-6 under the Integrated Child development Services (ICDS) programme. The impact of diminished nutrition on the affected children could continue to stay all through their lifetime. [18]

Its impact on the children's level of wellbeing, in the light of the closure of schools, is of critical importance. Most children no longer have access to regular and nutritious meals which is likely to further the burden on health services and impair critical health and nutrition interventions for children.[19] Combined with this is the fact that the services provided by the Anganwadi centres under the Integrated Child Development Services (ICDS) for supplementary nutrition have also been severely impeded. Pre-school children in the age group 1-6 have had to bear the brunt of this deprivation. There are some studies being carried out as to the extent of deprivation that the absence of these two programmes has had on the child, but no conclusive findings are as yet available in the public domain. The long-term effects of such deprivation, especially for children of poorer economic and social backgrounds are yet to be assessed and evaluated.

The need to restart the nutrition programmes as soon as schools re-open is of primary importance. Some States are providing dry, packed rations instead of the hot cooked meals as an interim measure during the closure of schools. The United Nations World Food Programme has noted that the mid-day meal scheme presents the lifeline for school children in the country, and its re-opening is critical.[20]

Yet another dimension adding to the criticality of educational shortfalls is the impact of COVID-19 on those at the bottom of the caste-ladder. Traditionally, these children have been comparatively more deprived when set against those from the 'upper castes'. With lesser financial capability to access online education, these children will fall further down the index of learning during the course of the pandemic, thus further threatening labour market inequalities in future.

The Azim Premji University carried out certain studies during its field studies, entitled 'Loss of Learning during the Pandemic'[21]. According to this study, the pandemic has resulted in complete disconnect from education for the vast majority of children. There are only inadequate alternatives such as community-based classes and online /mobile phone-based learning that have taken the place of regular school education. The expected regression in curricular learning – defined as 'forgetting' - by students from the previous classes, is surely going to be a major setback. "This includes losing foundational abilities such as reading with understanding and performing addition and multiplication, which they had learnt earlier and become proficient in, and which are the basis of further learning. These foundational abilities are such that their absence will impact not only learning of more complex abilities but also conceptual understanding across subjects." The study, carried out in more than a thousand schools spread over 5 states and 44 districts, focussed on four specific abilities in language and mathematics. The study revealed that in language there was a 92% loss in at least one specific language ability and about 82% loss in at least one specific mathematical ability. "Thus, this overall loss of learning – loss (regression or forgetting) of what children had learnt in the previous class as well as what they did not get an opportunity to learn in the present class – is going to lead to a cumulative loss over the years, impacting not only the academic performance of children in their school years but also their adult lives. "*(Ibid.)*

With specific reference to Karnataka, (although this does apply to all the states in the country), it was stated that "A dangerous cocktail of poor children being out of schools, denied mid-day meals and lacking access to online education is playing out in rural Karnataka as well as low-income pockets of urban areas. This has worried sections of education administrators and child right activists, but any feeble attempts at reviving classes in low-risk COVID-19 areas have been met with stiff resistance, officials said, not willing to be identified."[22]

With schools closed and social distancing keeping children apart from the rough and tumble of mutual playtime and learning, peer learning and socializing is not available anymore. This story is universal cutting across economic class and location. For children in the pre-primary and primary level, this has resulted in complete lack of interaction with other children in the same age group. Even interaction with children in the neighbourhood has been severely restricted. Undoubtedly, this has resulted in the almost complete lack of social interaction for the young children, an aspect so very essential for the wholesome development of the child's personality. At home too there have been serious repercussions: extended lockdowns have in many cases led to increased fights and physical and mental abuse in the domestic sphere. The lack of space, movement and exposure to the outdoors is on everyone's mind. This is especially true for adolescents. Such a mode of life enforces a type of isolation where unease, fear and suspicion preys on the minds of children. Younger children are full of anxiety and fear as their behaviour is dependent on the conduct and attitudes of their parents. For adolescents, who are already undergoing much physical, emotional and psychological changes, the pandemic period has been traumatic. There should be-at this stage of life-much brain development, sorely missing due tom there being no structured daily routine. Calibrated interaction with their parents may have helped, but they too have been very disturbed during the pandemic worrying over job loss, reduced incomes and internal family strife.[23]

Even before the pandemic, India's burden of child health and nutrition was more than any other country with casualties of about a million children (below the age of five) every year, along with a heavy stunting and wasting rate. Now, the situation has become far more complicated due to multiple stressors including COVID-19, impoverished economic status, loss of employment, poor and unhygienic living conditions, and lack of healthcare facilities. Overall, the combined impacts of all the stressors will further deteriorate the health and nutritional status of children and warrants immediate operationalization and implementation of MDM scheme across all the regions in coming days. A comprehensive solution would lie in enriching the nutritional contents of MDM by supplementing the existing menu with more fruits, milk, cereals and vegetables to compensate for the nutritional imbalance of the child. This necessitates additional funding from the government and decision makers. At a broader level, better coordination between mid-day meal providing agencies and the governmental agencies can strengthen this weak health and nutrition network for India and the globe.[24]

We have to keep in mind the possibility of impact on the mental and psychological aspects of the child. Researchers in a study published in Elsevier Public Health Emergency Collection, concluded that there is a pressing need for planning longitudinal and developmental studies, and implementing evidence-based elaborative plans of action to cater to the psycho-social and mental health needs of vulnerable children and adolescents during the pandemic and afterwards. According to some reports, there is a 42% rise in occurrence of depression. The absence of peer interactions and relationships means that children are not able to learn about cooperation, trust, loyalty and support. At the same time they do not learn about themselves and how to understand and express their own emotions. In fact, the pandemic has deprived them of two main sources of social interaction, the school and the neighbourhood, thereby depriving themselves of the simple everyday joys of walking to class together, sharing lunch or playing and creating together. [25]

ChildFund, a not-for-profit agency working in child development, in collaboration with Council for Social Development, has released an assessment report titled, 'Perception, Fears and Readiness for Reopening of Schools'*26* with the purpose of understanding the preparedness of the public education system vis-a-vis the perceptions and expectations of the important stakeholders with the aim to bring the voices from the field to inform the policy decisions in favor of the children on the margins. The survey was carried out in 20 backward districts in 10 States - Bihar, Chhattisgarh, Delhi, Jharkhand, Madhya Pradesh, Maharashtra, Odisha, Rajasthan, Uttar Pradesh, and West Bengal in November 2020. These States had witnessed the heaviest inflow of migrant labourers and their children faced immense challenges in re-enrolling in schools due to a lack of documents. The prolonged closure of schools further exacerbated their situation as it resulted in a decline in nutrition levels among the children, online learning came with severe challenges, and the psychological well-being of the children was majorly affected.

The key findings of the report are as follows: The majority of parents and children want the schools to reopen. It was noted that children of migrant parents were facing challenges in getting enrolled due to lack of documents. More than 50% parents witnessed increased negative behaviour and more than 60% children themselves also expressed experiencing these changes in their behaviour. These included an increase in anger and irritability, and lack of concentration. 64% children expressed the need for support regarding extra classes to cover the learning gaps and removal of the burden of exam for the year 2021.Teachers state that a further delay in opening of schools will increase the dropout rates of girls (47%), child labor (52%), and widen the learning gap (57%). The key recommendations included the need for financial allocations, in form of a COVID-19 rehabilitation package to be made to the public education system, by the Union and state governments for provisions like social and emotional learning sessions to help children overcome the pandemic induced emotional setbacks and special training/bridge classes for children who have not been able to follow during the online classes. Further, RTE norms for the pupil-teacher ratio will have to be met, especially considering the increased load on the public education system resulting from swelled up enrolment due to economic reasons and reverse migration. The report also recommended providing information to the parents and community about government schemes and programs so that they can avail them accordingly; partnership of the government with non-government organizations (NGOs) to bring back all children to school; and provisions for a financial package to help government schools for the COVID-19 related additional infrastructural needs, such as the implementation of standard procedures (physical distancing, WASH facilities and health screening) and appointing additional resources ensure regular sanitization and hygiene in the school according to the local need.[27]

Aekta Chanda, Senior Education Specialist, ChildFund India says, "In India, educational vulnerability is overlapped with socio-economic disadvantage. Reopening schools is a serious concern in the background of already lacking basic infrastructure of the public provision of school education in India, which is the only option available to cater to the educational needs of children from marginalized communities. It is important to understand the perceptions of various stakeholders before re-opening schools, to plan the process in an inclusive manner, because this group was worst impacted due to temporary closure of schools and the increased emphasis on online mode of education available during the pandemic. With this report, we hope to support the education system to be better prepared to welcome the children back with the reopening of schools."[28]

Going forward, the big question is what will the world in general, and the sector of education, look like post-pandemic. "Governments, education systems and school managements are ceaselessly engaging in dynamic interactions to chart the way forward. Around the world, they are urgently recalibrating outdated systems and modernising them for the 21st century. Educators have had an opportunity to reimagine learning and equip students with the cognitive, creative, social, emotional and physical skills required to navigate the future….[T]he integration of technology in classroom teaching has compelled educators to upgrade their technical skills. This has not been without its challenges, and more so has come at the cost of stressed-out educators."[29]

"We as a nation are not good at understanding our children's needs or fulfilling them. especially when it comes to mental health… The WHO started conducting large-scale surveys across different countries by October 2020 and found that there was a five-fold increase in reporting of anxiety and depressive symptoms, substance misuse and suicidal behaviours."[30]

UNESCO also set up an International Commission on the subject of the Futures of Education.31 This Commission was chaired by the President of Ethiopia, HE Ms Sahle-Woek Zewde and its report can be summarised in the following manner, articulating nine ideas for public action:

Commit to strengthen education as a common good. Education is a bulwark against inequalities. In education as in health, we are safe when everybody is safe; we flourish when everybody flourishes.

Expand the definition of the right to education so that it addresses the importance of connectivity and access to knowledge and information. The Commission calls for a global public discussion—that includes, among others, learners of all ages—on ways the right to education needs to be expanded.

Value the teaching profession and teacher collaboration. There has been remarkable innovation in the responses of educators to the COVID-19 crisis, with those systems most engaged with families and communities showing the most resilience. We must encourage conditions that give frontline educators autonomy and flexibility to act collaboratively.

Promote student, youth and children's participation and rights. Intergenerational justice and democratic principles should compel us to prioritize the participation of students and young people broadly in the co-construction of desirable change.

Protect the social spaces provided by schools as we transform education. The school as a physical space is indispensable. Traditional classroom organization must give way to a variety of ways of 'doing school' but the school as a separate space-time of collective living, specific and different from other spaces of learning must be preserved.

Make free and open-source technologies available to teachers and students. Open educational resources and open access digital tools must be supported. Education cannot thrive with ready-made contents built outside of the pedagogical space and outside of human relationships between teachers and students. Nor can education be dependent on digital platforms controlled by private companies.

Ensure scientific literacy within the curriculum. This is the right time for deep reflection on curriculum, particularly as we struggle against the denial of scientific knowledge and actively fight misinformation.

Protect domestic and international financing of public education. The pandemic has the power to undermine several decades of advances. National governments, international organizations, and all education and development partners must recognize the need to strengthen public health and social services but simultaneously mobilize around the protection of public education and its financing.

Advance global solidarity to end current levels of inequality. COVID-19 has shown us the extent to which our societies exploit power imbalances and our global system exploits inequalities. The Commission calls for renewed commitments to international cooperation and multilateralism, together with a revitalized global solidarity that has empathy and an appreciation of our common humanity at its core.

While the above recommendations are at the level of policy ideas, they can be converted into a plan of action that can be implemented at an international level, with changes where required at the country or sub-country levels. With inspired leadership and commitment amongst the countries of the world, this is an eminently do-able programme.

Realising the need to modify educational practices in the light of the pandemic, the World Bank too issued a guidance note on remote learning.[32] The overall approach is to develop a multi-faceted remote learning model. This is also a plan that can be adopted by any country, while keeping in mind the extent and level of resources available. The main thrust areas are:

Developing a short- and long-term remote learning plan: Policymakers should assess their systems' capacity and resources to support a multi-faceted remote learning model, including a combination of technologies and delivery mechanisms. In the short run, the aim is to keep students learning; in the medium term, the objective is to prepare for schools to reopen.

Create an inventory of existing content to be deployed via remote learning: Rather than developing new content, which takes significant time and expertise, the focus should be on curating existing (especially free, 'open') content and aligning it to the curriculum. For instance, older radio and television programmes may be repurposed.

Organize content to align with existing curricula, while ensuring that learning opportunities match educational objectives. Simply listing a large repository of materials is not enough. Existing content should be organized so that students, their caregivers, and teachers understand what is available and the sequence in which it should be taught.

Create a virtual helpdesk to support caregivers, teachers, and students. Helpdesks complement the remote learning model, enabling students and caregivers to ask questions. They are also a conduit to receive feedback and share mass media messaging. Virtual helpdesks can be established quickly through various cloud-based tools.

Implementing a broadcast remote learning model: Where broadband access is not available, online learning is simply not an option; educators can introduce additional learning materials such as text messaging supplements/reminders, digital downloads, and low-cost newspaper inserts.

Utilize educational radio. The radio medium reaches a wide audience and no prior skills are needed by caregivers/students. This is particularly useful in settings where other connectivity options are unavailable and education radio stations exist. Once established, radio programming schedules must be communicated to reach the appropriate audiences.

Utilize educational television. Television is the fastest way to deploy lecture-based classes, as high-quality teachers can be recorded without much additional training. Students can then watch recordings or re-runs of these lectures. This is particularly useful in settings where most of the population has access to a television and education channels exist.

Implementing an online/mobile remote learning model: In contexts that have the infrastructure, funding, and capacity to host the technology, these options should be considered:

Increase access to digital resources, by improving connectivity. For countries with the infrastructure and bandwidth, improving connectivity is the first step. Education administrators must partner with mobile operators, telecom providers, and other providers to increase access to digital resources.[33]

Provide a consolidated, one-stop-shop to access content. A central online portal can provide a consolidated listing of available content, tools, apps and platforms, together with supporting materials and guidance for students, teachers and caregivers.

Make content available through a variety of devices. Online learning tools and platforms should run on a variety of operating systems and software applications. Online learning opportunities can be accessed using mobile devices and can be critical to ensure access by the widest possible user base.

Support the use of low- bandwidth (including offline) solutions. Mandating that online learning opportunities be optimized for low bandwidth and poor-latency conditions is advisable. Promoting the availability of downloadable tools and approaches can be similarly quite useful, particularly when schools have the means to convert educational content into digital formats and load them onto devices.

Videos can offer valuable learning resources, provided the availability of sufficient bandwidth and engaging content. Simply recording a teacher giving a long lecture is not enough because students may not be able to absorb the content. Best practice holds that shorter content is more easily accessed by students.

Provide supplemental guidance and support on how to use and access remote- learning content to students, caregivers, and teachers. Simply making content available to students is not enough. Teachers and caregivers need to be able to easily understand how to access and use it. Ideally, families and teachers should be given written guidance on how to access content, what related expectations are, and where to find additional information. This information can be communicated through the virtual help-desk or advertised via newspaper.

Use multimedia to share information about remote and online learning opportunities. Even if learning materials are only offered in one way (e.g. printed materials, radio or TV, online learning content, phone-based apps), multiple media channels (including text messages) can be used to alert students, families, and communities of which materials are available and where to find additional support or guidance.

Early Childhood. The predominant remote-learning tools for young children are television and radio, including edutainment programmes. In contexts with high connectivity, television programmes and instructional videos can be streamed online.

Primary. The predominant remote-learning tools for primary-age children are television, radio, and online videos. Teachers tend to communicate with their students through SMS/Social Media. Learning Management Systems can also be used for communication, collaboration, and videoconference facilitated "check ins." More activities are online for upper primary.

Secondary. The predominant remote learning mode for secondary students is online. In some countries, radio and television are used to supplement online learning, and may play a more dominant role, depending on the country's digital infrastructure and connectivity.

The UNICEF also brought out a brief advisory on how to keep the children learning during the pandemic.[34] The five-point tip-sheet focussed on Planning a routine together which factors in age-appropriate education programmes, that can be followed on line or through TV or radio;

Having open conversations encouraging your child to ask questions, while acknowledging their feelings and comforting that it is natural to feel afraid in such circumstance;

Start with shorter learning sessions and make them progressively longer. Within a session, combine online or screen time with offline activities or exercises.

Be aware that while digital platforms provide opportunities for children to keep learning, increased access online brings heightened risks for children's safety, protection and privacy.

Stay in touch with your children's teacher or school and support each other in parents' or community groups.

In a sense, educators can look upon the present pandemic, despite its unbearable outcomes, as providing an opportunity to transform the sector into a stronger and more versatile instrument of social change in the days to come. A study carried out by Brookings entitled "Beyond reopening schools" presents a hopeful and practical methodology to strengthen education and make it stronger than it was before COVID-19.[35] This springs from the fact that today the world in general, and developing countries in particular, have a much greater appreciation for the importance of schools. Public recognition of the essential caretaking roles schools play has increased, as has the gratitude of parents towards teachers. " It is hard to imagine there will be another moment in history when the central role of education in the economic, social, and political prosperity and stability of nations is so obvious and well understood by the general population." Thus, this presents an opportunity to capitalise on the new-found support for education that is present in virtually every community. The study argues that "strong and inclusive public education systems are essential to the short- and long-term recovery of society and that there is an opportunity to leapfrog toward powered-up schools."[36]

As defined in the study quoted above, a 'powered-up school' places a strong public school at the centre of a community and leverages the most effective partnerships to help learners grow and develop a broad range of competencies and skills in and out of school. The central question addressed in the paper is this: Is it possible to realistically envision education emerging from the novel coronavirus pandemic stronger than it was before? The concept of a powered-up school envisages that the school would invite supports, including technology, allowing allies such as community, parents and employers to reinforce, complement and bring to life learning experiences both within and outside the school. The new allies would complement and support teachers and encourage the child's healthy mental and physical development. A diagrammatic representation of how this works in an enlightened society has been presented in this study, by adapting it from the Office of Elementary and Secondary Education in the United States. The representation presents a dynamic and constantly self-improving mechanism that is by no means impractical.

The interrelationship between various components of the school ecosystem can be seen in the diagram and how they work together to improve outcomes in the school both in scholastic and societal terms.

The rationale for the requirement of thinking in this innovative manner emerges from four trends that are emerging from the impact of COVID19 on education globally.

Figure 1: Health and Social Protection Agencies

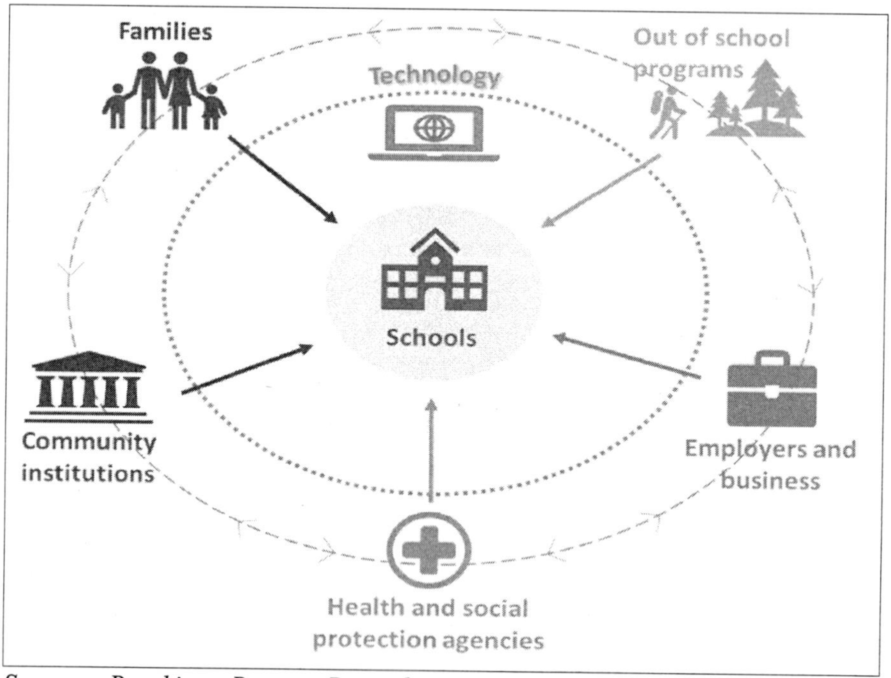

Sources: Brookings Report: Beyond re-opening schools: How education can emerge stronger than before Covid-19, September 8, 2020

a. The pandemic has resulted in accelerating educational inequality in an unprecedented fashion; and more so in areas where it was already high. It was a well-known fact reinforced by one study after another, that education systems in too many countries are not delivering quality education needed to ensure that children have all the skills necessary to thrive. As economist Lant Pritchett explained, "although countries in the developing world had largely succeeded in getting almost all primary-aged children into schools, too many students were not learning even the basic literacy and numeracy skills necessary to continue learning." [37]

On the other hand, we also see the presence of children in wealthy communities for whom schooling has never been better before: personalised teaching, the use of technology and creation of internet platforms, and the creation of learning pods, where a small group of children get the best education possible at exorbitant costs. While this may be good for these particular children, it represents a worrisome trend of the massive acceleration of education inequality.

The responses vary widely by level of income: Less than 25 percent of low-income countries currently provide any type of remote learning, and of these, the majority are using TV and radio. In contrast, close to 90 percent of high-income countries are providing remote learning opportunities, nearly all of which are provided online.[38] In low and middle income countries, only 36% of families have access to the internet. The learning gap, the report states, between rich and poor will likely grow during the pandemic, not just between hig and low income countries but also between high and low income regions and communities within countries. It is also evident that girls, refugees, migrant children and youth are likely to be severely impaired.[39]

b. The present moment is a 'leap-frog moment'. Innovation in education has suddenly moved from the margins to the centre. There is now an opportunity to identify new strategies that of sustained can help young people get an education that prepares them for these changing times. It should be argued that our goal for all children is to become life-long learners and develop the competencies that will make them constructive citizens in society. The new learning must include

1. innovative pedagogical approaches alongside direct instruction to help young people not only remember and understand but analyze and create;
2. new ways of recognizing learning alongside traditional measures and pathways;
3. crowding in a diversity of people and places alongside professional teachers to help support learning in school; and
4. smart use of technology and data that allowed for real-time adaptation and did not simply replace analog approaches.

c. The present moment is also demonstrating rising public support and recognition of how essential schools are in society, and that we can leverage a window of opportunity to make them stronger. "As teachers and school leaders around the world struggled with hardly any forewarning to pivot to some form of remote learning, parents and families around the globe who had relied on schools as an anchor around which they organized their daily schedule faced the shock of life without school." This recognition has helped gencratc a new wave of public support for strengthening education across the world.

d. The pandemic has galvanized new actors in the community—from parents to social welfare organizations—to support children's learning like never before. Education has developed new allies. The idea of children's education being powered by an ecosystem of learning opportunities in and outside schools, is not new; but has a new relevance and impetus that educators must leverage. The concept of a community school as the hub of children's education and development, with strong partnerships among other sectors from health to social welfare must gain ground: schools have the potential to remain open all day as centres for community engagement, services and problem solving. Schools can facilitate learning opportunities through a web of collaboration among them, community organizations, businesses, and government agencies that often pair direct instruction with innovative pedagogies allowing for experimentation.

The Brookings Report which we are examining at some length here provides five proposed actions to guide the transformation of the educational systems. There is no doubt that this role must be fulfilled by public schools (in the Indian context, government schools, funded by public money). It is only such publicly funded schools that can be identified by decision makers to transform systems to better serve all children and youth, especially the most disadvantaged. Public schools must be at the centre of any education system that seeks to close widening inequality gaps. The Report highlights the creative use of technologies, especially through mobile phone communication, as examples of strategies that if sustained could strengthen children's education. These five strategies are:

A. Leverage public schools: Put public schools at the center of education systems given their essential role in equalizing opportunity across dimensions within society. Public schools play a critical role in reducing inequality and strengthening social cohesion. By having the mandate to serve all children and youth regardless of background, public schools in many countries can bring together individuals from diverse backgrounds and needs, providing the social benefit of allowing individuals to grow up with a set of common values and knowledge that can make communities more cohesive and unified. This is not to decry private schools: in many countries, including India, Chile, Kenya etc, low cost private schools have also played a role in increasing universal access to primary education. It must also be kept in mind that in many places, it is the public schools that outperform private schools, both the subsidised private schools as well an independent schools.[40] Further, private schools tend to be less diverse in their admission policy, thereby excluding students from --- low income and coloured families. It is only public schools that can play multiple roles to serve communities, regions and entire nations, and have the greatest impact on the population of students.

B. A laser-focus on the instructional core: Public schools have to figure out how to identify strategies, based on hard evidence, of what works to improve student learning, with a heavy emphasis on the heart of teaching and learning processes, or the pedagogical core. This is based on the string evidence that educators are the most important school-side factor in student learning. Various studies have proven that it is the interaction among educators, learners and educational materials that matter most in improving student learning.[41] Even the brief experience gained after the pandemic hit, already identifies some clear strategies, involving learners, educators and parents in new ways using technology. Apart from technology, there will be too, the living experience of the people at the centre of education.

C. Harness education technology: Countries must deploy education technology to power up schools long term in a way that meets the teaching and learning needs of students and educators; otherwise, technology risks becoming a costly distraction. Countries are using whatever they have at their disposal: radios, televisions, computer, and mobile phones. Caution must be exercised since past experience shows that the impact of ed-tech interventions on student learning has been disappointing.[42] Yet ed-tech can help learning by supporting the scaling up of quality education, facilitating differentiated instruction, expanding opportunities for student practice and increasing student engagement. There are some sterling examples where good results have been achieved: La Radio Ensena in Chile and the Oak National Academy in the UK, and the Aprendo en Casa of Peru are good examples. In these examples, the role of the teacher willing to come forward and start the initiatives using such technology is very important; both online-learning as well as offline technology have contributed to the success. The supportive role of parents in encouraging these initiative by schools is also very important.

D. Parent engagement so as to forge stronger and more trusting relationships between parents and teachers is the fourth of the initiatives offered in the Report. Encouraging parents' engagement is often not given the required importance. It is a fact that building stronger parent-teacher relationship is not given the importance that it requires. The pandemic has forced a rethink in this regard. Where earlier the topic of parent-teacher engagement occupied a marginal place in discussions on education, now education leaders are discovering how powerful allies parents can be in the education of their children. Many countries are now forging new policies that place parents in a significantly more important role. In India itself, it has been observed that some State government, noticeably Himachal Pradesh known as the *Har Ghar Pathshala* (A school in every home) where about 48,000 teachers were deployed to connect to parents through WhatsApp. Over 92% of parents engaged with teachers through 'ePTMs' (Electronic Parent Teacher Meetings). Students' assessments are also being carried out through WhatsApp. As per all reports, these contact programmes have been quite successful. Even civil society organisations such as Pratham have been using a combination of WhatsApp and text messages and weekly phone calls. The capability of low-income or marginalised parents to become allies in support of the children's learning is quite significant. Ultimately, the pandemic has opened up an opportunity to forge stronger and more trusting relationships between parents and teachers.

E. An iterative approach: Embrace the principles of improvement of science to evaluate, course contents, document and scale new approaches. Rapid sharing of early insights complemented by documentation, reflection, feedback loops, etc., will have to be combined with traditional methods. Some institutions are working on Real-Time Scaling labs which learn, document, and. share emerging insights in rapid reiterative cycles, making sure that all stake-holders are included in the process and that both failures an successes are documented. the willingness and capacity to act on this learning so as to make changes is critical to the process.

In other words, the five-pronged strategy does not centre around the school structure alone. There are enough examples of education innovations that provide access to relevant learning for those in and out of the school building to set our sights higher. A powered in school in every community is possible if all stake-holders can collectively work together to harness the opportunities presented by this crisis.

A word of caution is necessary, and this has been mentioned earlier in this essay as well. The answer to the closure of the schools cannot simply be a higher dependence on digital education. We cannot be blind to the fact that this transition is fraught with serious repercussions. The nature of the societal disadvantage, especially in a country like India only compounds the digital disadvantage. An overview of this problem was attempted in Livingstone's article. [43] "In the race to get ahead in the digital age, some risk getting left behind." Disadvantaged families face great difficulties in supporting their children in our competitive society. Most studies ignore crucial forms of exclusion. The six potential inequalities which shape the child's chances at access to a digital education have been identified in this paper. They include gender (of both parent and child), ethnicity of the child, socio-economic status of the household, parental education, family composition (single-parent vs couple) and special educational needs and disabilities of the child. The study establishes that parents of children from higher socio-economics status or education are more digitally advantaged, using a wider range of devices to go online. On the other hand, those with just a secondary education or coming from coloured background or those requiring special education, have more barriers to face. Advantaged parents offer more forms of online support to their children and take part more in enrichment activities, such as language groups, video games, music technology, etc. But, they also face the risks associated with online systems. The findings of the Report highlight why digital inequalities matter in our increasingly digitalized and connected world. The most consistent findings concern forms of privilege – measured here by parental education or household socio-economic status. Differences in ethnicity, family composition or special educational needs are small and inconsistent, suggesting that parents are adopting some compensatory or alternative strategies to support their children. Parents shift between embracing, balancing and resisting the role of digital technologies in their children's lives.

"Some manage to mitigate disadvantage precisely by harnessing the potential of the digital, but the overall picture is one of persistent social stratification. New possibilities for teaching, learning and parenting need to be accessible to everyone, if digitalization is to have a positive impact on the inclusiveness, diversity and healthy growth of our society. Governments and policy-makers need to recognise and act on the digital inequalities, and provide the necessary economic and social support to less advantaged groups."[44]

Recommendations:

Thus, while we have many recommendations regarding providing a sustainable and complete menu of options to ensure that the child keeps learning during the pandemic, the response from the countries across the world have been differentiated by the economic status of its populations, the dynamism of their leadership and the nature of the inputs that go into the making of policy options.

UNESCO's Commission on the Futures of Education lays down the nine principles that will guide such a new world.[45] The Commission clearly pronounced that "we cannot return to the world as it was before". The nine principles are:

Commit to strengthen education as a common good. Education is a bulwark against inequalities. In education as in health, we are safe when everybody is safe; we flourish when everybody flourishes.

Expand the definition of the right to education so that it addresses the importance of connectivity and access to knowledge and information. The Commission calls for a global public discussion—that includes, among others, learners of all ages—on ways the right to education needs to be expanded.

Value the teaching profession and teacher collaboration. There has been remarkable innovation in the responses of educators to the COVID-19 crisis, with those systems most engaged with families and communities showing the most resilience. We must encourage conditions that give frontline educators autonomy and flexibility to act collaboratively.

Promote student, youth and children's participation and rights. Intergenerational justice and democratic principles should compel us to prioritize the participation of students and young people broadly in the co-construction of desirable change.

Protect the social spaces provided by schools as we transform education. The school as a physical space is indispensable. Traditional classroom organization must give way to a variety of ways of 'doing school' but the school as a separate space-time of collective living, specific and different from other spaces of learning must be preserved.

Make free and open source technologies available to teachers and students. Open educational resources and open access digital tools must be supported. Education cannot thrive with ready-made content built outside of the pedagogical space and outside of human relationships between teachers and students. Nor can education be dependent on digital platforms controlled by private companies.

Ensure scientific literacy within the curriculum. This is the right time for deep reflection on curriculum, particularly as we struggle against the denial of scientific knowledge and actively fight misinformation.

Protect domestic and international financing of public education. The pandemic has the power to undermine several decades of advances. National governments, international organizations, and all education and development partners must recognize the need to strengthen public health and social services but simultaneously mobilize around the protection of public education and its financing.

Advance global solidarity to end current levels of inequality. COVID-19 has shown us the extent to which our societies exploit power imbalances and our global system exploits inequalities. The Commission calls for renewed commitments to international cooperation and multilateralism, together with a revitalized global solidarity that has empathy and an appreciation of our common humanity at its core.

COVID-19 presents us with a real challenge and a real responsibility. It has been stated that big crises generates big ideas and opportunities. These ideas invite debate, engagement and action by governments, international organizations, civil society, educational professionals, as well as learners and stakeholders at all levels. One such response has been from the Alliance for #Right to Learn, which focussed its attention on issues related to the online learning models and how learning can empower the student and the teacher in the days ahead. One of the important recommendations of its Report46 is about blended learning models which include both synchronous and asynchronous learning. The first is where online education happens in real time and includes circle time (for connecting with student, sharing discussing, etc.), actual face-to-face teaching, sessions with small groups as well as co-curricular sessions (on art, yoga, dancing, etc.). The second occurs through online channels without real-time interaction. In both, there is provision for support from the teachers for the students after the online sessions as well. The objective of these models is to identify core concepts and skills for each grade and to develop "a three year curricular roadmap to ensure that long-term learning is not impacted". Simultaneously, the professional development for teachers is also required so that that they understand and adopt the paradigm shifts in learning occasioned by the pandemic.

The New Education Policy (NEP) announced by the Government of India in July 2020 makes no remarks or recommendations regarding the Covid situation, as it was completed prior to the onset of the pandemic. Yet, it would not be out of the way to seek a recommendation on the current situation. One possible approach to the current situation would be to reconstitute the very same committee to prepare an approach paper on the strategy to be adopted by the Centre and the States to tackle the situation and restore normalcy when we are through with the covid. This would give an all-India perspective to a national crisis of the highest order, affecting the lives and quality of our children and ultimately our human workforce. It would also act as guidelines for all the stakeholders to refer to with regard to their own particular issues arising from the pandemic. In fact, the additional recommendations in this regard can be brought out very quickly in view of the wide horizon of the NEP 2020 and the expertise of the members of the Committee on all issues related to education.

While this paper is intended to describe the situation in the school education sector which has been drastically and catastrophically affected by Covid-19, it also tries to prescribe some policy responses that governments both at Centre and the states, will have to initiate during the current phase of the Covid-19 pandemic as well as thereafter when we are in the recovery phase. If we revert to business as usual, then we will be blinding ourselves to the possible intergenerational crisis that this pandemic may have already created. Perhaps this is too early a reaction as the aftereffects of the pandemic are still not fully analysed for the educators to appreciate and prepare policy responses. Nevertheless, a prescription is attempted below. What we need now is nothing less than a national rejuvenation program; we should not reduce education to foundational literacy and numeracy, but treat children as they are, study the experiences they bring and address their nutritional, emotional and intellectual well-being as a whole. Without ourselves learning any lessons from the pandemic, how can we demand that our children learn their lessons.[47]

It is relevant to quote some actionable points that have been identified in this regard keeping in mind the seriousness of the situation in India. This seriousness in India can be measured by the indices available in the Stringency Index put together by the Oxford Coronavirus Government Response Tracker (OxCGRT)48. This Index is a composite of nine metrics, namely, school closures, workplace closures, cancellation of public events, restrictions on public gatherings, closures of public transport, stay-at-home requirements, public information campaigns, restrictions on internal movements and international travel controls. The school closure indicator for India shows that between 5 March 2020 and 20July 2021, schools were closed for 503 days. Of these days, 404 days were at the level of the most severe policy response. This can be contrasted with pandemic-hit Europe which within a few months of March 2020, began resuming in-person schooling for certain groups of children or localities. This came on the back of mounting evidence that learning losses and sociological stress was having a heavy cost on children and young adolescents. When hybrid schooling models were introduced in those countries, they prioritized children of younger ages, essential workers and those with special needs for in-person learning. In fact, by March 2021, most countries had resumed in-person education. Some of them followed multipole modalities such a rotation of children for in-person and remote learning. Similar strategies were not followed in India, even as relaxations were made for public gatherings. The poorest among the Indian children - Dalits, tribals and others with no electricity, struggled with on-line classes. Attendance data was ignored. Undoubtedly, existing education inequalities will increase. The recently formed ational Coalition on Education Emergency has indicated that teachers are unprepared for remote learning and are simply forwarding social medial links to the children through WhatsApp. Kerala stands out as by June 2020, it had provided educational TV channel KITE VICTER to about 4 million children. It was made clear that this was no alternative to regular schooling, but only an alternative to bridge the academic gap. The state took advantage of the investments made over the last two decades in information technology for schools, capacity building for teachers and teacher developed digital content. In most of the country, families are coping with more than issues of remote learning: they are ravaged by diseases, malnutrition, job losses. Interruptions in child health services, early nutrition and midday meals have affected growth and development of young children.

"The response to India's education emergency demands action on education, health and livelihood, focusing on every child as an individual. Each school should prepare a safe school opening and child support plan. Teachers must be vaccinated ion priority. Local adaptions and flexibility are essential. An 'Education Emergency Room' must be set up in each district to coordinate, implement and monitor plans. Many activities have to be coordinated: develop health and sanitation measures in schools and protocols for public transportation; encourage children who are not engaged with schools to come back; develop tools to help teachers make quick diagnoses of students' learning gaps; train teaches to use this as a guide to support children's recovery; offer additional classes or activities;

implement school health and nutrition; develop tools to accompany the educational trajectory of each student. Technology should be deployed safely for such purposes that identify and respond to children's needs."[49]

Keeping all these thoughts and suggestions in mind, an attempt is being made to recommend course of action to deal with the education emergency. Some of the key issues to consider are indicated below.

Creation of Advisory Committees at Central and State level: Both at the level of the Central government and the States, expert committees may be constituted, comprising of educators, administrators, teachers, social groups, parents and guardians etc. The membership of this committee may be extended to private schools as well. The committee should have access to all papers and other studies regarding re-opening schools and use their collective knowledge to prepare a strategy paper on the issues that reopening of schools will entail. The committees may be constituted at least 2-3 months before the schools are expected to be fully and formally reopened. They will make recommendations covering all aspects of education that may be accepted by the central/state governments and continue in place for a period of about a year after the formal opening of schools.

This is advised notwithstanding the fact that all schools may not open simultaneously. It is likely that the classes will reopen in a staggered manner, in different parts of the country, depending on the levels of recovery from the pandemic. It is perhaps likely that that the senior classes will open first and the junior classes later. Some States may open up the educational system earlier than other States. These committees will be guided by actual situation in the States and suggest the corrective action to be taken.

Objective criterion for promotion of children: The question of how the cognitive capabilities of the children can be evaluated for their admission or promotion to the next higher class has already engaged the attention of educators across the country. In classes lower to Class XII, the basis of such promotion or advancement will have to be their performance in the class just below. The no-fail policy largely adopted by many States under the Right to Education Act will be the norm for the rest. Even for promotion for secondary to senior secondary ie Class IX to Class X, or Class XI to Class XII, revised guidelines will have to be followed. In May this year, the Central Board of Education had announced a revised policy under which students of these classes, who appeared for their exams, were allotted grace marks to ensure they scored minimum marks required to pass ie 33%. Instead of giving weightage to annual exams, the revised promotion policy states that a student securing 33% marks in five subjects will be passed. The order stated that results will be calculated on the basis of annual exam, mid-term, and internal assessment or practicals. Previous promotion policies called for securing 25% in the 60-mark annual exams in the five main subjects. The department has also allowed schools to grant a maximum of 15 marks as "grace" to reach the 33% mark "in one or any number of subjects only for promotion to next higher class." It is expected that the similar procedure would be followed for children moving from primary to upper primary (i.e. Class V to Class VI) or from upper primary to secondary (ie Class VIII to Class IX). In the five levels of primary there may not be any problems because as a common rule these students are never failed or withheld. [50]

Each School is will be required to form a result committee of five persons. This committee will have to internally moderate the marks to account for the school level variations by using a reliable reference standard. The historical performance of the particular school, will be taken as the reference for moderating the marks accessed by the school for 2020 – 2021. The subject wise marks assessed by school for 2020 – 2021 will be taken in a range of +/-5 obtained by students in the reference year. 40% weightage will be granted to the student based on the marks obtained by her in the Unit Test or mid-term tests or pre-Board exams conducted by the school. 51 Another 40% will be calculated on the marks based on average theory component of the best three performing subjects out of the main five subjects. Finally, 30% will be awarded on theory component of the final pre-Board exams. It is gratifying to see that the CBSE has already issued these guidelines for the schools to adhere to.

A view may be taken that some of the criteria stipulated above for promotion without exams appear to be quite arbitrary. We may also keep in mind that the RTE Act 2009 provides for a no-detention policy for promotion, at least in terms of the classes covered under its ambit. What is needed is to strengthen the school-based and teacher-based assessments as detailed in the NEP to ensure that assessment of learning with a focus on the student's development, based on objective criterion and impartial evaluation is quickly put in place. The recommended practice of CBSE appears to be random tweaking of the numbers that already exist and to use the same for passing or failing the student. The philosophy behind the no-detention policy has to be understood and then interpreted in a positive manner. Not only this, the mere upwards movement of the student to the next higher level will not address the problems of cognitive development that would have been expected in a classroom situation when in the midst of his or her peers. It is therefore necessary to ensure that the actual mental development of the child does occur in a positive and non-threatening manner. When the student reaches the next level through this process, he will have to sit through a series of catching up classes which will have to be organized to ensure that gaps perceived are filled up.

Catching up: An objective criterion to assess the learning deficit will have to be arrived at, which while assessing and measuring this deficit, will also provide for state to state or even sub-state variations. This can be arrived at by conducting basic tests, standardizing them to at least the level of the state. It is bound to happen that such learning deficits will be more in the subjects of the sciences, mathematics or competence in languages. Across all levels of school education, from Class I to Class XII, the primary focus during the first six months after regular school opens, will be to ensure that the long absence from the brick and mortar school system, despite the best efforts attempted through digital classes, have not adversely affected the mental development of the students. This issue can be broken up into two parts:

- the treatment to be given to Students of Class X who are moving to Class XI and those who are moving from Class XII to collegiate level, ie those who have been deemed to be passed (based on their performance in regular classes) and who are just about to enter the under graduation level. We have examined this aspect in the preceding paragraphs. Indeed for entry at the collegiate level, the admission authorities may devise their own entrance exams to screen the applicant students. However, it is to be expected that such admission tests will take into account the most extraordinary situations that the students have gone through.
- The manner in which the educational processes are to be handled with reference to all the other classes.

As far as the first of these groups is concerned, it appears that the colleges where these students will enter will have no option but to decide to accept these students, based on their class performance. The question of how these admission authorities can recommend promotion to the under-graduation level will tackle the situation without a formal testing of their capabilities at the Class XII level is yet to be ascertained. Such a system based on class performance is subject to many imponderables: the absence of a rigorous examination system may result in biases and prejudices by the teacher at the class level, the lack of effort by the student that she would have otherwise put in, aggregation of earlier performances into the final class level assessment etc. Indeed, we now have the National Testing Agency (NTA), already set up as a recommendation of the NEP that should create standardized assessments in various subjects which the students can take according to their convenience.

The students will also be giving their preferences for arts, or science or commerce, and this may pose another problem for the colleges not admitting these students. Would they be able to conduct some tests to assess the preferences of the student s for the various branches of college education? The NEP has recommended a multi-disciplinary liberal arts frame work, which will enable the students of senior secondary level of the future to choose a host of subjects based on what is on offer or even available through distance learning or open schools.

Based on these choices, in the future the colleges can, if deemed necessary conduct their own entrance exams. In any case, for professional courses, institutions do have their own admission exams. Although the number of students applying is expected to be higher much this year in view of the promotion policy adopted.

As for the lower classes from Class I to Class XI, the gap in their current levels of education, both in terms of cognitive development and understanding concepts, will have to be identified and addressed through intensive and reiterative classes. For the lower classes, the focus will have to be on numbers, language, science, mathematics, expression etc. For the higher classes, these reiterative exercises will necessarily cover the standard syllabus for the entire period during which the schools were closed which may as well be about two years, as per indications now. That is to say, a student who enters Class X as an example, will be instructed in all the subjects that would have been taught to her in Class VIII and IX. The six-month period would enable the teachers to compress the two year gap into a series of bridge courses that will intensively address this learning gap.

Teacher training is bound to be a major challenge in the days ahead. The stresses that the teachers are currently facing has not been fully appreciated and possibly overlooked, because of the emphasis on the students. There have not been any teacher development courses over these last two years. The issues thrown up by the pandemic have underlined the need for many short-term crash course for teachers that address the issues of deficit in learning, mental health issues of students and teachers, etc. Courses will have to be conducted for teachers to re-orient them to the changed circumstances and to revive pedagogical practices in teaching, communication, classroom transactions etc. This must be done at least for a couple of months prior to the formal opening of the schools. Even though many of them have been involved in the digital classes during the pandemic, it is necessary to make them aware of the problems that students may be facing both at the cognitive level as well as in the social and emotional equations they have with their classmates. This may require behavioural experts who can inform these teachers during this exercise for teachers. The system as such may aim for a hybrid model of teaching post covid as well, where the digital mode will co-exist with the traditional methods in the future. The development of the teacher's capabilities to handle such a situation is an essential part of the strategy for the future. It will not be out of place to mention that over the years, development of the teachers' capabilities have not received the attention that it deserves. Fr several decades now. The District-level Training Centres have been lying defunct even in the best of times. The emphasis given by NEP for teacher education is significant and we can use this crisis to revive and rejuvenate this essential part of teacher training. In fact, the subject of teacher training requires a more complete and exhaustive treatment in a separate paper only for itself. Be it suffice to state that in the task of ensuring that the child does not lose out on his true learning potential in the course of the pandemic, equal importance is required to address issues of the teachers with respect to improving their capabilities during these trying times and to reorient them towards the new pedagogical needs that have arisen now.

Identification of students without access to digital education, who were not able to participate in zoom classes, especially those students on government schools. It is quite possible that such students deprived of digital learning processes may have slipped down into a knowledge gap that would be very difficult to make up. Invariably experience teaches us that these students are likely to belong to economically and socially backward and underprivileged sections of society, including girls, SCs/STs or minority and disabled students. Once such an identification exercise has been carried out, the teacher will have to ensure that during the catching up bridge course, personal attention is paid to such belonging to such students. On a national level, it is necessary for the government to develop digital capabilities at school level and then at the level of the homes of these students across the length and breadth of the country. Fortunately, we have a fairly extensive digital system with reasonable internet penetration.[52] The more important requirement is to make available the technology physically to the students who are presently unable to access it. Admittedly, this may be difficult to establish in each home. However, the cost gap for setting up such facilities at least at the panchayat level, for the families of such students who have been deprived of the benefit of such digital education, is likely to be substantial and for this a policy decision that will have to be taken in the long-term interests of the students of this country. The development of educational technology across the country is a requirement that cannot be put off anymore. Strengthening panchayat level facilities for this purpose, perhaps with incentives to the service delivery providers, can be an option that has to be considered. The use of radio technology has not been fully utilized for this purpose: the fact that the Prime Minister addresses the nation periodically on this facility can be leveraged for the purpose of developing edutech facilities for far flung areas of the country.

The natural corollary to the above is to identify children whose age-appropriate knowledge is lacking. We are aware that a sizeable proportion of the students, especially whose studying in rural schools may not have had access to any form of education during the pandemic period. This may be especially true of less privileged students in the public school system. It is also likely that even after regular schools reopen, they would continue to be deprived of educational practices in keeping with the digital mode. The children of disadvantaged social groups such as the Scheduled Castes and the Scheduled Tribes will have to face this problem which will only increase the learning gap between them and children from better social and economic backgrounds. Further, it is quite probable that the majority of such students will be girls arising out of the natural biases existing in our societal order. It is also quite probable that a significant percentage of such students may opt to drop out of the formal educational systems, in view of the two-year gap to the regular educational calendar. They may disappear out of our view and never be able to re-enter the educational stream. The task of ensuring that they remain within the formal educational system must be taken up by the school authorities as well as the community and the organization in the voluntary sector. Our country has an unenviable record of children who drop out of schools, even in normal times. This phenomenon is particularly true amongst girls from rural and backward areas as well as from disadvantaged sections of society. A mass movement has to be ensured throughout the country to bring back these children to the formal educational sector.

Engaging with parents and guardians as well as the community becomes very crucial at this stage. The long absence of children from schools would have had a severe impact of parents and guardians of children. This may be particularly true of older children who may have developed certain personality and behavioural changes that are required to be taken care of. Involvement of the parents can be particularly useful for this. The Parent-Teacher Associations present in most school have to be revived and made more active. The need for parents and guardians, working together with the community to be in close touch with the students during the critical period has to be impressed on them. All children who have fallen out of the school system have to be identified before schools formally re-open. The village panchayats and the urban wards of municipal bodies must get into the act and identify each such child who have dropped out and /or have missed out from the digital system of education of the covid pandemic period. If required, state governments must provide incentives to ensure that such children are back in their classes. In fact, if the school assumes a central role in the community life of the students, the benefits of such an interaction can be productive and useful to create a well-integrated local society and will also aid in the role of nation building.

Psychological evaluation of children adversely affected during this period. This is a sensitive task which an average teacher may not be able to perform. Further, the necessary facilities to address these issues in a decentralized manner may also not be available, especially in sub-urban and rural schools, mainly because such qualified persons may not be universally available. The almost complete disruption of the normal social interaction for young children both at school and the neighbourhood may have severely affected the normal social skills required for a child's psychological developmment.It is here that we have to take recourse to the wisdom of the community around the school, which will necessarily have to get involved into the critical question of the mental health of their children. Arranging for group activities during afternoon breaks or on holidays, will enable the affected students to re-establish contact in a healthy and positive manner with their peers and the society in general.

The blended or hybrid model of education is likely to be the new normal, even in a post-pandemic world. The national and state level educational and research organizations, known as NCERT and SCERTs can take up detailed exercises to roll out an educational format for all ages and classes that will integrate the physical brick and mortar school model with a digital model to which all students of whatever social and economic background can gain access. Even though the current pandemic may be a once in a generation, or once in a century, event, it is clear that the education sector has been impacted in such a manner as to make necessary such innovations in the future. A future-ready educational paradigm has now become the need of the hour. It would be an error to think that during the covid, teaching simply switched to online mode and that we can simply restart where we dropped off. "The post-Covid-19 situation is far too complex to respond to the wooden pedagogy stuck to the chapters of the prescribed textbook. A team of subject specialist must sit together to look at the syllabus designed for every grade level and deliberate on ways to reorganize it for this unusual academic session."[53]

The Azim Premji Foundation has developed a strategy that can be, mutatis mutandis, considered by the states of Indian while readying themselves for the reopening of schools.54 The basic thought in the rolling out of this practical methodology is to do the best that we can for the restoration of learning for the children who may have lost two full academic years by the time we come out of the shadow of the virus. The longer the schools stay closed, the loss of learning will only deepen, particularly for the younger students and those from economically and socially disadvantaged communities. Despite the video classes that many, though certainly not all, schools have resorted to, the process of learning together in a classroom has debilitated the task of learning. Technology based learning, as an alternative to classroom learning can only compromise equity and quality. The strategy envisages two scenarios, where schools open fully or partially. A sustained and concerted campaign will have to be initiated by the school and the community in general to ensure that children return to classes. And when they do, the focus must be on recovery of foundational learning and to ensure grade level learning.

And if schools continue to be closed, efforts must be made to reach the children through some face-to-face interaction where teachers visit children's homes, meet small groups of children in open spaces etc. supplemented with materials with which children can work on their own. Continuous, contextualized teacher support and decentralised decision-making will create an enabling environment for this. Undoubtedly, teachers are central to good education - in times like these, their role is even more important. This is especially so since many families have had to face extreme loss, both because of deaths of family members and also due to the deprivation of income and employment. The tasks that the schools and the community face are complex and solution defying. Getting children back to schools, the first priority, is itself a formidable task. The second is the evaluation of the loss of learning that the children in these two years have had to face. Children can be segregated into groups based on their levels of learning. Once there is a realistic evaluation, then the curriculum will have to be redesigned to suit the situation and the needs of the individual child. This may involve the designing o the annual calendar of thew school, and even perhaps the reorganisation of the school year.

Simultaneously, teachers will have to be brought back to the centre of the stage. Professional career development plans will have to be put into place factoring in the critical issues arising from the closure of the schools for these two years. It is vital to address issues of social and emotional well-being of both learners and teachers. The entire hierarchy of the School Education system will require to be recalibrated in the current context. The State Council for Education and Training (SCERT) and Boards of Examinations must relook at the curriculum while prioritising learning outcomes. The School Education Department at state level must develop standard operating procedures, fix minimum number of days, provide extra funds for enabling the school to follow safety protocol etc. At the district level, schools must be monitored for safety protocol etc and must have the flexibility to open, operate and close schools according to the priority determined by the District Collector. District Institutes of Education and Training (DIETs) can facilitate in-service training in both face-to-face as well as online models. Block and Cluster Coordinators must closely monitor all schools, recommend opening, closing and operations of schools as per prevailing conditions and also ensure safety and hygiene norms.

We have our work cut out for us. The impending third wave of the pandemic is surely to further exacerbate the malaise affecting school education. The asymmetry in learning capabilities of the children of India, that has always been a feature of the Indian School education system has only deepened in this crisis. This asymmetry runs across the various divides that have been existing in our social and cultural fabric: urban vs rural, government vs private schools, rich vs poor, upper caste vs lower castes, digital access vs limited or no access, boys vs girls etc. It is certain that those who have always been at the lower end of the learning spectrum, would have fallen further below the national averages on all counts in the wake of the pandemic. An appreciation and acceptance of these realities will be the first step towards creating a newer and more just and humane educational paradigm. Not only will this involve heavy expenditure in setting up digital technology where they do not now exist infrastructure across the country, but it will also involve a reset in the mental attitudes and mores of behaviour of education administrators and teachers as well as the political leadership of the country at national and sub-national levels. The enhanced involvement of the community, including local bodies in urban and rural areas, and the active prodding of parents will become the new normal. The traditional school management committees, now working perfunctorily, will need to adopt a sense of purpose and accept heavier responsibilities.

The task cannot be completed in any short frame of time. It is likely to take several years of concentered work for the effects to be visible. The mandate of the administrative and academic commissions and committees conceived of by the NEP 2020 will have to be amended to this effect with the directions that they would coordinate their activities. The main objective of these collective actions will be to heal the damaged structures of school education. Any lapse or lack of will and commitment will have long terms effects that will not be repairable. We can see the outlines of what must be done in this regard, as this paper has attempted to do. The question is do we have the collective will to make it happen.

ENDNOTES

1. Jean Dreze and Amartya Sen, *An Uncertain Glory: India and its Contradictions,* Allan Lane (Penguin Group) edition 2013

2. Emmerich Davies, *Absence: Electoral Cycles and Teacher Absenteeism in India*, paper prepared for Workshop on the Political Economy of Education, Nufflield College, University of Oxford 2018. Accessible at : http://barrett.dyson.cornell.edu/NEUDC/paper_90.pdf

3. Ibid, Dreze and Amartya Sen. Pl see Chapter 'Integrating Growth and Development' pages 17-44)

4. *School Choice in Low-Information environments: A study of Perceptions and Realities in Four States, published by the Azim Premji University November 2018 accessible at* https://archive.azimpremjiuniversity.edu.in/SitePages/pdf/SchoolChoices_Web.pdf

5. Educational Statistics At a Glance, Government of India, Ministry of Human Resource Development, Department of School Education and Literacy, Statistics Division, 2018, accessible at: https://www.education.gov.in/sites/upload_files/mhrd/files/statistics-new/ESAG-2018.pdf

6. Ibid: Table 24 (C)

7. Covid 19 fallout: The impact on Education In India: India Today: Kaushik Deka and Shelley Anand, January 3, 2021: Issue date January 11, 2021

8. Report from the Department of School Education and Literacy, Ministry of Education, Government of India accessible at https://udiseplus.gov.in/#/home

9. List of references: in keeping with the times, all these resources are available online.
Millennium Development Goals: Final Country Report of India, published by Social Statistics Division of the Central Statistics Office under the Ministry of Statistics and Programme Implementation, available at: http://mospi.nic.in/sites/default/files/publication_reports/MDG_Final_Country_report_of_India_27nov17.pdf

10. Report of the United Nations on Sustainable Development Goals. Accessible at https://www.un.org/sustainabledevelopment/education/

11. 'This is what is Needed to Meet the Sustainable Development Goals, published by the World Economic Forum: accessible at : https://www.weforum.org/agenda/2021/05/sustainable-development-goals-global-effort/

12. Sahu, P. (2020). Closure of universities due to Coronavirus Disease 2019 (COVID-19): Impact on education and mental health of students and academic staff. *Cureus*, *12*(4), e7541.

13. Unicef Data Hub report of March 2020, accessible at https://data.unicef.org/covid-19-and-children/

14. Unesco's Report 'Education: From disruption to receovery, accessible at https://en.unesco.org/covid19/educationresponse

15. https://www.worldbank.org/en/news/immersive-story/2021/01/22/urgent-effective-action-required-to-quell-the-impact-of-covid-19-on-education-worldwide

16. Accountability India provides figures related to the Mid-Day Meal programme which is available at https://accountabilityindia.in/wp-content/uploads/2021/01/Mid-day-Meal_2021-22.pdf

17. State Survey of School Meal Program: India 2020, accessible at https://gcnf.org/wp-content/uploads/2021/05/State-Survey-of-School-Meal-Programs-in-India-Report-with-Annexes.pdf

18. 18 Jayashree, B and Gopinath R. *As India's children miss mid-day meals due to anganwadi closures, jow n nutrition be ensured. Article in Scroll dated 5/10/2020, accesible at https://scroll.in/article/973716/as-indias-children-miss-midday-meals-due-to-school-closures-how-can-adequate-nutrition-be-ensured*

19. Report of Centre for Budget and Governance Accountability: https://www.cbgaindia.org/wp-content/uploads/2021/01/Impact-of-COVID-19-on-Child-Nutrition-in-India-What-are-the-Budgetary-Implications.pdf

20. Report from the Hindu dated 31 January 2021. Accessible at https://www.thehindu.com/news/national/mid-day-meals-lifeline-for-millions-should-be-re-activated-as-schools-re-open-un-food-agency/article33709490.ece

21. Loss of Learning during the Pandemic: Field Studies in Education February 2021, Research Group, Azim Premji University.

22. Article in the Economic Times of 7th May, 2021accessible at https://economictimes.indiatimes.com/news/politics-and-nation/no-school-no-mid-day-meals-or-ration-covid-19-deals-double-blow-to-kids-in-karnataka/printarticle/78694080.cms

23. Beyond Walls and Mirrors, by Sood, Jyotika, Roy, Lachmi Deb and Nayar, Lola. Outlook June 28, 2021.

24. https://poshan.outlookindia.com/story/poshan-news-india-faces-nutritional-crisis-for-school-children-dependent-entirely-on-midday-meals-amid-covid-19/360433

25. Refer xvii.

26. Report of ChildFund published in easypresswire dated 30 March, 2021 entitled 'Perception, Fears and Readiness for Reopening of Schools accessible at https://easypresswire.com/release/2978-childfund-releases-assessment-report-titled-perception-fears-and-readiness-for-reopening-of-schools.html

27. Ibid

28. Ibid

29. Sharma, Manika, Director Shri Ram Schools: *The Text Books Do Not tell us.* Editorial Content pg 22 Outlook dated 28 June 2021.

30. Sen, Amir Dr. Child and Adolescent Psychiatrist and Director & Co-founder of Children First. *Lonely Eyes fixed on the screen.* Outlook 28 June 2021, pg 30.

31. Education in a post-Covid world: Nine ideas for public action: International Commission on the Futures of Education, chaired by HE Ms Sahle-Woek Zewde (President of Ethiopa). The report is accessible at:https://en.unesco.org/sites/default/files/education_in_a_post-covid_world-nine_ideas_for_public_action.pdf

32. The World Bank Education Global Practice: Guidance Note: Remote Learning and Covid-19. Accessible at https://www.worldbank.org/en/topic/edutech #covidedtech

33. We have already seen earlier that digital access to learning cannot compensate for the loss of learning occasioned by the closure of schools. This may seem to fly in the face of the demand for enhanced digital mode of education. Not only will this digital education aggravate the present divide between the students from different social and economic groups, it will leave the deprived children with severe learning deficits. In a country such as ours, the traditional classroom education is likely to deliver better learning outcomes.

34. From the desk of the UNICEF Global Chief of Education accessible at https://www.unicef.org/coronavirus/5-tips-help-keep-children-learning-during-covid-19-pandemic

35. Beyond reopening schools: How education can emerge stronger than before Covid-19. By Emiliana Vegas, Co-director Centre for Universal Education, and Rebecca Winthrop , Co-director Centre for Universal Education (8 September 2020)) accessible at https://www.brookings.edu/research/beyond-reopening-schools-how-education-can-emerge-stronger-than-before-covid-19/

36. Ibid

37. Pritchett, L. *The Rebirth of Education: Schooling Ain't Learning*. Center for Global Development, Washington, Published by Brookings Institution Press, 2013

38. https://www.brookings.edu/research/school-closures-government-responses-and-learning-inequality-around-the-world-during-covid-19/

39. ibid

40. Chris Sakellariou: Department of Economics, Nanyang Technological University, Singapore. *Private or Public School Advantage: Evidence from 40 countries using PISA 2012-Mathematics*. Published in Applied Economics Volume 49, 2017- Issue 29. Accessible at https://www.tandfonline.com/doi/abs/10.1080/00036846.2016.1248361

41. One of the many studies relevant in this context is Cohen, David K.Bal, Deborah Loewenberg, *Instruction, Capacity, and Improvement*. Consortium for Policy Research in Education, Philadelphia, PA. Office of Educational Research and Improvement (ED), Washington, DC, 1999

42. Ganimian, Alejandro J; Vegas, Emiliana and Hess, Frederick M: Realising the Promise: How can education Technology improve Learning for all. Accessible at https://www.brookings.edu/essay/realizing-the-promise-how-can-education-technology-improve-learning-for-all/
Inequalities in the home influence children's digital opportunities

43. By Sonia Livingstone: January 9th 2019, Prof of Social Psychology, LSE's Dept of Media and Communications : accessible at https://blogs.lse.ac.uk/parenting4digitalfuture/2019/01/09/inequalities-in-the-home-influence-childrens-digital-opportunities/

44. Ibid

45. Report of 'Education In A Post-Covid world: Nine Ideas for Public Action from the Report of the International Commission on the Futures of Education: https://en.unesco.org/sites/default/files/education_in_a_post-covid_world-nine_ideas_for_public_action.pdf

46. White Paper: Online learning & Community Building in the COVID-19 Age: Narayanan, Dr Sowmya; Fazal, Nooraine; Wahbi, Mary: accessible at: https://docs.google.com/document/d/1v5hx-QtfEmSrdPOEf0Y7tBNdj-5H632p2mKpRkgLyI4/edit?ts=60ed1a98

47. "The crisis ahead, from learning loss to resumption" by R Ramanujams in the Indian Express 20th July 2021 pg 6.

48. https://ourworldindata.org/covid-stringency-index: The Hindu editorial on August 13, 2021 pg 6: Squaring up to India's education emergency by Sajitha Bashir and Anvar Sadath.

49. Ibid

50. From the website of the Central Board of Secondary Education: https://www.cbse.gov.in/cbsenew/Examination_Circular/2020/FAQpdf10042020.pdf

51. School of Data Science and Business Intelligence reporting on the CBSE promotion criteria https://sdbi.in/cbse-announces-the-promotion-criteria-after-the-cancellation-of-class-12th-boards-2020-2021-batch/

52. Report on Internet Penetration published by Statista accessible at https://www.statista.com/statistics/792074/india-internet-penetration-rate/

53. Kumar, Krishna. Returning to school 17 months later, The Hindu, editorial of 14 September, 2021.
https://www.thehindu.com/opinion/lead/returning-to-school-17-months-later/article36441808.ece

54. Note of Azim Premji University on Reopening of Schools in Pandemic Times:
https://apfstatic.s3.ap-south-1.amazonaws.com/s3fs-public/Reopening%20Schools%20in%20Pandemic%20Times.pdf?ESx3kpNfOBXS_HRWaB.hk_FGFK1YBfj_

The diagram at Fig 1 was reproduced from the Brookings Report (pl. see end notes xxx).

4

POST-COVID ECONOMIC CHALLENGES AND ENVIRONMENTAL REGULATION

Kanchi Kohli and Manju Menon

Abstract: *This paper outlines and analyses the slew of environmental regulatory changes introduced by the Indian government during the covid pandemic. The paper introduces the main environmental regulations and how their legal and policy standards have been lowered by successive governments in the name of national development and economic growth. It then outlines the regulatory changes undertaken by the government during the pandemic. The government engaged in extensive and frequent regulatory changes to accommodate the Covid protocols of social distancing. But more importantly, these changes were meant to create incentives for economic recovery at the cost of greater environmental and livelihood damage and destruction. The paper concludes by suggesting some steps based on the long-term experiences of environmental regulation for a post-Covid future.*

Key Words: Environmental regulation, policy standards, economic recovery.

INTRODUCTION

The spread of the Covid-19 pandemic globally is an unprecedented experience in our lives. It ripped through entire populations causing large numbers of deaths and prolonged illnesses. The environmental causes and consequences of the pandemic have been a subject of discussion during this period. Research studies have found correlations between biodiversity loss and new diseases (Tollefson, 2020)1. Experts have stated that we have been risking virus attacks due to human activities affecting nature at a massive scale. Agriculture, deforestation and other industrial activities have increased animal- human contact resulting in the growth of zoonoses (Jameel, 2020)2. Researchers also found that the most polluted places had the highest number and most severe cases of Covid-19 (Jefferson,

2020)3. These studies show that industrial scale land use change is responsible for climate change, environmental degradation and pandemics.

The state management of the pandemic impacts in India laid bare the long-term failures of governmental institutions to protect citizens and provide for their needs, especially the vulnerable sections of society that are also the largest sections of our population like rural households and informal migrant workers in cities. The lockdown as a primary means of controlling the spread of the Covid pandemic has affected the economy deeply. At the same time the lockdown also provided a surreal experience of pollution free environment in several parts of the world especially urban areas. The shutdown of global economic production and movement of goods and people resulted in the highest ever fall in carbon emissions.

These experiences and discussions during the first wave, provoked the question of whether a post-Covid green future was possible. As philosopher Bruno Latour notes, the pandemic showed the world that we could finally imagine something being more important than the global economy. He said that the pandemic made us question what was necessary and what was possible. According to Latour, "The pandemic has shown us the economy is a very narrow and limited way of organising life and deciding who is important and who is not important." (Watts, 2020)4 These reflections were in line with the long standing work of heterodox economists who have been working to convince governments to reorganize the economy and development sectors within the limits of environmental and planetary well-being (Wittenberg-Cox, 2020[5]; Boehnert, 2018[6]).

India's environmental regulations are understood to be the only firewall between ecologically important land and waterscapes and aggressive policies for economic growth. The regulatory procedures that are to be followed by infrastructure and industrial projects involve scientific assessments and public participation. This paper outlines and analyses the slew of environmental regulatory changes introduced by the Indian Central government during the Covid pandemic. The first section of the paper introduces the main environmental regulations and how their legal and policy standards have been lowered by successive governments in the name of national development and economic growth. Section 2 outlines the regulatory changes undertaken by the Central government during the pandemic. The government engaged in extensive and frequent regulatory changes to accommodate the Covid protocols of social distancing. But more importantly, these changes were meant to create incentives for economic recovery at the cost of greater environmental damage and destruction. Section 3 suggests some lessons and steps based on the long term experiences of environmental regulation for a post-Covid future.

SECTION 1

Environment regulation of economic development in India

Environment regulation in India is a shared responsibility of Central and State governments .This shared jurisdiction is framed and operationalized by web of laws that are enforced through expert regulatory institutions. At the national level, the ministry upholding the mandate to protect India's environment is the Ministry of Environment, Forests and Climate Change, established in 1985. The ministry's website lays out its five-point objective as "Conservation and survey of flora, fauna, forests and wildlife; Prevention and control of pollution; Afforestation and regeneration of degraded areas; Protection of the environment and Ensuring the welfare of animals".

The legal and regulatory measures for environmental protection have evolved since the 1970s. They have been prompted by India's commitments to international treaties, the state of environmental degradation or industrial accidents. Post-1990s, legal and regulatory frameworks have been introduced to mediate environmental protection, natural resource use and neoliberal, private sector led economic development. This was justified in the light of:

- The increased demand for land and water resources for growing sectors such as power, mining, roads, industries, ports and commercial forestry that were seen to contribute to India's GDP.
- The conversion of forests, coasts, wetlands and rivers to fulfill economic demands would necessarily cause pollution, ecological degradation and social impacts such as displacement and livelihood loss.
- International commitments to include public participation and grievance redressal protocols as part of environmental regulations.

Therefore, procedures for information disclosure, impact assessments, project approval protocols, public hearings, compensatory and offset schemes were introduced to the environmental decision-making framework. These were meant to act as a firewall between the economic priorities and environmental damage. Industrial, infrastructure and extractive projects were to be approved only after their potential environmental impacts were assessed and legally mandated mitigation measures were recommended. Some laws also required taking the view of project affected people through public hearings before final decisions were taken by expert technical bodies. Over the years, the past environmental performance of a project also needed to be disclosed while seeking approval for expansion.[7]

Four legal processes form the fulcrum of the central government's decision making for the conversion of natural resources for economic development. These are popularly known as *Environment Clearance, Forest Clearance, Wildlife Clearance and Pollution Consents.* These processes draw their mandate from Acts and Rules and are enforced through a series of executive orders, circulars and notifications which regularly alter the scope of their influence. (See Table 1)

Table 1: Prior environmental approval requirements for industrial and infrastructure projects in India

	Environment Clearance	**Forest Clearance**	**Wildlife Clearance**	**Pollution Consent**
Law	EIA and CRZ Notifications under Environment Protection Act (EPA), 1986	Forest Conservation Act (FCA), 1980	Wild Life Protection Act, 1972	Air (Prevention and Control of Pollution) Act, 1981 Water (Prevention and Control of Pollution) Act, 1974
Objective	Prior Assessment and scrutiny of environment impacts of certain industrial, infrastructure projects	Forest Conservation by regulating conversion of forests for non-forest use.	Conservation of wildlife by creation of Protected Areas (PAs); Prevention of damage to wild life and its habitat	Prevention, Restriction and Control of Pollution
Regulatory Institutions	Central level: MoEFCC and Expert Appraisal Committees (EACs) State level: State Environment Impact Assessment Authorities (SEIAA) and State EACs Regional Level: Regional Offices of MoEFCC	Central level: Forest Advisory Committee (FAC) Regional level: Regional Empowered Committees (REC) Regional Offices of MoEFCC	Central level: National Board for Wild Life (NBWL) and its Standing Committee, State Level: State Board for Wild Life (SBWL), Wildlife Division of State Forest Departments	Central Level: Central Pollution Control Board State level: State/UT Pollution Control Boards and their regional offices

Public Participation	Yes, through public hearing and written comments	Consent of Gram Sabha (Village Assembly) for forest diversion	No	No
Offset and Mitigation Measures	Conditions for mitigating and managing specific impacts	Compensatory afforestation against felling of trees; payment of NPV value against loss of forests; Conditions to prevent encroachment and damage	Conditions and mitigation measures to avert damage to wildlife and its habitats	Pollution Control Standards; Conditions for mitigating and managing pollution impacts

Source: Authors

These laws are meant to govern the environmental impacts of mainstream economic sectors. This puts the environment ministry in a position to determine tradeoffs between the protection of the environment and allowing for its damage to enable economic growth. This is a major responsibility and the Ministry's role has not been without controversy. While social movements and environmental organisations have called out the economic bias of the environment ministry[8-9], industry associations have sought greater leniency in regulatory procedures. Successive governments have relied on high level committee reports calling these regulatory procedures as roadblocks and causing delays in investments.[10] In its approach for process related reforms, the National Environment Policy, 2006 recorded that "The recommendations of the (The Govindarajan Committee) which identified delays in environment and forest clearances as the largest source of delays in in development projects, will be followed for reviewing the existing procedures for granting clearances and other approvals under various statutes and rules."[11] This issue of environmental procedures delaying economic projects re-emerged before the 2014 general elections with manifestoes of leading political parties assuring policy reforms including for "ease of doing business".

In 2014, when the new National Democratic Alliance (NDA) government led by the Bhartiya Janata Party (BJP) came to power the regulatory firewall was already considerably thin. Several exemptions from and exceptions to the approval processes were already in place[12_13] and there existed a feeble monitoring protocol[14] to ensure compliance with environmental safeguards. Within months, the incumbent government set in place two high level committees[15-16] to recommend changes to all major environmental laws except the Wild Life Protection Act. These committees presented proposals and recommendations for lowering the standards for environmental scrutiny in several ways. They emphasised on the enforcement of environmental safeguards through the principle of "utmost good faith", i.e. a belief in the inherent goodness of project authorities to abide by the law and that in case of a breach, the violator could be penalised through monetary fines.

This new phase of environment regulation also focused on regularizing projects operating in violation of prior environmental approvals. In 2017, the Union Environment Ministry rolled out an amnesty scheme for all projects operating in violation of the environment and forest approvals. This resulted in a process set up to review over three thousand proposals and regularize their operations. A special expert committee was set up to review proposals, and regularize their operations through a payment of compensation and additional environment management measures. This process, which was to be a one-time measure with a six month window, became a routine affair within the ministry. It has continued to be in operation till June 2021. Even though this process was in existence for three years prior to the Covid-19, it became a flashpoint when three massive industrial accidents took place in April and May 2020, at projects operating without environment approvals (Nandi, 2020a).[17] There was massive public outcry when a draft notification proposed amendments to the environment clearance process which included the regularization of violations.[18-19]

SECTION 2: CHANGES TO ENVIRONMENTAL REGULATION DURING COVID-19

The nation-wide lockdown was announced on March 23, 2020 with the justification that National Disaster Management Authority (NDMA) was *"satisfied that the country is threatened with the spread of COVID-19 epidemic."*[20] The lockdown meant:

- All state and regional institutions regulating environmental impacts or engaged in forest, wildlife management officially stopped operations as government offices including social justice departments were allowed to function with "bare minimum staff" [21]
- All Courts, the National Green Tribunal[22], State-Level Pollution Appellate Authorities announced adjournment and postponement of hearings.
- Meetings of Expert committees looking at environmental approvals and project violations were deferred for at least ten days (Press Trust of India, 2020a)[23] and then set up as virtual meetings.
- Central Pollution Control Board issued various guidelines including those for "Handling, Treatment and Disposal of Waste Generated during Treat-

ment/Diagnosis/ Quarantine of Covid-19 Patients". These guidelines were sent to all SPCBs.

Within four days of the first national lockdown in the first wave, offices of the forest department particularly required for wildlife patrolling, managing forest fires and plantations, were included in the essential services exemptions. However, wildlife conservation organisations reported that poaching and illegal wildlife trade doubled between March-June 2020[24] (Traffic, 2020).

Even as environmental institutions were non-functional and grievance redressal mechanisms were closed, *"manufacturing of drugs, pharmaceutical, medical devices, their raw material & intermediates"* and *"coal and mineral production, transportation, supply of explosives and activities incidental to mining operations"*, power plants and ports were allowed to function as "essential services" during the lockdown. Public and private sector companies were required to follow Covid-appropriate protocol (Ministry of Coal, 2020)[25]. But the compliance with the same could not be monitored and the Covid-19 challenged district administration was stretched beyond capacity to enforce the norms. There was no regulatory oversight available to adhere to project-level environmental conditions and parameters (Kohli et al, 2020)[26]. Reports from different parts of the country linked this lack of institutional oversight to violations of environmental safeguards and increased health risks including to the Covid-19 pandemic (Krishna Chaitanya, 2020)[27] .

The response to this chaos caused by unregulated industrial activity differed from State to State. In the first few phases of the lockdown, State governments did not have flexibility to design Covid-19 protocols that were different from those prescribed by the Central government. So there were no directions to resume the functions of environmental institutions, especially in areas where large-scale industrial operations and mineral extraction transportation were being carried out undeterred. Some State -level politicians and the State governments took notice of news reports and directed that special care be taken to curtail violations and not increase risks (Press Trust of India, 2020b)[28]. In effect there was a complete breakdown of the limited regulatory architecture entrusted with the responsibility of monitoring the compliance with environmental safeguards.

Lowered legal standards for project approvals

Immediately after the announcement of the March 2020 lockdown, India's environment regulatory framework was ostensibly adapted to Covid-19 restrictions and protocols. But in effect, a number of substantive and procedural changes were made that lowered the already weak legal standards and procedures for project approvals. Some immediate changes were:

EXEMPTION FROM ENVIRONMENTAL APPROVALS: On March 27, the environment ministry recategorized *"Projects or activities in respect of bulk drugs and intermediates manufactured for addressing ailments such as Novel Corona Virus (COVID- 19) and those with similar symptoms"*. This allowed the environment ministry to grant quick approvals to these projects without environment impact assessments or public hearings.

VIRTUAL APPRAISALS AND APPROVALS: Expert and Advisory committees tasked with scrutinizing environment, forests and wildlife-related approvals started meeting virtually to review projects.[29] Some of these meetings lasted only ten minutes and others went up to five hours.[30] However, approvals were granted to several high profile and controversial projects including for the construction of the new Parliament building in New Delhi, new hydro power projects in North East India (Nandi, 2020b)[31] and the Statue of Unity in Gujarat (Gokhale, 2020)[32]. None of these activities were in the MHA's list of essential services (Nandi, 2020c)[33]. An office memorandum was issued in November 2020, emphasized that EAC meetings should be held twice a month to avoid any delays in approvals.[34] In April 2020 the Standing Committee of the National Board for Wild Life (NBWL) approved infrastructure projects that could affect wildlife habitats, through its "first ever video-conferencing meet" (Koshy, 2021)[35].

Table 2: Number of Expert or Advisory Committee virtual meetings between November 2018-February 2020

Environment Clearance (EACs)	Forest Clearance (FAC)
135	17

Source: Authors

Table 3: Number of Expert or Advisory Committee virtual meetings between March 2020-june 2021

Environment Clearance (EACs)	Forest Clearance (FAC)
216	18

Source: Authors

- EXTENSION OF POLLUTION CONSENTS AND ENVIRONMENT CLEARANCES: State Pollution Control Boards gave three-month extensions to the "Consent to Operate" to all industries, irrespective of whether they were in Ministry of Home Affairs' list of essential services. The reasons included the need to allow for uninterrupted operations and inability to "process some applications for renewal."[36] The Ministry of Environment, Forests and Climate Change (MoEFCC) also issued an Office Memorandum (OM) to extend the validity of ECs expiring between March 15 2020 and April 30 April, 2020 till June 30, 2020.[37] This Office Memorandum specifically cited *"the outbreak of Corona Virus (COVID-19) and subsequent lockout declared"* as its justification.

- CANCELLATION OF PUBLIC HEARINGS AND VIRTUAL PUBLIC HEARINGS: Several State Pollution Control Boards entrusted with the task to conduct public hearings as part of the environment clearance process, postponed or cancelled them citing Covid-19 reasons. Applications for these projects could not be scrutinized under the EIA notification, 2006 until these hearings were conducted. In response, there were demands from project proponents that these public hearings be conducted through virtual mode[38] (Press Trust of India, 2021). Project-affected communities and environmental groups objected to this and protested (Nandi, 2020d)[39] and initiated litigation (Plumber, 2020)[40] challenging the public hearings held during the Covid-19 pandemic and the holding of virtual public hearings as they were not effective to ensure public participation.

The environment ministry issued executive orders that allowed for the virtual implementation of regulatory procedures like expert committee meetings and public hearings in a manner that did not have meaningful use. These clarifications or legal changes were issued on a monthly basis either through OMs, executive orders or through amendments of Environment Protection Rules. In all cases these amendments were given effect by exercising legal clauses that allow dispensing the requirement of public comments citing "public interest". [41]

During this time the environment ministry gave environment clearances to hundreds of projects, and approved forest diversion proposals of vast areas. Independent studies have pointed to the scale and impact of these approvals both on forest rights and wildlife protection (Pinjarkar, 2021)[42], (Sharma, 2021)[43]. During the lockdown, expert committees recommended approvals to 120 projects, a quarter of which were located in Constitutionally recognized Fifth Schedule areas where *Adivasi* communities reside.[44] Another study shows that in 2020, the wildlife board approved the use of 1792 hectares of wildlife habitat for 48 projects, most of which were for linear projects like roads and transmission lines.[45] (Mohan, 2021).

While the Central government paid so much attention to granting project clearances through the Covid lockdown even to non essential projects and activities, three accidents within the first three months of the Covid lockdown highlighted the effects of the failures of this weakened environmental regulatory architecture.

On April 10, the dyke of a coal ash pond of the Sasan Ultra Mega Power Project in Singrauli, Madhya Pradesh, collapsed. This plant is considered to be one of the largest integrated power projects in the world. This collapse swept away six people, two of whom were reported to be dead. The slurry from the ash pond contaminated nearby agricultural fields. (Menon et al, 2020)[46] . Local villagers had complained that the plant was operating without adherence to pollution control and dyke maintenance procedures. The district administration had routinely issued notices against non-compliance but the project operations and pollution control consent had neither been suspended or revoked. In its letter and notice dated April 13, the Madhya Pradesh pollution control board observed that the breach had occurred due to uncontrolled discharge without adhering to the safeguard conditions listed in the pollution consent (Dutta, 2020)[47].

In the early morning hours of May 7, 2020, villagers living around the LG Polymers industrial plant in Vishakhapatnam smelt a toxic gas leak. Inhaling colourless and inflammable styrene monomer gas allegedly led to the death of 12 people and over 50 people were hospitalized. News reports indicate that *"over 2000 people were evacuated between 5 a.m. and 9 a.m"*. The joint committee of the National Green Tribunal (NGT) observed that the leak could have been a result of faults caused while the plant was shut during the nationwide lockdown and a chemical reaction that would have occurred in the storage tank when the operations restarted (Bhattacharjee, 2020)[48]. The investigations also brought to light that the plant had expanded its operations without seeking mandatory environment clearance. The Company had admitted to the same in its application while seeking post facto regularization of the violation. The decision on this was pending when the gas leak took place. Neither the state regulatory authority nor the MoEFCC had restrained its expanded operations, till the breach took place.

On May 27, an oil well belonging to Oil India Limited (OIL) blew out in a small village near Dibru Saikhowa National Park and the Maguri Motapung beel in Tinsukia, Assam. Soon after on June 9, a fire broke out at the oil well risking lives of the surrounding villages and threatening the biodiversity of the Dibru-Saikhowa National Park (Madhusudhan and Bindra, 2020)49. This incident brought to light that in 2016, OIL had requested for an exemption from conducting a public hearing for further exploration of hydrocarbons in the National Park. The reason cited for this request was conflicts with the local population. This environment ministry's expert committee permitted OIL this request stating that OIL had held a hearing for setting up one of its oil wells five years ago, and therefore the concerns of the local population are on record (Kalita, 2020)[50]. After this explosion, two erstwhile members of the standing committee of the NBWL disclosed that during their site visit to assess the OIL's proposal for laying a crude oil pipeline they found that the company had "already completed most of the pipeline-laying work, leaving only a small unfinished stretch across the Dibru river and Maguri beel.". In their article in *The Wire* the two members stated they had reported the matter to the environment ministry and sought that this be reported to the Supreme Court. They wrote, " the NBWL and other regulatory bodies are routinely presented with such *fait accompli*" situations Madhusudhan and Bindra, 2020)[51]. It took until November 2020 for the fire to be controlled, but the impacts were being felt by the villages well into 2021 (Mondal, 2021)[52]. Recent reports indicate that the biodiversity loss from the blowout could take atleast a decade to recover (Goswami and Ghosh, 2021)[53]

Post-Covid-19 Economic Revival and Environmental Regulation

Months before the second wave hit India, India was celebrating its victory over the pandemic. The lockdown was lifted and the focus shifted to state level electoral politics and economic revival even as the vaccine production and vaccination of the population was ridden with challenges. Many countries in the world started implementing Covid-19 economic stimulus packages amidst the demands from environmental institutions to "build back better" (OECD, 2020; UN Department of Economic and Social Affairs. 2020)[54]. But India remained fixated with a V-shaped recovery.

In May 2020, the Union Finance Minister, Nirmala Sitaraman delivered a five-part presentation on a plan for economic revival through the government's *Atmanirbhar (self-reliance)* Package. India's first economic recovery proposal did not involve corporate bail outs at the scale of some Western countries and it failed to put money in the hands of the poor or provide for the needs of large sections of unemployed people. But the Central government pushed for more environmentally damaging mining and infrastructure projects as these were seen as a palliative for the economy. The Covid relief package rearticulated support for the expansion of airports, ports and highways and greater privatisation of the mining sector for which legal reforms were introduced in mid-March[55].

The March 2020 Mineral Laws (Amendment) Act, 2020 & Coal Mines (Special Provisions) Act, 2020 had already set the stage for the fresh auctions for 41 new coal blocks by Prime Minister Narendra Modi, in June 2020 (Ministry of Coal, 2020)[56]. These amendments introduced the concept of *"pre-embedded clearances,"*[57] *allowing for* automatic transfer of environment and forest clearances to new allottees of coal mines for two years. In March 2021, the government also enacted The Mines and Minerals (Development and Regulation) Amendment Act , 2021[58] to encourage commercial mining by removing restrictions on specifying the end use of mined ore (Grover, 2021)[59]. It also allowed the Central government to intervene and auction mines if "state governments face challenges in conducting auction or fail to conduct it". The Act also sought to ease transfer of mines from old owners to the new successful bidders, with an assurance to address legacy issues including that of taxation, stamp duties, etc (Mishra, 2021)[60]. India's push for new coal projects through these amendments and justification for the economic recovery would result in more carbon emissions.

In August 2020, the Ministry of Road Transport and Highways issued a press release to announce that the Covid-19 outbreak had not slowed down highway expansion. In fact the National Highway Authority of India (NHAI) would exceed its target for construction of 4500 km of highways during 2020-21. The press release stated, *"Despite challenges due to the outbreak of the novel coronavirus pandemic, the National Highways Authority of India (NHAI) has awarded highest length of projects during FY 2020-21 till date as compared to the projects awarded during same period in last three years."* 26 new projects of 744 km length were awarded with the capital cost of *"over Rs 31,000 crore, which includes cost of civil construction, land acquisition, and other pre- construction activities"* (Ministry of Road Transport & Highways. 2020)[61].

These announcements established that the Central government would continue to focus on opening up new and greenfield areas for mining and related infrastructure expansion.

In 2021, the Central government's economic revival plans involved the takeover of India's most ecologically fragile coastal and island ecosystems, in particular the Lakshadweep and Andaman and Nicobar group of Islands. Plans for tourism and port infrastructure in the two islands had been envisioned even prior to the Covid-19 pandemic. Niti Aayog, India's highest planning body, had released a Vision Document back in May 2019 for *'Transforming the Islands with Creativity and Innovation'*. The vision document build the justification for the creation of Exclusive Economic Zones, deep sea mining, trans-shipment terminals and tourism (Niti Ayog, 2019)[62]. During the first wave of the Covid-19 pandemic the implementation of this vision was delayed.

The big push for these proposals came once again through the announcements in the 2021 Budget. Infrastructure projects, in particular national highways and ports, were the important focus of this budget. The budget offered to spend big on infrastructure which spans across roads, power generation, bridges, ports & so on (Kumar, 2021)[63]. Several of these projects were justified for the creation of livelihoods for coastal communities (Chandrababu, 2021)[64]

In the last quarter of 2020, the NITI Aayog, issued a request for proposals (RfP) to select a technical consultant to prepare a Master Plan for "holistic development of Great Nicobar Island" (Press Trust of India, 2020c)[65]. In the first half of 2021 news about the "Rs 75,000 crore plan that includes an international container trans shipment terminal, a greenfield international airport, a power plant and a township complex" (Sekhsaria, 2021a)[66] emerged. Before that in early January 2021, the Standing Committee of the National Board for Wildlife (NBWL) *"denotified the entire Galathea Bay Wildlife Sanctuary to allow for the port there"* (Sekhsaria, 2021b)[67].

By mid 2021 the environment ministry had started receiving proposals to grant environment coastal regulation zone and wildlife related approvals for "luxury tents and resorts on some islands; two water aerodrome projects in Shaheed and Swaraj islands (formerly Neil and Havelock islands, respectively); two major township and area development projects on the Great Nicobar Island and Little Andaman, one of which is also likely to involve denotification of a tribal reserve" (Nandi, 2021a)[68-69]

During the peak of the second wave, the Central government announced several administrative measures "for large-scale beachside tourism and infrastructure development" in the Lakshadweep Archipalego (Shaji, 2021)[70]. This included the controversial draft Lakshadweep Development Authority Regulation 2021 (LDAR), which gave the newly appointed administrator of the Union Territory powers to acquire land and remove or relocate islanders from their property for town planning or development purposes. This led to local protests by the Islanders, demanding the removal of the newly appointed administrator and the withdrawal of the draft LDAR (Unnithan, 2021)[71].

Environmental regulatory changes to approve these projects at a greater pace and scale were a necessary part of this plan. The regulatory apparatus for project approvals was set up to conduct virtual meetings and Covid-defined protocols were already in place for carrying out approval linked public hearings. At the Central level the expert committees met routinely and approved projects in every meeting (Dutta, 2021)[72] ((Nandi, 2021b)[73].

The Central government also continued with the process of overhauling environment law reforms and introduced fresh proposals. Some of these included:

- *Review of Draft Environment Impact Assessment (EIA) Notification 2020:* The ministry appointed NEERI-CSIR to review the two million (Biswas, 2020)[74] comments received for the draft EIA, 2020. While the ministry held back the issuance of the final notification, office memorandums and circulars were routinely issued to introduce changes to the environment clearance regime.
- *New Environment Management Law:* The ministry appointed consultants to design a new environment management law merging the three central

level environment laws, i.e. Air Act, 1981, Water Act, 1974 and EPA, 1986.

- *Amendments to the Indian Forest Act:* In April 2021, the ministry issued an Office Memorandum inviting proposals for the amendment of the Indian Forest Act, 1927 (Nandi, 2021c)[75]. This law governs the reservation and protection of forest lands by forest departments and regulates the collection, use and transit of forest produce.

The effects of the breakdown of institutional response to manage environment impacts continued to show. The Covid-19 protocols designed to facilitate unhindered functioning of economic sectors without any attention to environmental monitoring and mitigation resulted in serious local conflicts.

- In Odisha there were major street protests against unregulated transportation of minerals and inter-State movement of trucks through village roads. The inability of district authorities and pollution control boards restraint incessant dust from transportation led to violent protests (Menon, 2021) [76].

- Adivasi communities in Gujarat took to the streets to protest at a public hearing being organised as part of the environment clearance process world's biggest zinc smelter complex in Tapi, Gujarat. According to news reports the project affected people demanded that the public hearing be deferred/postponed (Times News Network, 2021[77]. Officials incharge of the public hearing told the media that they had planned to "take complaints from 200 people at a time due to Covid protocols However, those who came first and made submissions did not leave. This caused the crowds to swell " (Express News Service, 2021)[78].

- In Karnataka, hundreds of fishermen jumped into the sea demanding that the construction of a port- linked road be stopped (Express News Service, 2021)[79]. The fisherfolk had written to the district administration that demolition activity not be undertaken in the light of the Covid-19 pandemic and also the pendency of court proceedings related to environmental approvals.

SECTION 3: RECOMMENDATIONS FOR A POST-COVID ENVIRONMENTAL REGULATION

India's economic growth policies have been based on large-scale resource grabs, lowering environmental regulatory standards for projects and condoning their environmental violations, increasing economic and social inequality and putting poor people, especially natural resource dependent people, workers and children at risk to the impacts of environmental degradation and climate change. The environmental regulatory framework has come undone through years of political posturing on environmental matters while prioritizing natural resource extraction for private capitalist growth. But the Covid pandemic has just shown us all that environmental and health protection for all is in private and public interest. Ecologists have argued that the modern world has invited this covid pandemic with its nature damaging policies and that we have not seen the last of these. They have also warned that the singular focus on vaccination to protect humanity from pandemics is like "treating the symptoms without addressing the underlying cause" (Tollefson 2020)[80]. We may all not agree that environmental degradation was responsible for the pandemic and therefore the need of the hour is to restore nature. But many may agree with Professor Bruno Latour that this frightening form of nature is already within us and therefore we can only manage our present condition. Irrespective of what approach we take to guard ourselves and be prepared against future pandemics, a different approach to environmental regulation would be helpful towards this effort.

To make our environmental response matter to this threat of pandemics that we face as humanity, it is necessary to reorient environmental regulations to the objectives of public health and safety rather than to more economic growth. Until now, environmental laws and policies may have given some consideration to economic livelihoods that are based on natural resources[81] but the role of environmental regulations in actively preventing death and disease and in enhancing public health and safety is largely ignored. This has resulted in huge numbers of industrial and mining accidents, man-made disasters and chronic illnesses such as cancers and respiratory diseases and deaths among certain sections of the population. These were accepted as the costs of development and economic growth. Now, having experienced the health and economic catastrophe of the pandemic at a global scale, it would be sensible to not overlook the potential of environmental regulation to protect public health and to prevent making populations already exposed to the covid pandemic more vulnerable due to air pollution and other forms of environmental degradation. If forest conservation, coastal and marine regulation, infrastructure expansions and land use changes are to be measured against these metrics, we could expect different forms of impact assessments and regulatory decisions.

Environmental regulations can play a major role in reducing and preventing more deforestation, habitat fragmentation and rapid land use change. Regulatory decisions could not only help us move away from development projects that result in these forms of environmental impacts but new regulatory procedures could also establish the significance of setting up of long-term conservation projects with environmental justice as the organizing principle.

These regulations need to be mainstreamed into economic sectors to ensure that society's needs of affordable housing, water, sanitation and food are met with by enhancing natural ecologies rather than disrupting them. India's development effects has been extremely lopsided as it has taken resources from rural, forest dependent and urban worker communities and provided them to a small section of caste and class privileged Indians. As a result we have not only lost precious natural resources but also widened the gap between the rich and poor. Social and economic inequality is a huge threat in itself to the wellbeing of our society. It is necessary now more than ever to design environmental and other sectoral policies and processes that reduce inequality in material terms.

The progressive policy principles of transparency and public participation have nearly disappeared from environmental regulations in the last two decades. This is despite a growing interest among affected communities to engage with regulatory processes to influence decisions and obtain remedies for project impacts. During the covid pandemic too, when public participation was nearly impossible, there were a number of mobilisations through social media to demand better environmental policies and resist the dilution of environmental standards to accommodate the central government's economic plans. The mobilisation of 2 million responses to the draft EIA 2020 is symbolic of the heightened public sentiment in favour of environmental issues in the context of the covid pandemic and climate change. Environmental regulations need to provide ample opportunities for deliberative processes and public participation so that ecologists, health professionals, scientists and economists can ideally work together to confront environmental threats like pandemics.

The Covid pandemic and its impacts on human systems and institutions should be seen as a wake up call to governments, environmental institutions and civil society that we cannot unreflexively go back to old positions or demands. While there was plenty wrong with India's environmental regulations even before covid, the new norms and procedures that we set up to respond to future threats should prioritise planetary wellbeing over economic growth (Table 4 and Table 5). This requires us to build deeper connections between environmental sustainability principles and democratic institutions of governance.

Table 4: Key changes to the environment, forest, wildlife clearance and pollution consent procedures between March 2020-December 2020

	Environment Clearance (EC)	**Forest Clearance (FC)**	**Pollution Consents (CTO)**	**Wildlife Clearance (WC)**
March 2020	25.3.2020 [EC] Extension of validity of ECs expiring between 15 March-30 April extended till June 30, 2020 28.3.2020 [EC] and 31.3.2020 [FC]_ Amendment to allowing for new mine owners to apply for environment clearance within two years. No time frame specified for grant of EC. This amendment was introduced to align with concept of "Pre-embedded clearances" introduced through Mineral Laws (Amendment) Act, 2020. The amendment also allows already mined out material to be evacuated and transported by previous lease owner, and will not be part of the mine capacity of new bidder.		31.3.2020: Several pollution control boards including Punjab, Odisha, Karnataka ?? gave three month extension to industries to whose pollution related Consent to Operate were expiring in end March 2020	No specific legal changes or procedural reforms. However, several proposals for the denotification of wild life sanctuaries and national parks protected were denotified or under consideration for denotification as (ref ???) . These proposals were linked with projects in the A&N islands, etc etc.??
April 2020	29.4.2021 Office Memorandum (OM) on the reconciliation of *"Pre-embedded clearances"* for EC and FC with mining law amendments			
May 2020	14.5.2020: OM allowing for change of calendar plan for mining *(coal and non-coal)* activity based on previous which EC. No fresh EC required for change.			
	21.5.2020 Amendment to the Environment Protection Rules, 1986 related to washing of coal. The MoEFCC replaced the January 2014 notification that required TPPs to use of coal that has less than 34% ash content. TPP were allowed to use low-grade Indian coal that produces more fly ash. But, TPPs will have to comply with emission norms, fly ash utilisation norms and use transportation with safeguards or means that are less polluting.			

June 2020	16.6.2020: Launch of Single Window clearance portal of EC, FC, CTE/CTO applications for *"transparent, technology driven & non-intrusive monitoring system"*			
July 2020		27.7.2020: Exemption from compensatory afforestation for laying of underground Optical Fiber Cables (OFC), telephone lines, drinking water supply pipelines, electricity cables, CNG/PNG and Slurry pipelines within the RoW of existing roads *(with conditions)*		
August 2020		9.8.2020 MoEF-CC agrees to the request of Ministry of Mines for lump sum payment of NPV by the user agency up to March 31, 2021 or within two months from the time COVID pandemic ends, whichever is earlier. 12.8.2020: Central Government power to reject FC proposal if response to additional information not received within 90 days		

		18.8.2020: MoEFCC allows for dispensation of Compensatory Afforestation (CA) land on double the degraded forest land instead of equivalent non-forest land for the National Highways projects irrespective of the User Agency. This is for Central Sector Projects where the project is owned, developed and maintained by Central Government but the execution is carried out by a state agency.		
September 2020	14.9.2020: OM on public hearing protocol during Covid *(more than one PH with ceiling of 100 people, use of virtual platforms)*			
November 2020	11.11.2020: OM allows TPPs to change source of coal without an amendment to the EC 12.11.2020: OM clarifies that if PH for a project is exempt as per EIA Notification, no additional Public Hearing in cases where project is in violation of EIA notification, 2006			

Table 5: Key changes to the environment, forest, wildlife clearance and pollution consent procedures between January-June 2021

	Environment and CRZ/IPZ Clearance (EC)	Forest Clearance (FC)	Pollution Consents (CTO)	Wildlife Clearance (WC)
January 2021	28.1.2021: Expansion of distillery units for production of Ethanol intended for blending with petrol to be considered as B2 projects (no EIA or public hearing) provided there is a certificate from any competent authority certifying this end use.			
February 2021	16.2.2021: OM no additional Public Hearing for "legacy cases" mining projects where EC was granted for 5 years under EIA 1994 19.2.2021: OM laying out procedure for dealing with violations arising due to not obtaining a prior CRZ clearance for permissible activities. Application for post facto approval to be made to the MoEFCC along with a the assessment and recommendation of the State Coastal Zone Management Authority			

<table>
<tr><td>March 2021</td><td>2.3.2021: Amendment to EIA notification granting exemption from EC for a project where there is a change in change in product mix/ capacity and where the project proponent can self certify that there will be “no increase in pollution load”</td><td>22.3.2021 State governments cannot impose additional conditions after Stage I (in principle) FC by central government</td><td></td><td></td></tr>
<tr><td>April 2021</td><td colspan="3">1.4.2021: Amendment to Environment Protection Rules related to compliance of TPPs with emission standards. Timelines for compliance expended timeline extended till 2022 for TPPs within 10km from NCR or non-attainment cities with population of 10 lakhs+. Extension till 2023 for TPPs in “non attainment” cities and within 10 km of critically polluted areas) or December 2024 for others.

22.4.2021: Draft Flyash Utlisation Notification opened for public comments. The modifications include allowance to TPPs to dispose flyash upto 300 km. Time frame to address “Legacy” flyash concerns within 10 years. Introduction of a new system of fines to be collected by the CPCB and used for environment restoration in case of violations.</td><td></td></tr>
<tr><td>May 2021</td><td></td><td>10.5.2021: Guidelines to Regional Offices to expedite forest clearances for “critical infrastructure projects” LWE districts and those related to defence and security in border areas</td><td></td><td></td></tr>
<tr><td>June 2021</td><td>9.6.2021: Inclusion of a central government institution for approving the extraction of sand from ICRZB areas in Lakshwadeep and A&N Islands</td><td></td><td></td><td></td></tr>
</table>

ENDNOTES

1. Tollefson, Jeff. 2020. *Why deforestation and extinctions make pandemics more likely* accessed from https://www.nature.com/articles/d41586-020-02341-1 on January 9, 2022

2. Jameel, Shahid, 2020. On Ecology and Environment as drivers of human disease and pandemics, ORF Issue Brief, Issue No 388. July 2020.

3. Jefferson, Brandie. 2020. Pollution and pandemics: A dangerous mix, accessed from https://source.wustl.edu/2020/11/pollution-and-pandemics-a-dangerous-mix/ on January 9, 2022

4. Watts, Jonathan.2020. *Bruno Latour: 'This is a global catastrophe that has come from within, accessed from* https://www.theguardian.com/world/2020/jun/06/bruno-latour-coronavirus-gaia-hypothesis-climate-crisis on January 9, 2022

5. Wittenberg-Cox, Avivah.2020. *5 Economists Redefining... Everything. Oh Yes, And They're Women, accessed from* https://www.forbes.com/sites/avivahwittenbergcox/2020/05/31/5-economists-redefining-everything--oh-yes-and-theyre-women/?sh=3e5a9831714a on January 9, 2022

6. Boehnert, Joanna. 2018. *Anthropocene Economics and Design: Heterodox Economics for Design Transitions,* She Ji: The Journal of Design, Economics, and Innovation, Volume 4, Issue 4, 2018, Pages 355-374, Accessed from https://www.sciencedirect.com/science/article/pii/S2405872618300856 on January 9, 2022

7. MoEFCC Circular No. J-11013/6/2010-1A.II (Part) regarding Environmental Clearance to the expansion projects / activities under the EIA Notification, 2006 - Certified Compliance Report regarding dated 7 September 2017

8. Kothari, Ashish. 2004. Draft National Environment Policy 2004: A Critique. Economic and Political Weekly ,Vol. 39, No. 43 (Oct. 23-29, 2004), pp. 4723-4727

9. Menon, Manju and Kohli, Kanchi. 2009. From Impact Assessment to Clearance Manufacture, Economic and Political Weekly, Vol. 44, Issue No. 28, 11 Jul, 2009

10. GoI (2002): Report on Reforming Investment Approval and Implementation Procedure (Part II), Government of India, New Delhi.

11. Ministry of Environment and Forests, National Environment Policy, 2006, Government of India, New Delhi

12. Goswami, Urmi. 2014. Environment Minister Veerappa Moily to focus on forest clearance system
accessed from
https://economictimes.indiatimes.com/news/economy/policy/environment-minister-veerappa-moily-to-focus-on-forest-clearance-system/articleshow/28812755.cms?utm_source=contentofinterest&utm_medium=text&utm_campaign=cppst on August 13, 2021

13. Kohli, K. and M. Menon. 2005. Eleven Years of the Environment Impact Assessment Notification, 1994. Kalpavriksh, Just Environment Trust, Environment Justice Initiative (HRLN). pp 94

14. Menon, Manju and Kohli, Kanchi. 2019. Regulatory Reforms to Address Environmental Non-Compliance IN Policy Challenges 2019-2024: The Key Policy Questions for the New Government and Possible Pathways, Centre for Policy Research, New Delhi

15. Ministry of Environment Forests and Climate Change (2015), "Report of the Committee to Review the issues relating to the Coastal Regulation Zone, 2011

16. Ministry of Environment, Forest and Climate Change Office Memorandum (OM) No. 22-15/2014-IA.III dated 29th August, 2014

17. Nandi, Jayashree. 2020a. *Vizag polymer unit didn't have environmental nod, accessed from* https://www.hindustantimes.com/india-news/vizag-polymer-unit-didn-t-have-environmental-nod/story-CSMrE8I36C3k5T-TR2fVsDM.html on January 9, 2022

18. EIA Legitimised Environmental Destruction. Now, Govt 'Renovates' it for the Worst, https://science.thewire.in/environment/eia-2020-environmental-degradation-draft/

19. The Draft EIA Notification, 2020: Reduced Regulations and Increased Exemptions Part I & II, Centre for Policy Research, https://www.cprindia.org/research/reports/draft-eia-notification-2020-reduced-regulations-and-increased-exemptions-part-i-ii

20. Ministry of Home Affairs Order No. No. 40-3/2020-DM-l(A) Government of India dated March 23, 2020

21. Addendum to Guidelines annexed to the Ministry of Home Affairs Order No. 40-3/2020-DM-l(A) dated March 24, 2020

22. NATIONAL GREEN TRIBUNAL PRINCIPAL BENCH Circular dated March 31, 2020

23. Press Trust of India.2020a. *Coronavirus: Environment Ministry suspends meetings of its green panel till March 31,* accessed from https://www.business-standard.com/article/pti-stories/coronavirus-environment-ministry-suspends-meetings-of-its-green-panel-till-march-31-120032100155_1.html on January 9, 2022

24. Traffic. 2020. *Indian wildlife amidst the COVID-19 crisis accessed from* https://www.traffic.org/publications/reports/reported-wildlife-poaching-in-india-more-than-doubles-during-covid-19-lockdown/ on January 8, 2021

25. Ministry of Coal. 2020. *Ministry of Coal working to ensure maintenance of critical coal supplies during the COVID-19 lockdown period: Pralhad Joshi accessed from* https://pib.gov.in/PressReleasePage.aspx?PRID=1608754 on July 7, 2021

26. **Kohli, Kanchi, Nayak Sampada and Dora, Santosh.** 2020. *Has the coronavirus lockdown increased health risks in mining areas?, accessed from* https://en.gaonconnection.com/has-the-lockdown-increased-health-risks-in-mining-areas/ on January 9, 2022

27. Krishna Chaitanya, SV. 2020. *Tamil Nadu: Pollution puts Ennore locals at risk of COVID-19 pandemic?, accesse from* https://www.newindianexpress.com/cities/chennai/2020/apr/12/tamil-nadu-pollution-puts-ennore-locals-at-risk-of-covid-19-pandemic-2128940.html on January 9, 2022

28. Press Trust of India. 2020b. *12% population in polluted Korba industrial area highly vulnerable to COVID-19: Chh"garh minister, accessed from* https://www.outlookindia.com/newsscroll/12-population-in-polluted-korba-industrial-area-highly-vulnerable-to-covid19-chhgarh-minister/1797983 on January 9, 2022

29. The meeting agenda and minutes recorded, "*meeting of the Expert Appraisal Committee (EAC) for coal mining projects was held on 17th April, 2020 through video conferencing with support NIC team due to Covid-19 lockdown.*"

30. Analysis by Aditi Pinto and Van Adhikar Media Team How The Government Diluted Forest Rights Of Adivasis During Lockdown available on https://behanbox.com/2020/07/20/how-the-government-of-india-used-the-lockdown-to-dilute-the-forest-rights-of-communities-voices-of-the-people-affected-by-coal-mining-projects/

31. Nandi, Jayashree. 2020b. 2.7 lakh trees to be felled for hydropower project in Arunachal's Dibang Valley, accessed from https://www.hindustantimes.com/india-news/2-7-lakh-trees-to-be-felled-for-hydropower-project-in-arunachal-s-dibang-valley/story-i0GVuHt8nHF4JbxeM4birM.html on January 9, 2022

32. Gokhale, Nihar.2020. *Despite COVID lockdown, environment ministry's expert panels race to clear projects, accessed from* https://india.mongabay.com/2020/05/despite-covid-lockdown-environment-ministrys-expert-panels-race-to-clear-projects/ on January 9, 2022

33. Nandi, Jayashree. 2020c. Environment ministry on project clearance spree, activists wary, accessed from https://www.hindustantimes.com/india-news/environment-ministry-on-project-clearance-spree-activists-wary/story-vv0oGyPPmtPlL6E8mIpZMJ.html on January 9, 2022

34. Ministry of Environment, Forests and Climate Change Office Memorandum F. No. 22-35/2020-IA.III dated November 18, 220

35. Koshy, Jacob. 2021. Parliament proceedings | Lockdown reduced number of environment clearances, accessed from https://www.thehindu.com/sci-tech/energy-and-environment/parliament-proceedings-lockdown-reduced-number-of-environment-clearances/article34076504.ece on January 9, 2022

36. State Pollution Control, Odisha Office Order No. 4029/IND-I-CON(M)1377 dated March 31 2020

37. Ministry of Environment, Forests and Climate Change Office Memorandum F.No. 22-25/2020-IA.III dated March 25, 2020

38. Press Trust of India. 2021. *Odisha Mining industries seek public hearing through online mode,* accessed from https://www.outlookindia.com/newsscroll/odisha-mining-industries-seek-public-hearing-through-online-mode/2078655 on January 9, 2022

39. Nandi, Jayashree. 2020d. *Public hearings on crucial infrastructure projects compromised due to pandemic*, accessed from https://www.hindustantimes.com/india-news/public-hearings-on-crucial-infrastructure-projects-compromised-due-to-pandemic/story-tNFni2lJU3qXk1X1BIznLL.html on January 9, 2022

40. Plumber, Mustafa. 2020. *Law Students Move Karnataka HC Seeking To Stay Virtual EIA Public Meeting For Peripheral Ring Road Project [Read Petition], accessed from* https://www.livelaw.in/news-updates/law-students-move-karnataka-hc-seeking-to-stay-virtual-eia-public-meeting-for-peripheral-ring-road-project-163300 on January 9, 2022

41. These amendments cite "the Central Government, under sub-rule (4) of rule 5 of the Environment (Protection) Rules,1986, in public interest dispenses with the requirement of notice under clause (a) of sub-rule (3) of rule 5 of the said rules" to allow for the amendments to be issued without prior notice and seeking public comments.

42. Pinjarkar, Vijay. 2021. 'Tiger habitats overlooked in rush to grant nod for infra projects accessed from .. http://timesofindia.indiatimes.com/articleshow/84840063.cms?utm_source=contentofinterest&utm_medium=text&utm_campaign=cppst on August 14, 2021

43. Sharma, Richa. 2021. 1,800 hectare wildlife habitat diverted for infra projects in 2020: Report, accessed from https://www.newindianexpress.com/nation/2021/jun/05/1800-hectare-wildlife-habitat-diverted-for-infra-projects-in-2020-report-2312203.html on August 14, 2021

44. Analysis by Aditi Pinto and Van Adhikar Media Team How The Government Diluted Forest Rights Of Adivasis During Lockdown available on https://behanbox.com/2020/07/20/how-the-government-of-india-used-the-lockdown-to-dilute-the-forest-rights-of-communities-voices-of-the-people-affected-by-coal-mining-projects/

45. Mohan, Vishwa. 2021. *In 2020, wildlife board cleared land diversion for 48 projects*, accessed from http://timesofindia.indiatimes.com/articleshow/84129084.cms?utm_source=contentofinterest&utm_medium=text&utm_campaign=cppst on January 9, 2022

46. Menon, Manju, Gupta Debayan and Kohli, Kanchi. 2020. *The criminality of fly ash management, accessed from* https://en.gaonconnection.com/the-criminality-of-fly-ash-management/ on January 9, 2021

47. Dutta, Arup. 2020. *Fly ash slurry in Singrauli contaminates water reservoir after taking lives and homes, accessed from* https://india.mongabay.com/2020/04/fly-ash-slurry-in-singrauli-contaminates-water-reservoir-after-taking-lives-and-homes/ on January 9, 2022

48. Bhattacharjee. Sumit. 2020. *Visakhapatnam gas leak | How negligence and violations led to a deadly disaster, accessed from* https://www.thehindu.com/news/cities/Visakhapatnam/visakhapatnam-gas-leak-how-negligence-and-violations-led-to-a-deadly-disaster/article31761949.ece on January 9, 2022

49. Madhusudhan, M.D. and Bindra, Prerna Singh. 2020. *Lessons from Baghjan: India's Environmental Regulatory Processes Are Broken, accessed from* https://science.thewire.in/environment/baghjan-oil-well-national-board-for-wildlife-oil-india-limited/ on January 9, 2022

50. Kalita, Jayant. 2020. *Oil India Skipped Public Hearings Before Expanding Drilling in Assam's Baghjan, accessed from* https://thewire.in/environment/exclusive-oil-india-skipped-public-hearings-before-expanding-drilling-in-assams-baghjan on January 9, 2022

51. Madhusudhan, M.D. and Bindra, Prerna Singh. 2020. *Lessons from Baghjan: India's Environmental Regulatory Processes Are Broken, accessed from* https://science.thewire.in/environment/baghjan-oil-well-national-board-for-wildlife-oil-india-limited/ on January 9, 2022

52. Mondal, Manisha. 2021. *How villagers in Assam's Baghjan are rebuilding lives after 5-month-long oil well fire accessed from* on January 9, 2022 https://theprint.in/in-pictures/how-villagers-in-assams-baghjan-are-rebuilding-lives-after-5-month-long-oil-well-fire/619061/

53. Goswami, Roopak and Gosh Sahana. 2021. *In Assam, biodiversity loss due to the Baghjan oil blowout could take at least a decade to recover,* accessed from https://scroll.in/article/999437/in-assam-biodiversity-loss-due-to-the-baghjan-oil-blowout-could-take-at-least-a-decade-to-recover on January 9, 2022

54. OECD. 2020. Building back better: A sustainable, resilient recovery after COVID-19 accessed from https://www.oecd.org/coronavirus/policy-responses/building-back-better-a-sustainable-resilient-recovery-after-covid-19-52b869f5/ on January 9, 2022; UN Department of Economic and Social Affairs. 2020. Building back better after Covid-19 through risk-informed development cooperation, accessed from https://www.un.org/development/desa/financing/post-news/building-back-better-after-covid-19-through-risk-informed-development-cooperation on January 9, 2022

55. On March 13, 2020, the central government introduced Mineral Laws (Amendment) Act, 2020 & Coal Mines (Special Provisions) Act, 2020 which allowed for companies with no prior experience can auction for coal/lignite mining blocks. Companies did not require to disclose any end use required for coal/lignite mining.

56. Ministry of Coal . 2020. *Unleashing Coal: New Hopes for Atmanirbhar Bharat (Government of India to launch auction for commercial coal mining on 18th June 2020)*, accessed from https://pib.gov.in/PressReleasePage.aspx?PRID=1630919 on January 9, 2022

57. Ministry of Mines Order No.16/4/2020-M.VI dated June 3, 2020

58. The Mines and Minerals (Development and Regulation) Amendment Act, 2021 accessed from https://mines.gov.in/writereaddata/UploadFile/mmdr28032021.pdf on January 9, 2022

59. Gover, Samarth. 2021. *Will India Be Able to Mine Its Way to a $5 Trillion Economy?, accessed from* https://www.thequint.com/explainers/mines-and-mineral-law-explained#read-more on January 9, 2022

60. Mishra, Richa. 2021.*Mining sector — unburdening the legacy issues, accessed from* https://www.thehindubusinessline.com/opinion/mining-sector-unburdening-the-legacy-issues/article33637030.ece on January 9, 2022

61. Ministry of Road Transport & Highways. 2020. *NHAI awarded Highest Length of Projects during FY 20-21 till date as compared to last three years during the same period , accessed from* https://pib.gov.in/PressReleasePage.aspx?PRID=1650030 on July 7, 2021

62. Niti Aayog, 2019. '*Transforming the Islands with Creativity and Innovation',* Government of India, New Delhi https://niti.gov.in/sites/default/files/2019-07/Transforming-the-Islands-through-Creativity-%26-Innovation.pdf

63. Kumar, Ravi Prakash. 2021. *Union Budget: Here is a quick look at the highlights, accessed from* https://www.livemint.com/budget/news/union-budget-2021-live-updates-nirmala-fm-sitharaman-budget-speech-highlights-11612144454923.html on January 9, 2022

64. Chandrababu, Divya. 2021. *Budget 2021: Infra push, extra income for coastal communities in poll-bound TN, accessed from* https://www.hindustantimes.com/budget/budget-2021-infra-push-extra-income-for-coastal-communities-in-poll-bound-tn-101612172848268.html on January 9, 2022

65. Press Trust of India. 2020c. *Niti Aayog to hire consultants to prepare development plan for Great Nicobar, accessed from* https://economictimes.indiatimes.com/news/economy/policy/niti-aayog-to-hire-consultants-to-prepare-development-plan-for-great-nicobar/articleshow/78367382.cms?utm_source=contentofinterest&utm_medium=text&utm_campaign=cppst on January 9, 2022

66. 66 Sekhsaria. 2021a. *Mystery Deepens: NITI Aayog Says It Has No Vision Document for Great Nicobar, accessed from* https://science.thewire.in/environment/great-nicobar-island-niti-aayog-75000-crore-plan-denial-rti/ on January 9, 2022

67. Sekhsaria. 2021b. *NITI Aayog vision for Great Nicobar ignores tribal, ecological concerns, accessed from* https://www.thehindu.com/sci-tech/energy-and-environment/niti-aayog-vision-for-great-nicobar-ignores-tribal-ecological-concerns/article34120093.ece on January 9, 2022

68. Nandi, Jayashree. 2021. *Experts fear biodiversity loss in Andaman, Nicobar Islands, accessed from* https://www.hindustantimes.com/india-news/experts-fear-biodiversity-loss-in-andaman-nicobar-islands-101622415141217.html on January 9, 2022

69. MINUTES OF 61st MEETING OF THE STANDING COMMITTEE OF NATIONAL BOARD FOR WILD LIFE HELD ON 18th FEBRUARY, 2021 http://forestsclearance.nic.in/writereaddata/Order_and_Release/3119125812141Minutes61stSCNBWL.pdf on January 9, 2022

70. Shaji, K.A. 2021. *The development plan that could end up sinking Lakshadweep islands, accessed from* https://india.mongabay.com/2021/06/the-development-plan-that-could-end-up-sinking-lakshadweep-islands/

71. Unnithan, P S Gopikrishnan. 2021. *Lakshadweep residents on hunger strike to protest against draft regulations, accessed from* https://www.indiatoday.in/india/story/lakshadweep-residents-hunger-strike-protest-praful-khoda-patel-1811900-2021-06-07 on January 9, 2022

72. Dutta, Anisha. 2021. *PM house in new Central Vista given green clearance, accessed from* https://www.hindustantimes.com/cities/delhi-news/central-vista-v-p-pm-residences-to-be-ready-by-2022-101620026340743.html on January 9, 2022

73. Nandi, Jayashree.2021b. *Centre allows expansion of Odisha's Kulda coal mine despite air pollution fears, accessed from* https://www.hindustantimes.com/india-news/centre-allows-expansion-of-odisha-s-kulda-coal-mine-despite-air-pollution-fears-101613187028676.html **on January 9, 2022**

74. Biswas, Soutik, 2020.*The environment law that mobilised two million Indians, , accessed from* https://www.bbc.com/news/world-asia-india-53879052 on January 9, 2022

75. Nandi, Jayashree. 2021c.*Centre seeks expression of interest for draft amendment to Indian Forest Act, accessed from* https://www.hindustantimes.com/environment/centre-seeks-expression-of-interest-for-draft-amendment-to-indian-forest-act-101619761427171.html on January 9, 2022

76. Menon, Meena. 2021. *A "do or die" agitation against coal pollution in Odisha, accessed from* https://india.mongabay.com/2021/05/a-do-or-die-agitation-against-coal-pollution-in-odisha/ on January 9, 2022

77. Times News Network. 2021. *Gujarat: Violent protest at Vedanta's project in Tapi*, accessed from http://timesofindia.indiatimes.com/articleshow/84153491.cms?utm_source=contentofinterest&utm_medium=text&utm_campaign=cppst on January 9, 2022

78. Express News Service. 2021. *Gujarat: Villagers 'resort to violence' during public hearing on zinc plant in Tapi, accessed from* https://indianexpress.com/article/cities/ahmedabad/gujarat-villagers-attack-police-vandalise-vehicles-during-public-hearing-on-zinc-plant-in-tapi-7390557/ on January 9, 2022

79. Express News Service, 2021

80. Tollefson, Jeff. 2020. *Why deforestation and extinctions make pandemics more likely* accessed from https://www.nature.com/articles/d41586-020-02341-1 on January 9, 2022

81. The National Environment Policy, 2006 states "*that while conservation of environmental resources is necessary to secure livelihoods and well-being of all, the most secure basis for conservation is to ensure that people dependent on particular resources obtain better livelihoods from the fact of conservation, than from degradation of the resource*".

5

COVID-19 AND VULNERABLE GROUPS

Aditi Mehta

Abstract: *This paper attempts to understand the intersection of caste and poverty keeping the pandemic-induced stigmatization in mind. The analysis is based on the study conducted among the population of De-Notified Tribes (DnT) inhabiting peri-urban areas adjoining Udaipur city and in a mofussil town called Dabok. The paper looks at the material condition prevailing in various DnT communities which made it virtually impossible for them to follow public health advice. The gendered impact of Covid-19 is also explored in the paper. There has been a specific impact on women and children. Caste and class added to the travails of Dalit and tribal women apart from the issues that they face along gender lines. Access to food and nutrition, access to essential commodities, access to basic healthcare also suffered during the pandemic. The increase in cases of child abuse and domestic violence were alarming throughout the pandemic which saw intermittent regional shutdowns or State-wide lockdowns. While listing out the issues specific to the marginalized communities in India, this paper brings out how different factors like caste, class and gender have played a role in their suffering. Digital divide also added to the misery of the vulnerable groups. The paper lists out a set of measures focusing on what local self-governments can do in terms of providing basic citizens' rights to the DnTs and other marginalized communities. Need for the government to focus on protecting livelihoods of the marginalized communities is stressed in the policy suggestions. Addressing gender gap issues, providing sexual and other healthcare services during crisis are suggested.*

Key Words: De-Notified Tribes, Dalit, Tribes, Child abuse, Domestic violence, livelihood, health care.

"Jiske paas kuch nahi hai, woh kya khoyega?"

(What will she lose, she who has nothing?)

Babulal Bhaat, ex-member, Rajasthan Board for Semi-Nomadic, Nomadic and De-Notified Castes and Tribes

I. Background and Context

The Corona pandemic hit Indian shores through Kerala in January 2020 and since then there is nothing in the economy, society or polity that has remained unaffected by the virus and which has not suffered its consequences. Crucial to our understanding of Covid impact is the lived experience of the pandemic by the marginalized, the poor, and those the caste system has excluded. Covid has exposed the iniquitous fault lines of our social system which through its intersecting dissections of caste, class, and gender, differentially impact the poorest and the most vulnerable, especially women.

This paper attempts to grapple with the intersection of caste with poverty in the context of Covid and to arrive at some tangible policy instruments. It is, in part, an essay, attempting to describe the impact on the most disadvantaged, and in part an analysis of some sectoral trends.

The analysis presented in the paper is situated in the geographical areas of selected Denotified Tribe (DNT clusters in the peri-urban areas adjoining Udaipur city and another mofussil town, Dabok. These populations are generally engaged in service occupations, with no land to their name, often not even their house-sites. We will also discuss in addition, some issues of the Bhil tribals of Udaipur district in Rajasthan of north-west India.

II De-Notified Tribes (DNTsDnTs): Their origins and vulnerabilities

The DNT is a class of people who are traditionally objects of "othering" by wider society irrespective of the pandemic. They constitute the Bhats, traditional drummers, puppeteers and entertainers; Kalbeliyas, traditional snake-charmers and dancers; Banjaras, traditional agriculturists, salt-sellers and purveyors of goods; Gadilya Lohars, who wield the hammer and tongs to fashion iron implements for use in agricultural operations and Mogiyas, those who were traditionally occupied in distilling desi liquor, and undertook miscellaneous agricultural duties such as shooing peacocks and wild animals from farmers' fields. Except for the Banjaras and the Gadilya Lohars, all the above are still considered to be belonging to unclean castes. They are excluded from mainstream society on account of their criminal and inferior caste status, are generally bone-poor and have been precariously and perilously subsisting on the sharp edge of survival. They are found on village peripheries, local leaders shying from issuing them residential pattas (title deeds), as these tribes are commonly stigmatized to be criminalized, attracting opprobrium for bringing in their wake prostitution and thievery. It must also be borne in mind that the DNTs do not comprise a fringe population group.

The Renke Commission, appointed by the government in 2008 to recommend policies for the socio-economic upliftment of these communities, had estimated that about 10 % of the general population in India belonged to NT-DNT DnT communities. Rajasthan had a population of 6.6 crores as per the 2011 Census. Hence, the population of DnTs in Rajasthan alone may be estimated at around 66 lakh adults, about a decade ago. These are not small numbers.

DnTs and Social Stigma: A common urban middle-class fallout of the Covid pandemic is found to be the social stigma attendant on the contracting of the virus, leading to attitudes of discriminatory behaviour towards those who have the disease. This "othering" while attempting to distance the healthy from the ill, subordinates the ill in terms of a socially defined category. The physical distances mandated are also couched and accompanied by a societal psycho-social value-judgment wherein the infected person is considered to be unclean or to have undertaken irresponsible behaviour for having contracted the virus. This commonplace prejudice brings in its wake the implicit creation and normalization of hierarchical categories amongst those suffering, not just towards the common societal enemy of an unknown virus. Here the othering demarcates the healthy superior from the unhealthy inferior, the blamer versus the blamed, the hygienic versus the non-hygienic and the clean versus the unclean, leading to forms of discrimination and distance-enhancing attitudes.[1]

In fact, NGOs such as Human Rights Watch have red-flagged instances of vigilante intimidation and violence where people are publicly shamed, even confined and arbitrarily punished in several states of India including Rajasthan.[2] Health workers in urban centres, including Udaipur city also faced taunts and threats of eviction. The Jan Swasthya Abhiyan-India, in their letter to Dr. Harsh Vardhan, the then union health minister, had condemned some measures such as marking homes of those with COVID and marking the finger of those tested positive with indelible ink and cautioned that these would cause fear, isolation and stigmatisation[3].

The reason for this small discussion on Covid-induced stigmatisation is to draw out parallels and tangents from the medically induced stigmatisation of the Covid-struck, sufferers of the pandemic situation, and the social stigmatisation of those who are struck by caste, who are socially stigmatised from birth due to their accidental inherited position as lower-caste, erstwhile criminals. The point essentially is that Covid-induced stigmatisation, while now recognised and commonly condemned is a transient stigmatisation, and relatively benign, compared to the deep-rooted and systemic stigmatisation faced by the DNT population.

DNTs and economic precarity: Before dwelling deeper into a discussion on the impacts of the pandemic on vulnerable groups, a brief word regarding the special circumstances of the DNTs and its contribution to their economic precarity is in order. In 1871 the British notified about 150 tribes as "criminal" under the Criminal Tribes Act, since these tribes were unamenable to the regulatory and social norms and mores of the ruling dispensation. These "criminals" could be arrested and bound down on the slightest suspicion and were often subjected to the most inhuman indignities. They were also widely and publicly stigmatised to ensure the acquiescence of wider society in their collective arraignment. After Independence, the Government of India repealed and replaced the Criminal Tribes Act (CTA) with effect from 31 August 1952, by the Criminal Tribes (Repeal) Act, 1952 (Act No XXIV of 1952).[4] This led to the origin of the term "Denotified" communities. Unfortunately, the subsequent Habitual Offenders Act and the Goonda Act cloned the mindset of the CTA and even today these criminal tribes often constitute the default suspects whenever crimes, heinous or petty, are investigated at the local level.

A sub-group of the DNTs is the Banjara community, dealing with bullocks—their purchase and sale- and the use of bullocks in transporting goods. In recent years, the business of bullocks has suffered a hit, partly due to harassment by activists of the Bajrang Dal, who seized many trucks of bullocks being transported on suspicion of their being readied for slaughtering, and also due to the fact that the use of bullocks in agricultural operations has been steadily replaced by tractor use. Now Banjaras take to the work of selling miscellaneous home-use items, like blankets, used clothes, chilies, vegetables, etc. Community members also reportedly started the practice of *dhayari-mazdoori*, or daily physical labour to earn wages and supplement their food supplies with oils, spices, salt and vegetables.

Another sub-group are the Kalbeliyas. An area of visible and naked deprivation, the entire community of Kalbeliyas seems immersed in a profoundly degrading poverty. Their *kaccha* and *pucca* structures were made of tarpaulin, tin, cloth, paper and plastic sheets, all in evidence to protect and enclose the small and rude area that constitutes their home. The Kalbeliyas of the Udaipur division, unlike their counterparts in Jaipur and Jodhpur divisions, are not engaged in dance and music. The traditional occupation of the Kalbeliyas was snake-charming and snake-catching, and the hewing and scraping of rocks and stones to make *ghattis* or *okhals*, and *khads*, stone grinders of various dimensions for kitchen usage. Understandably, their traditional services where the caste had a niche skill and comparative community advantage are hardly required today, household snakes being a rarity and the traditional stone grinders also being relegated to the class of curious and charming antiquities, rarely used.

Today the women of the Kalbeliya caste do *kachhra-been'na* (rag picking), the sorting and segregation of rubbish, to sell recyclable bottles, bits of twine, rope, string, plastic sheets, bottles, tins, receptacles, and other possibly useful items from domestic refuse. The men do daily labouring, standing at important cross-roads that serve as labour *mandis* in the hope of being picked up for a day's labour at the daily rate. All of the women are reported to be eating only the evening meal. Even children were given a single meal in a day, in the evening. When I looked visibly appalled, I was apprised of the grim reality that even during non-Covid times, community members would generally partake of a single meal.

Women typically leave the home early, sift through garbage piles at self-allocated dumps, sell the reusable refuse to authorised contractors, then return homes after stopping at a merchant's shop to purchase their daily amounts of *atta, dal* or vegetables, oil and condiments to cook their evening meal, their hearths being fired on twigs and sticks gathered en-route. Their economy functions on what is called *tak-lai na tak-khai*, literally earning at the ready and eating at the ready, or to put it simply, hand to mouth.

Another focus of this study are the Bhil tribals residing in villages around Udaipur. The Bhils largely live in mixed tribal and non-tribal habitations, except those tribals who reside in the far-flung villages of Kotra and Jhadol. While in all indices of nutrition and health, education, income and wellbeing, tribals score below their non-tribal counterparts, their position is significantly better than those of the DNTs, NTs and SNTs discussed earlier. Unlike the DNTs, tribals possess small strips of land, live in cohesive communities and enjoy a social status. The incidence of Covid cases in the second wave of Covid in the latter part of 2021 was also significant.

III. Methodology

The paper relies on printed reports, grey literature and my own field trips into the habitations of the selected respondents. I was specifically interested in studying the lived experience of these excluded groups during the pandemic and the survival and coping mechanisms brought into play by these communities to counter the worst ravages of the pandemic. I contacted Babulal Bhat, a DNT leader and ex-Member of the De-Notified, Nomadic, and Semi-Nomadic Tribes Board of Rajasthan. Accompanied by Ramlal Banjara and Partha Kalbeliya, the four of us went to one of the residential sites of the community at village Dhuni Mata, off Dabok, home of the famous zinc smelter, Hindustan Zinc. There are about 200 homes of the Banjara community in Dhuni Mata, some residing in unauthorized occupation of half-finished brick and thatch homes on plots of forest department land, while the rest reside in allocated house plots in the Banjara Basti, called 'Banjaron ka Khera', about 2 km from the JK cement factory. I also visited the Kalbeliya basti, adjacent to the Banjara basti of Dhuni Mata, with another pool of approximately 200-odd houses. Even though I physically visited the sites, Covid restrictions prevented me from interacting more closely with the respondents, and I necessarily curtailed myself to the most basic and rudimentary of questions.

In addition, the paper relies on analysis of previously available primary data from the National Family Health Survey and other sources to give an overview of the larger context within which some of the inequalities and vulnerabilities described below have unfolded.

IV. Impact of COVID-19

The COVID-19 pandemic affected different groups very differently. The section below looks at the findings with respect to four large population groups, based on both primary and secondary data.

Covid-19 and the DNTs

During Covid and the lockdown, the Banjara community occupied itself in crop-cutting and harvesting. Despite being a semi-Nomadic community, most families had access to small tracts of agricultural land. As situations of food shortage are were a part of their collective memory, most members of the Debari Banjara community believed in keeping adequate food stocks in their homes and fortuitously had wheat for the year in store. However, most families also reported having pawned their women's jewellery and taking loans to meet their non-wheat food consumption demands during the pandemic. There were also, reportedly, intra-community contributions of packets of dry rations for those who were lower down on the economic scale. The hunger that stalked the other DNT communities did not visit the Banjaras, as most were ration-card holders, and thus had access to the 10 kgs of grain/per capita per month that the government provided during the Covid.

Surprisingly, there was only one case of Covid reported in the entire close-knit Banjara community of Dhuni Mata, comprising about 500 homes in two separate habitations and it led to the subsequent mortality of Sajana Bai, wife of the earlier Sarpanch, Gorilal Banjara. There was only one other case of Covid-related mortality in the entire district, an unnamed woman in village Jalara, gram panchayat Sambora, near the town of Salumber, Udaipur. While the exact number of Banjaras in the Udaipur district is unknown (there has been no caste Census in India since 1931, the socio-economic and caste census of 2011 being non-granular and non-differentiating of different SC and OBC castes) the Banjara jati-samaj, of which Ramlal is an important member, estimates about 10,000-12,000 homes of Banjaras in the entire district. If one was to take these assertions at face value, this is nothing short of astonishing, being an example of the successful physical isolation of the community, or alternatively, the comprehensiveness of the social boycott of these communities ordinarily practised. It is pertinent to note here, that none of the communities lived in any special isolation due to the Covid. Covid-like physically-isolationist restrictions applied on the majority of these castes as a matter of course in their daily lives.

Among the Kalbeliyas, none of the women had been out over the last few weeks except sporadically due to the uncertain nature of curfews, even over weekends. A brief visit inside their huts was mute witness to nothing remotely edible at hand. The heaps and mounds of rubbish that these women were used to going through in order to forage enough reusables to sell for a square meal for the family and children was a thing of the past. As public foraging was disallowed, and the quantities of waste considerably diminished during the phases of lockdown, there was scarcely anything for them to eat and they reported that they had been eating on *udhaar*, eating on loan, from different suppliers, as their regular grocery supplier, the village Bania, had refused them loans apprehending their insolvency. With occupational opportunities virtually ceased ever since the period of lockdown, the community subsisted on food charity and small doles of dry rations from a few NGOs and other welfare organisations. There was no MNREGA (Mahatma Gandhi National Rural Employment Guarantee Act) work undertaken in their panchayat to tide over the time of scarcity during both the lockdowns and when asked, the women said that MNREGA payments were both meagre and tardy.

There is a cruel irony at the objective situation of the Kalbeliya camp or dera counterpoised by the strictures of frequent hand-washing with soap and physical-distancing written on the buses, billboards and hoardings enroute. Ironically, one of the huts in the camp had a handwritten slogan posted for all to see, exhorting '*do gaz ki doori*'. These advisories were virtually impossible to administer, and outside the realm of possibility for the Kalbeliyas, although the younger women were using face-masks. What is obvious is the deeply exclusionary nature of the most rudimentary public health advice for the poorest of our citizens for this most universal of all viral afflictions.The handpump at the edge of the dera was dry and had reportedly been dry for the last two years. The small earthen pots of drinking water in the huts were brought by the women on their heads from a distance of about two kilometres. There was no food or foodstuffs anywhere to be had in the middle of the day, and to spend on soap seemed an unimaginable luxury when hands were habitually scrubbed with dry sand and soil, the cycle of infection being perpetuated possibly due to the fecal load in the loose soil. These populations were so off the social radar that it was clear that even the requirements of hand hygiene and social distancing was further cementing the social and economic deprivations of our society. These two fundamentals of hygiene could be credibly implemented by only the privileged social classes.

On asking Devli Bai and Sita Bai, two women of the Kalbeliya basti of Dhuni Mata village, about their main survival issues, both cited that certainly they had no earnings, but almost in the manner of pointing to a temporary roadblock, difficult but not insurmountable. The women seemed more concerned about their issue of subsistence on land that belonged to the Forest Department, despite their habitation having been in existence for several decades. Thus, even with the prospect of starvation and disease staring them in their faces, the community was kept on constant tenterhooks, perpetually at risk of eviction or removal. Even the Forest Rights Act of 2006 is of no succor for them, as Kalbeliyas and other DNTs are not traditional forest dwellers but seen as interlopers and their long-standing occupation over such forest land is not seen as a traditional, occupational right, but the pestilent squatting of undesirable persons.

What seemed to turn all common knowledge on its head was the counter-intuitive situation of not a single Covid case in the entire community of the Dhuni-Mata Kalbeliya Dera, comprising upwards of 200 homes. When I asked what they thought comprised the reason for their greater immunity to Covid, the women seemed to almost brush away my query, stating they had bigger worries than the *bukhar*, which would be faced, should it come. The high burden of disease these women carried, instead of being the host for further vulnerabilities, almost seemed to serve as an armour against further infections. Living such exposed lives in such openly hostile, unhygienic and unhealthy conditions seemed to predispose those living in such conditions to their own "bubble," wider society shunning them even further. While all of these populations were untested, there is no doubt about the enormous viral load and disease burden of TB, diarrhea and other diseases silently and incipiently carried by these populations exacerbated by endemic malnourishment. But these populations residing in tapris or makeshift hutments with no access to clean water and no sanitation facilities, were residing perforce in wide open spaces.

Another visit to Naal ka Bhilwara, a *kacchi basti* of over 450-500 households right off Tiger Hill, an exclusive colony in the heart of Udaipur city revealed a now-familiar sameness. The Bhat community was the majority community here, along with Kalbeliyas, Mogiyas and Bhils and certain communities of the SCs, but the issues, and even the physical geography of the slum-like structures were similar. Here too, there were no cases of Covid reported and no reported Covid-deaths, although the levels of poverty were abject and degrading. Thus, Covid did not penetrate the enormous blanket of poverty enveloping these communities, possibly because these communities are barely allowed any interaction with other castes of society, the physical distancing medically stipulated automatically occurring due to the physical distancing of their lives from most others. While the immunity through squalor argument is partially plausible, it is not convincing, being untested and scientifically unsubstantiated. The medical literature on coronaviruses (flu, Sars, etc.) does not give any backing to the immunity claim. There has been under-testing of these communities, possibly due to the stigma.

When I visited the basti of the Gadilya Lohar community in Dang village of Dabok, I was informed that again, there was not a single case of Covid in the community of 30 households of Gadilya Lohars and 17 households of the Banjara community. Nor had there been any demand for the iron tools the Lohars produced, and so no employment. Their felt impact of the Corona virus was on their livelihoods, not on their health. All the women in the group meeting asserted rhetorically that they would work for daily wages now for the first time in their history of 700 years. But they would later return to their livelihood and work as Lohars, despite the fall in demand for their wares. The entire community was resident on panchayat land, but without formal pattas, squatting informally, prone to eviction should some other more pressing demand for land arise or if the village leadership should choose to evict them.

A feisty Kalbeliya woman, Gainda Bai, spoke to me with a hint of challenge when I asked about Covid and its impact. ``We are Covid, I am Covid. What will this Covid do to us that has not already been done!" She was right. Her life possibly could get no worse.

Impact on Tribal Communities

A quick study of 42 community representatives and frontline NGO workers of Seva Mandir undertaken during the second wave of Covid showed that the tribal population still evinced resistance to testing, even as they were accustoming themselves to Covid-appropriate behaviour.[5] People were reportedly covering up their symptoms and hiding illnesses, visiting quacks instead of going to doctors at the health facility in the apprehension that they would be forcibly admitted to the hospitals. The covering up of symptoms, avoidance of vaccination and fear of forcible incarceration all link up with the issue of stigma and the general persecuted status of these groups. This could be a candidate explanation for the apparently low rates of Covid experienced in the DNT communities, but the fact that very few individuals, if any, spoke of experiencing any symptoms, or felt the need to address health, also gives pause to the above possibility.

In the tribal areas, village and gram panchayat Dhayla experienced 20 deaths among the age group of 30-55 years, and while there was no testing, it is widely presumed that the deaths were due to Covid. Again, misconceptions that the vaccine itself was causing death, and in some cases, male infertility, were reportedly causing villagers to shoo away medical workers in Umaidpura village of Thamla gram panchayat. The one positive in all the stories of negative Covid impact was the re-dedication to local based employment of some migrant workers, who having returned from the cities, were actively seeking local employment, working on the MNREGA sites, and working their own agricultural fields. But all such attempts are not positive. Youth from Khatmala gram panchayat, reportedly all laid off from their work in the local marble mines, are yet to successfully retool themselves and find alternative employment.

An analysis[6] of nutritional levels in the highly stratified, food-insecure zone of southern Rajasthan, the same tribal belt discussed above, suggests that like the Dalits and OBCs, tribals too suffered exponentially due to the lockdown. The lockdown caused a lack of migration avenues and the food basket of the tribals was strongly imperiled. The study included a total of 211 respondents including community volunteers, family members of tuberculosis patients and malnourished children, pregnant women, and some influential members of village society. The short conclusion of the study was that fully two-thirds of the respondents reported that food in their households was insufficient for the amount they wanted to eat, and 97% of the respondents reported that not having money to buy food was the reason for their not having sufficient food. The study highlighted the widespread food insecurity among tribal, migration-dependent communities in southern Rajasthan.

Gendered impacts of COVID-19

Covid has had severely gendered impacts on society which have widened pre-existing gender gaps along with reversing decades of efforts towards gender equality. Across every sphere, from health to the economy, women and girls are bearing the amplified impacts of the disease outbreak.

With the sudden announcement of the nation-wide lockdown contingent on the Covid, the informal labour sector including migrant women workers was the worst affected, leading to an enormous humanitarian crisis in the country. Millions of migrant women were on the streets, unemployed and starving for food. This has been documented widely in our press, even as the lockdown was initiated. A recent report by the Centre for Sustainable Employment, Azim Premji University, suggests that 47% women lost their jobs in the first lockdown in comparison to only 7% of the men. The recently released report by *United Nations Women* (UN Women) shows that the pandemic will push 96 million people into extreme poverty by 2021, 47 millions of whom are women and girls.[7] Women typically earn less and hold less secured jobs and past epidemics such as the Ebola outbreak have suggested that quarantining can have a significant impact on the economic and livelihood activities of women.

The pandemic has increased the unpaid domestic chores of women by nearly 30% thus pushing more women out of employment and into poverty.[8] The second wave of the crisis has furthered the losses as girls and women proved more vulnerable in absorbing the economic shocks. The Seva Mandir study clearly states that the pandemic has escalated the home-caring duties of girls and young women, towards the elderly and all others who have suffered any form of illness.[9] During the lockdowns, due to restricted mobility, women are unable to work, suffering the double brunt of reduced family incomes, and increased familial workloads of cooking, cleaning, fetching water and firewood, including home farm agricultural operations. Results from a recent PFI study to assess the knowledge and impact of COVID-19 on young people in three Indian states of Uttar Pradesh (UP), Bihar and Rajasthan show that 51% female adolescents experienced an increase in workload during the nationwide lockdown, as compared to 23% male adolescents. In UP 96% females experienced an increase in workload, with 67% being below 18 years of age.[10]

The impact of Covid on the health crisis was no different. Pregnant women were rendered further helpless with limited access to routine health care and access to essential ante-natal medical supplementation interrupted as was nutrition supplementation. This includes pre- and post-natal healthcare, access to quality sexual and reproductive health services, and life-saving care and support in the event of gender-based violence.

Women make up a significant force of more than 80% of nurses and midwives of all healthcare workers. Along with that, women have greater involvement in caring for children, the elderly and sick family members and ironically have to resort to cheaper measures of protection like low-quality masks. The gender gap is also visible in the vaccination drives as 1.2 crore more men than women have received at least the first shot of the vaccine.[11] The pandemic limited women's access to regular anganwadis and local public health centres which has caused a notable reduction in their nutrition, especially during their pregnancies. The U.N. Population Fund warns of up to 7 million unintended pregnancies worldwide. Furthermore, in India, 56.56% of women revealed that they conceived during the lockdown. While some of these were planned pregnancies, 40% of these were not planned pregnancies.[12]

Covid also triggered what is known as the 'sanitary pad crisis' in India. With the closing down of schools which constitute a major portion of the supply chain, only about 15% of adolescent girls had access to sanitary napkins.[13] Older women also complained of not getting access to sanitary pads due to their limited access to the market, thus having to take recourse to using pieces of waste cloth. In addition, if without access to toilet facilities at home, women necessarily have to go out into the open or the woods to defecate, being further exposed. The DNT women I spoke to did not speak of this issue, probably due to the fact that very few outreach interventions reached them.

The *Mint* analysed the latest All-India Health Ministry data which exhibits major disruptions in a range of basic health services in March as local administrations focused on containing the spread of Covid-19[14]. Based on data recently released by the National Health Mission (NHM), the survey included for March, 2021, data for all sub-centres, primary health centres, community health centres, district hospitals and sub-district hospitals, as well as some private facilities, ie 150,000 facilities across 627 districts, which means that data for roughly 40,000 facilities in 75 districts was not reported, presumably on account of lockdown-related disruptions in the administrative machinery. The results briefly are as follows:

- Maternal health care services have been severely curtailed, often to the extent of 36% for certain services.
- Children's immunisations fell across the board, to the extent of 69% in the case of MMR.
- Outpatient registrations for all major non-communicable diseases declined, upto 70% for oncology and 50% for heart diseases.
- In-patient treatments for all communicable diseases fell.
- Fewer emergencies reached the medical facilities.
- TB and HIV treatments fell.

All these above documented statistics paint an alarming picture where above the general picture of hunger and malnutrition, there has been a breakdown of essential medical services, boding ill for the health status of the public. This can destabilise the long efforts underway in tackling some endemic diseases like TB.

Increased violence against women was another major social impact of the health crisis. According to the WHO, violence against women remained a major threat during emergencies. As the Covid lockdowns trapped women at home to survive with their abusers, the National Commission of Women in India reported 2.5 times increase in domestic violence between February and May 2020.[15] The 68 days period of lockdown reported more complaints of domestic, intimate-partner abuse than those received between March and May in the previous 10 years. What is important to note here is that this alarming rise in the complaints was witnessed despite the fact that 86% of women who experienced violence never sought help. A report released by UNICEF also suggests that Covid has threatened the risk of an additional 10 million child marriages by the end of this decade.[16]

Keeping in line with the issues discussed above, impacts on women remain incomplete without an analysis of the impact on Dalit women who face the triple burden of caste, class and gender that has been multiplied several-fold due to the pandemic. Dalit women constitute a significant percentage in the total workforce of sanitation workers in India, who due to the Covid protocols are one of the most vulnerable and infection-prone groups of workers. However, ironically, these women are struggling to survive between irregular contractual incomes and furthered 'social distancing' during this period. There have been reports of violence (both physical and mental) against these women from the 'upper' caste population for raising their demands of hygienic working environments and health care kits for their jobs. With the reduced re- employment of domestic workers in urban and peri-urban centres, families suffering from caste prejudice have cut loose their lower caste workers, especially those residing in joint families. "*Dalit women have been waging their struggles against the pandemic of caste and now they have to fight against silence of the sociopolitical institutions that carry out all forms of violence in the period of the lockdown culture.*"[17] In the proclaimed 'modern lives', when women continue to fight for their basic rights, issues of caste, furthered by the pandemic, have made them the 'most vulnerable of the vulnerable.'

Impact of COVID-19 on Children

Although children have so far been largely spared the direct health impact of the pandemic, they are without doubt one of the biggest victims of its socio-economic impacts. Physical distancing, lockdown measures, and surveillance strategies are all affecting children in numerous ways. Their basic necessities like schooling and immunization services, newborn care services, community-based child protection programs, including those programmes for those living with disabilities have either been completely halted or severely truncated. Among the most vulnerable castes and the poor, the need for supplementary nutrition has been voiced, yet there have been only sporadic attempts to deliver nutrition at the doorstep to pregnant women and those children covered under the ICDS, especially during the lockdown. No systematic study on the extent of under-nutrition and malnutrition during the Covid lockdown period has yet been undertaken, even though the rural areas of Rajasthan are in the throes of a deep crisis of hunger and unemployment.

Earlier we saw how caste is an intersecting and significant causal factor in poverty and its perpetuation in the case of the DNTs. Due to the lack of empirical evidence, these have remained largely in the realm of observations and due to restrictions attendant on Covid, the traditional survey methods of data collection could not be employed. Likewise, there have not been studies on the virilogical incidence of Covid on the most marginalised caste groups, a lacunae which, it is recommended, must be filled by epidemiological studies on the incidence of Covid. In the following section, we will take the single index of childhood stunting as a proxy for underdevelopment, signifying the extent of development or its lack amongst selected groups of the population.

Under-nutrition and the prevalence of hunger is widely known in India. However, a shocking fact is that India is home to nearly one-third of all stunted children in the world, where age-related comparative height is below a global medically accepted range of variation. Again, 1 in 5 of these children come under the category of wasted. Among adults, 1 in 5 women as well as men are malnourished[18]. Thus, it is not an exaggeration to hold that widespread hunger and malnutrition hold sway. To add to the picture of a silent nutritional emergency is the evidence which suggests that the consumption of nutritious foods among the rural population has actually declined in the past 3 decades.[19]

While stunting in childhood flows into adulthood, and is associated with adverse consequences for morbidity and mortality, it also leads to lowered learning capacity and productivity. But the most revelatory aspect of this analysis arises when we see that nearly 40% of the SC-ST, 36% of the OBCs and 35% of the UC-Muslim children, respectively, are stunted. Thus, the SCs-STs, OBCs and UC-Muslim children are 14, 10 and 9 percentage points, or 35-50%, more likely to be stunted compared to the UC- Hindu children.[20] The evidence indicates that differences in the environment, such as sanitation and intra-familial literacy, that upper-caste and Dalit children grow up in, contribute to this inequality; and this is further compounded by socio-cultural factors: '*...gaps between "Hindu UC and Dalit (SC) children is affected by societal discrimination, manifested in the illegal but widespread practice of untouchability and all its ramifications. The incidence of Dalit children's shorter height increases in districts where the self-reported practice of untouchability is higher. We use data from the India Human Development Survey (IHDS 2012) to estimate the association between the practice of untouchability and child height".*[21]

The case being made therefore is for positive discrimination in practices that positively impact service delivery to pregnant and nursing mothers especially from stigmatised groups to build the health outcomes of lower-caste children. This important argument ties in with the earlier section on caste being a determining factor in the incidence or otherwise of Covid. Here we emphasise the importance of caste as a determinant of nutrition, health, survival and individual development. This is where the circularity of the issue of the DNTs, their being treated as societal pariahs and low nutrition and backwardness also ties in. Lower caste children would then be more susceptible to disease in general, although the lack of testing and diagnosis due to distance-enhancing stigmatisation points to the erroneous conclusion that the DNTs are less susceptible.

Although until now the number of Covid cases has been lower among children compared to other age groups, other health impacts on children have been significant. The nationwide lockdown and loss of jobs have taken a great toll on the nutrition level of children. Covid has aggravated the malnourishment levels in children which certainly includes wasting, stunting, and being underweight, worsening the health status of those already health-stressed. What is even more unfortunate is that India has been unable to provide for the needs of children equally. Caste, class, and religion play a major role even in an issue so fundamental as the basic nourishment of children.[22]

The closure of anganwadi centers and schools due to Covid resulted in halting the already thin-on-the-ground healthcare initiatives of the government, like the mid-day meals program which served as extra nourishment for millions of nutritionally-deficient school-aged children. Another major cause of concern is that according to the WHO report, India registered the largest drop in routine childhood immunization coverage in 2020. These are semi-permanent and debilitating losses, as the window of opportunity for childhood immunisations is fixed and specific, once missed, the backlog only getting multiplied. Water, sanitation, and hygiene (WASH) services are also at risk of disruption by lockdown measures, posing further threats to children's health through water-borne diseases.[23] Physical distancing, being trapped inside a house in small tenements and overcrowded homes has caused anxiety in urban children which is another concern. Facing extreme deprivations, uncertainties related to the future has triggered severe mental-health challenges.

India reported a huge spike in child abuse cases between March and May 2020. Where children are already vulnerable, loss of contact with teachers and friends has further pushed them into silence to report crimes against their violators. The economic burden caused by Covid too plays a huge role in hampering children's safety as it has compelled them into child labour and child marriage. Cases of high exploitation are also reported amongst children without parents or children who recently lost their parents to the disease outbreak.

The worldwide closure of schools has shifted the entire education system to online modes. According to UNESCO, by the end of April 2020,186 countries have implemented nationwide closures, affecting about 73.8% of the total enrolled learners. We have all experienced in the past years that online learning is no substitute for immersive school education. However, adhering to the covid protocols, all schools have created online structured learning modules irrespective of their infrastructural capacities. Although the right to equitable education is every child's right, the measures adopted clearly indicate that a child's learning experience is completely decided by his/her accessibility to technology and gadgets.

We are also deeply aware of the digital divide in the country. In India only 27% of Indian households have access to the internet and only 47% have any access to the internet or a computing device, that too, contingent on interrupted and intermittent power supplies. The issues of accessibility to technology and computing devices and hardware has created a huge gap in digital literacy. The key findings of the Household Social Consumption on Education in India, 2017-18 National Sample Survey (NSS)1 show the digital divide not only between the rural-urban, and private-public educational institutions but also the divisions based on caste. Out of total enrolled students, 96% of Scheduled Tribe students and 96.2% of Scheduled Caste students did not even have access to a computer, leave alone own one.[24] This one fact then, seals many fates for the future and predictably it is the SC and ST that are predisposed to have to suffer the wages of our enormous digital divide as well.

UNESCO released a projection in August 2020 covering 180 countries, estimating that 24 million children may not return to education in 2020 due to the pandemic. Ten million girls in India could drop out of secondary school due to the COVID-19 pandemic, according to a Right to Education Forum policy brief. The impact of COVID-19 on children's poverty, survival and health, learning, and safety are far-reaching. However, its effects will not be distributed equally. As we have seen, those on the lower edge of the caste divide are destined to bear the greatest costs in the absence of mitigating actions.[25]

Recommendations[26]

The right to life with dignity is the right of every human being. However, the pandemic has not further revealed the nature of the lives of the DNTs and their like. If anything, it has further disguised and further exacerbated the ostracisation of these groups. Thus, there is the additional human rights challenge of making visible the stigmatisation, poverty and destitution as the rest of the population perforce stays at home for safety and protection. It is essential to address these matters of the most basic human rights of our marginalised DNT populations, as the label "criminal" or 'denotified" further contributes to this ostracisation. People who are otherwise not casteist tend to steer away and work less or refuse to cohabit with those who are known to have criminal antecedents, even perhaps proclivities. Most DNT communities lack the most rudimentary of entitlements, right from voting cards and documented authentication, to house sites and livelihoods. Their access to second order entitlements like education and health are likewise completely fraught. But small steps must be taken.

The formation of empowered and decentralised panchayat level committees would enable a mapping of the social and economic deprivations of the communities as they reside, enabling the architecture of universal entitlements for the DNTs, NTs and SNTs including special provisioning by providing rations under free PDS, vaccination services, anganwadi services and work under MGNREGA, etc. These committees would also be best suited to address homelessness, joblessness, mobile education for children and record the cases of atrocities which are experienced by them with the object of their redressal. As has been suggested in policy documents presented by government agencies, independent commissions and NGOs like Action Aid, the allotment of land to these households would help them cope with the most abject forms of vulnerability and homelessness. Formulation of an empowered and separate grievance redressal and monitoring cell for DNTs at the state level is necessary to record cases of atrocities against them as also the issues of periodic inter-district travel and temporary, livelihood induced migrations of these peoples. The government should review its progress periodically and also set up a separate department at the state headquarters to look into the issues of these most vulnerable sections. Schooling of children belonging to these communities are the worst affected and access to mobile education and anganwadi units will help children and families to complete their education despite their constant migration.

The government needs to act urgently to protect and promote livelihood opportunities of the marginalised sections and folk artists, who are losing jobs and access to employment, even exacerbated further due to the digital divide. The DNTs require promotional support and deserve representation in the forums of government for them to raise their disparate voices and enable affirmative and effective action for their very particular issues and concerns. Recognition and encouragement to the world-famous artists of the Bhat, Kalbeliya, Behupuriya castes and other groups like the Manganiyars will help dignify their livelihoods, increase their income streams and help to increase their profile within the community. Efforts should be made to support mobilization and increase political participation of the community to represent their issues within society and the government. Today, community-based institutions are lacking at the state, district and even local level to raise voices regarding DNT issues and concerns. These communities must demand a rightful say in local governance bodies, to help in removing stigmas by bringing together different stakeholders to demand and work towards an inclusive society. In addition, special provision must be made for the capacity building and training of government officials to help the community address their issues more effectively.

Way forward to address the widened gender gap

This brief glimpse into the plethora of reports on the gendered impact of Covid highlights the urgency of the need to address the regressive gender gaps in society, further exacerbated and brought to the fore during the pandemic. The literature is exhaustive and the way forward with recommendations have been discussed in several previous publications on the issue.

I intend to categorize these under the overarching themes: application of gender lenses in policy formulation, interventions towards financial inclusion, ensuring social security and interventions to address attitudinal behaviours. The importance of reducing the gender imbalance in society is obvious and cannot be emphasised enough. The objective condition of the position of women will witness a noticeable change only when women get an equal representation in the process of policy formulation. For example, with 80% women constituting the healthcare workforce, only 13% of the members of the National COVID-19 task force are women. Therefore, it is important to have an explicit gender-lens to the policy-making process to identify the disproportionate burden of impact of Covid on women. This can be supported by decentralized, sex-disaggregated data on various dimensions of gendered impact. Financial inclusion of women plays a significant role in their empowerment. Ensuring control of women over their resources through direct benefit transfers for the foreseeable future and sustainable implementation policies of 'equal pay for equal work' can enable women in vulnerable positions to become economically independent. MNREGA can be extended to urban centres to provide work opportunities for women which can also be supplemented by increased investment in the scheme for both person-days worked and wages during Covid.[27] The Integrated Child Development Services (ICDS) network can also be supplemented and leveraged to provide full-time childcare services for working mothers.

It is also crucial to recognize and respect the tasks of unpaid care, value it and make serious attempts to rebalance it within the family, especially in families existing at the subsistence level. The demands for access to basic household infrastructure has been long pending, including providing infrastructure for household chores, such as easy and accessible water supplies and provisioning of cooking gas instead of firewood. These two changes will reduce women's unpaid work time. Along with legal and financial empowerment, social security plays a key role in making a gender equal environment. Classifying reproductive and sexual health services as essential can improve their access for women. There is a need to improve the interventions in family planning. Safe family planning and sustainably improved access to reproductive health care through ASHA workers and local public health centres can prevent unsafe abortions and reduce the infant and maternal mortality rates. Investment in our 3.3 million strong female frontline workers would ensure continuous efforts at the grassroots. Even in the post-pandemic world, this would help in continuous diagnosis of the health status of the country, working as a preventive along with curative measures.[28] It is also important to work towards an integrated decentralized helpline services for women to report violence against them and also get medico-legal and psychological support in cases of suffering and violence. Lastly, all of this will only be able to bring about change if there are efforts towards attitudinal change in people. Gender-sensitivity training of people in authority, medical and legal staff, counsellors and of course people from all socio-economic backgrounds require focused attention.

Mitigating the Impact of Covid on Children

As the disease outbreak has had serious consequences on the lives of children the need of the hour is to focus on collective action. Lack of studies about the catastrophic repercussions of the pandemic on children is proving to be one of the biggest hindrances in working on an optimal response formulation that captures all the dimensions of the impact. This should be followed by united efforts by stakeholders across sections: government officials, child rights advocacy groups, medical and legal teams, etc., come together to strategize the way forward for reversing the impact of the pandemic on the education sector. Immediate reinforcement of food and nutritional support is of crucial importance. As schools, which are a major source of food for most children, are closed, India, like many other countries, needs to come up with supplementary nutrition assistance programmes targeting children belonging to vulnerable groups.[29] Most middle class and parents tend to think of schools as places where children learn, so their closure can be compensated for by online or home schooling. But for marginalised groups, they are critical sources of food, sanitary pads and childcare, The administrative response to Covid in closing these institutions with little regard to replacing these functions further immiserates these groups.

As children continue to stay in confined areas, an increase and improvement in family support and child protection services are important. Local authorities and NGOs can play a major role in surveillance and provide closer support to children to report their problems.[30] This should be supported by legal-medical-psychological integrated helpline services which would help reduce the distance between children and governance. Lastly, as the pandemic has severely impacted the education system, governments can collaborate with civil society organizations working in the education sector to enhance the distance-learning and physical-learning education infrastructure, while acknowledging that nothing, simply nothing can compete with the physical presence of committed teachers. Adoption of these policy measures can help mitigate the risk and accelerate the efforts which were reversed by Covid.

Conclusion

In this essay I have focused on highlighting the catastrophic impact of the health crisis on the poor and marginalised, who exist at the cusp of caste, class and gender. The pernicious, wasteful and unjust societal cleavages of caste have penetrated and suffused the virtually watertight divisions of class and gender. But this pandemic, while exposing without camouflage the fault lines in our health and education sectors have blanketted over the caste marginalisations, making less visible the brutal impacts of government and private responses to the pandemic, such as lockdowns, online shopping and learning, staying inside homes wherever possible, closing key institutions in health, education and food supply chains, raising doubly the spectre of exclusion to those already stigmatised and so on. A further consequence of these responses is the way in which they disguise the creeping negative impacts of the responses on the livelihoods of and services for the poor.

At the last, it is equally important to emphasise that these clefts have not appeared overnight. These are the result of years of daily violence, structural violence. As Hannah Arendt had said, "Equality is the result of human organization. We are not born equal." This paper, through the exploration of Covid attempts to explore the regressive impact of caste in colouring most of our development initiatives and highlights the failure of our human organization to bring about a social equality that permeates to the sections of the poor and marginalised. Covid made the most vulnerable further vulnerable. These groups have been the victims of disguised structural violence that limits their very existence, leave alone allowing individual actors any semblance of individual agency to achieve their capacities and capabilities. As Veena Das puts it, "it's a crime without a criminal."[31] But the victims whose everyday sociality of life is violated are visible, despite the invisibilisation practiced daily by society. Such enquiry raises several complex conceptual and methodological issues which cannot be raised within the ambit of this short piece. But an understanding of the lives of the marginalized and vulnerable is central to our own understanding of where we stand as a nation.

Acknowledgments

In the writing of this paper I have received support and assistance from various people.

I am grateful to Shreelata Rao Sheshadri for her insightful and detailed comments. I would like to acknowledge the collaboration of Babulal Bhat, Ramlal Banjara and Partha Kalbeliya in conducting the field visits. I would also like to express my appreciation to Yashasvi Kumud for her contribution in data collection and analysis and providing writing assistance. This paper would not have been possible without the opportunity given to me by the Azim Premji University and the Constitutional Conduct Group.

BIBLIOGRAPHY

1. Bhattacharya P, Banerjee D, Rao TS. The “Untold” Side of COVID-19: Social Stigma and Its Consequences in India. *Indian Journal of Psychological Medicine.* 2020;42(4)

2. Human Rights Watch.“Human Rights Dimension of COVID-19 Response”.2020 <https://www.hrw.org/news/2020/03/19/human-rights-dimensions-covid-19-response>

3. Jan Swasthya Abhiyan: http://phmindia.org/wp-content/uploads/2020/03/jsa-breach-confidentiality.pdf (2020)

4. Sarthak. “Revised Report:Socio-economic Status of Women of the DNT and Nomadic Communities in Delhi”.National Commission for Women. 2016

5. ActionAid Association. Sphere of Exclusion: A Policy Document. ActionAid Association, Jaipur Regional Office, 2016 <https://www.actionaidindia.org/wp-content/uploads/2018/06/Sphere-of-Exclusion-NTDNT-policy-advocacy-folder-Flier.pdf>

6. Rathore V., Impact of COVID-19 on Women, *Seva Mandir*. Udaipur and Rajsamand. 2021(unpublished monograph).

7. Saxena A, Amin A, Mohan B S, Mohan P. Food Insecurity in Tribal High Migration Communities in Rajasthan,India. Food and Nutrition Bulletin,SAGE Publications.2020

8. Azcona G, Bhatt A, Encarnacion J, Seck P, Staab S, Turque L. ‘From Insights to Action: Gender Equality in the Wake of COVID-19’. *United Nations Women.* 2020

9. Basole A, Abraham R, Lahoti R, Kesar S, Jha M, Nath P, Kapoor R, Mandela S, Shrivastava A, Dasgupta Z, Gupta G, Narayanan R. ‘State of Working India 2021: One Year of COVID-19’. 2021

10. Population Foundation of India. Impact of COVID-19 on Young People:Rapid Assessment in Three States. New Delhi*: Population Foundation of India.* 2020

11. Ramesh M. More Men Than Women in India are Getting COVID Vaccine, But Why?. The Quint. 2021

12. https://www.thequint.com/neon/gender/why-are-more-men-getting-coronavirus-vaccine-than-wome

13. Economic Time Edge. Pandemic Fuels Baby Boom in India. The Economic Times. 2020 <https://economictimes.indiatimes.com/industry/miscellaneous/pandemic-fuels-baby-boom-in-india-says-latest-report-by-momjunction/articleshow/80013971.cms?from=mdr>

14. Rukmini S. How COVId-19 Response Disrupted Health Services in Rural India. *Mint*. 2020 <https://www.livemint.com/news/india/how-covid-19-response-disrupted-health-services-in-rural-india-11587713155817.html>

15. Garikipati S, Only 15% Girls in India had Access to Sanitary Pads During Lockdown. Scroll.in. 2020 <https://scroll.in/article/965984/only-15-girls-in-india-had-access-to-sanitary-pads-during-lockdown>

16. Advisory on Right of Women in the Context of COVID-19. *National Human Rights Commission*. 2020 <https://nhrc.nic.in/sites/default/files/Advisory%20on%20Rights%20of%20Women_0.pdf>

17. United Nations Children's Fund, COVID-19: A threat to progress against child marriage, UNICEF, New York, 2021 <https://data.unicef.org/resources/covid-19-a-threat-to-progress-against-child-marriage/>

18. Patil M S. Gender Equity and COVID-19: Dalit Standpoints. *Economic and Political Weekly.* 2021 <https://www.epw.in/engage/article/gender-equity-and-covid-19-dalit-standpoints>

19. Bagai A, Sukumar A, Puri S. Women in India: COVID-19 Impact, Response and Policy Environment. Sattva. 2021 <https://www.sattva.co.in/wp-content/uploads/2021/03/Sattva_Insights_Gender_COVID-19-Response-and-Policy-Environment.pdf>

20. Population Foundation of India. Policy Brief: The Impact of COVID-19 on Women. Population Foundation of India. 2020

21. International Institute for Population Sciences (IIPS) and ICF. National Family Health Survey

22. (NFHS-4): 2015-16. 2017.

23. World Food Program and National Statistical Office. Food and Nutritional Security Analysis.2019.

24. Deshpande A, Ramachandran R. How Caste Discrimination Impacts Child Development and Stunting in India. The Wire. 2021 <https://thewire.in/caste/caste-discrimination-child-development-stunting-malnutrition-india>

25. United Nations Sustainable Development Group. Policy Brief: The Impact of COVID-19 on Children,2020

26. Key Indicators of Household Social Consumption on Education in India, NSS 75th round. Government of India, *Ministry of Statistics & Programme Implementation*. 2017-18

27. OECD. Combatting COVID-19's Effect on Children. Tackling Coronavirus (COVID-19):Contributing to a Global Effort. 2020 <https://www.oecd.org/coronavirus/policy-responses/combatting-covid-19-s-effect-on-children-2e1f3b2f/>

28. Gupta A. Red Tape: Bureaucracy, Structural Violence and Poverty in India. Duke University Press. 2012

ENDNOTES

1. Bhattacharya P, Banerjee D, Rao TS. The "Untold" Side of COVID-19: Social Stigma and Its Consequences in India. *Indian Journal of Psychological Medicine*. 2020;42(4):382-386.

2. Human Rights Watch."Human Rights Dimension of COVID-19 Response".2020 <https://www.hrw.org/news/2020/03/19/human-rights-dimensions-covid-19-response>

3. Jan Swasthya Abhiyan: http://phmindia.org/wp-content/uploads/2020/03/jsa-breach-confidentiality.pdf (2020)

4. Sarthak. "Revised Report:Socio-economic Status of Women of the DNT and Nomadic Communities in Delhi".National Commission for Women. 2016: Pg-16.

5. Rathore V., Impact of COVID-19 on Women, *Seva Mandir*. Udaipur and Rajsamand. 2021(unpublished monograph).

6. Saxena A, Amin A, Mohan B S, Mohan P. Food Insecurity in Tribal High Migration Communities in Rajasthan,India. Food and Nutrition Bulletin,SAGE Publications.2020: 06

7. Azcona G, Bhatt A, Encarnacion J, Seck P, Staab S, Turque L. 'From Insights to Action: Gender Equality in the Wake of COVID-19'. *United Nations Women*. 2020: 08-09

8. Basole A, Abraham R, Lahoti R, Kesar S, Jha M, Nath P, Kapoor R, Mandela S, Shrivastava A, Dasgupta Z, Gupta G, Narayanan R. 'State of Working India 2021: One Year of COVID-19'. 2021: 21-22

9. Rathore V, Ibid

10. *Population Foundation of India*. Impact of COVID-19 on Young People:Rapid Assessment in Three States. New Delhi: *Population Foundation of India*. 2020: 16-17

11. Ramesh M. More Men Than Women in India are Getting COVID Vaccine, But Why?. *The Quint*. 2021 https://www.thequint.com/neon/gender/why-are-more-men-getting-coronavirus-vaccine-than-women

12. Economic Time Edge. Pandemic Fuels Baby Boom in India. *The Economic Times*. 2020 <https://economictimes.indiatimes.com/industry/miscellaneous/pandemic-fuels-baby-boom-in-india-says-latest-report-by-momjunction/articleshow/80013971.cms?from=mdr>

13. Garikipati S, Only 15% Girls in India had Access to Sanitary Pads During Lockdown. Scroll.in. 2020 <https://scroll.in/article/965984/only-15-girls-in-india-had-access-to-sanitary-pads-during-lockdown>

14. Rukmini S. How COVId-19 Response Disrupted Health Services in Rural India. Mint. 2020 <https://www.livemint.com/news/india/how-covid-19-response-disrupted-health-services-in-rural-india-11587713155817.html>

15. Advisory on Right of Women in the Context of COVID-19. *National Human Rights Commission.* 2020 <https://nhrc.nic.in/sites/default/files/Advisory%20on%20Rights%20of%20Women_0.pdf>

16. United Nations Children's Fund, COVID-19: A threat to progress against child marriage, UNICEF, New York, 2021 <https://data.unicef.org/resources/covid-19-a-threat-to-progress-against-child-marriage/>

17. Patil M S. Gender Equity and COVID-19: Dalit Standpoints. *Economic and Political Weekly.* 2021 <https://www.epw.in/engage/article/gender-equity-and-covid-19-dalit-standpoints>

18. International Institute for Population Sciences (IIPS) and ICF. National Family Health Survey (NFHS-4): 2015-16. 2017.

19. World Food Program and National Statistical Office. Food and Nutritional Security Analysis.2019.

20. Deshpande A, Ramachandran R. How Caste Discrimination Impacts Child Development and Stunting in India. The Wire. 2021 <https://thewire.in/caste/caste-discrimination-child-development-stunting-malnutrition-india>

21. Ibid

22. Deshpande A, Ramachandran R. How Caste Discrimination Impacts Child Development and Stunting in India. The Wire. 2021 <https://thewire.in/caste/caste-discrimination-child-development-stunting-malnutrition-india>

23. United Nations Sustainable Development Group. Policy Brief: The Impact of COVID-19 on Children,2020: 09-10

24. Key Indicators of Household Social Consumption on Education in India, NSS 75th round. Government of India, *Ministry of Statistics & Programme Implementation*. 2017-18

25. United Nations Sustainable Development Group. Policy Brief: The Impact of COVID-19 on Children,Ibid

26. ActionAid Association. Sphere of Exclusion: A Policy Document. ActionAid Association, Jaipur Regional Office, 2016 <https://www.actionaidindia.org/wp-content/uploads/2018/06/Sphere-of-Exclusion-NTDNT-policy-advocacy-folder-Flier.pdf>

27. Bagai A, Sukumar A, Puri S. Women in India: COVID-19 Impact, Response and Policy Environment. Sattva. 2021 <https://www.sattva.co.in/wp-content/uploads/2021/03/Sattva_Insights_Gender_COVID-19-Response-and-Policy-Environment.pdf>

28. *Population Foundation of India*. Policy Brief: The Impact of COVID-19 on Women. Population Foundation of India. 2020

29. OECD. Combatting COVID-19's Effect on Children. Tackling Coronavirus (COVID-19):Contributing to a Global Effort. 2020 <https://www.oecd.org/coronavirus/policy-responses/combatting-covid-19-s-effect-on-children-2e1f3b2f/>

30. United Nations Sustainable Development Group. Policy Brief: The Impact of COVID-19 on Children,Ibid:14-17

31. Gupta A. Red Tape: Bureaucracy, Structural Violence and Poverty in India. *Duke University Press*. 2012: 26-27

PART II

Pandemic, Cities and Technology: Governance Questions

6

URBAN DEVELOPMENT AND PANDEMIC: A TIME TO RESET THE PRIORITIES

P. Joy Oommen

Abstract: *Administrators want their cities to be more resilient in the wake of the Covid-19 crisis, but it can be achieved only by making the poor and vulnerable sections of the population more resilient to unanticipated shocks. Providing a cleaner and more hygienic environment, adequate and safe housing, access to reliable and affordable healthcare for them should form the core of this effort. This in turn will call for an all-out effort to regularize and upgrade slums and other illegal colonies where the economically or socially weaker sections live or provide them alternate accommodation. Increasing the stock of affordable rental housing is another priority. Availability of land is often mentioned as a constraint, but we see that many Government departments and PSUs are making plans to monetize the 'excess lands' in their possession. This should stop and all excess lands should be handed over to Local Governments with a mandate to use them primarily for developing civic amenities and housing for the weaker sections. A reliable and efficient public transport system with coordination among all players - public and private- is surely a priority for any city. It would help the cause of a cleaner environment while saving money and time for the commuters. Helping more people to get jobs and livelihoods is another major challenge. Ease of doing business is best achieved when local governments facilitate investments and new enterprises. Special efforts would be needed to help those in the informal sector to get their jobs and livelihoods back. Targeted skill development and retraining, setting up of orderly and well-maintained markets, facilitating bank loans and ensuring support of civil society organizations are needed to achieve this. Overall, it is the opportune time to reset our priorities and move forward.*

Key Words: Urban resilience, excess lands. Ease of doing business, Livelihood, Skill development. Vulnerable population.

Introduction

India is among the countries worst affected by the Covid-19 pandemic in terms of the total number of infections and deaths. And as we have moved into the second half of 2021, we are making a slow and painful recovery from a much more lethal version of the pandemic, described as the second wave. Going forward, it appears reasonable to prepare ourselves, individually and collectively, to live with the pandemic of varying degrees of severity for some more years into the future. In the meantime, we also realise that the pandemic has done as much devastation to the health of our economy as it has to the health of millions of people. A Pew Research Report of 2021 estimated that about 33 million people belonging to the middle class in India had slipped into poverty during 2020. Another Research Agency, the Mumbai- based Centre for the Monitoring of Indian Economy (CMIE) has estimated the number of people who have suffered fall in incomes during 2020-21 to be as high as 97 percent. Meanwhile urban unemployment is at an all-time high of 17 percent according to their report for May 2021. There are reports in many States of people from all walks of life--- businessmen, farmers, professionals and young people committing suicide on account of mounting debts, failed businesses, lost jobs.

It is clear that if we have to put a halt to the human tragedy that is continuing to unfold before us, we would need to look at urgent and radical changes not just in the way we deal with natural or man-made disasters like a pandemic but also how we pursue socio- economic development of the people in our country. Since the resources available to individual sectors are limited, it also becomes imperative to prioritise the plans and projects to achieve the objectives in a time-bound manner. This paper attempts to undertake this task of resetting the goals and priorities for India's urban sector.

It needs to be kept in mind that irrespective of the sector, the principles that would govern or determine the objectives would be common for all of them. Elimination of hunger and poverty, creation of employment and livelihoods, provision of hygienic physical environment and shelter along with physical and social security, access to affordable health care and education are among the most important of those objectives. Every sector has to directly address these objectives or support others in achieving them. Pursuing economic growth in terms of GDP growth rates or setting targets like achieving $5 trillion GDP by 2025 cannot save large sections of our population descending further into abject poverty, disease and squalor. There is also overwhelming evidence to show that through the pandemic period, income inequalities in India, which were already at alarmingly high levels, have worsened.

The first section of this paper provides an overview of India's urban landscape, their contribution towards India's economy and the tremendous pressures that they sustain due to massive migration which leads to the lack of basic civic amenities for large sections of the poor who live in the city. The second section of the paper draws attention to the migrant labour crisis witnessed by India in 2020 soon after the government announced a lockdown to contain the spread of COVID-19 and draws attention to the challenges to urban planning while suggesting a set of recommendations with regard to how the urban poor can be helped with provisioning of housing facilities, land, rental agreement schemes, public transport, social infrastructure and livelihoods schemes. The third section presents the conclusions.

I

India's Urban Landscape: The Fading Golden Lights

India is not among the more urbanised countries of the world. In 2021, the estimated urban population stood at 34.93 percent. In the case of China, the only comparable country in terms of total size of population, it is 60 percent. However the projections for 2036 indicate a much sharper growth of urban population with as many as six States- Kerala, Tamil Nadu,Telangana, Gujarat, Maharashtra and Delhi--- emerging as 'urban states' with over 50 percent of population in urban areas. Many of the larger cities of the country are already among the most populous in the world as also among the most congested and polluted. About 35 percent of the population live under tarpaulin or tin shelters in slums which lack almost all civic amenities other than perhaps a few common water taps. The majority of them wait for water tankers to come from the municipal bodies (or from private suppliers who sell water at very high prices). Many of these slum areas report major disease outbreaks every year especially during rainy seasons on account of contaminated water. It is also true that cities being the main transportation hubs, especially with their airports and some with seaports, are the entry points for new infections coming from other States and countries. The high population densities and cramped living conditions make spread of infections faster too. A crowd-sourced survey of the National Institute of Urban Affairs showed that in the first wave of Covid-19, as much as 90 percent of the total infections happened in the 100 most populous cities of the country. Even the advantages that the cities have in terms of better health infrastructure and access to information and support systems proved inadequate especially during the second wave of COVID-19 pushing up the death toll to alarming levels. We have also witnessed the soul-crushing effects of country-wide lockdowns on low-income groups,daily wage labourers, street vendors, migrant labour and semi-skilled workers in the informal sector.

Whose City is it?

Whether in times of a crisis or in normal times cities and even smaller urban centres are looked upon as leaders for their rural hinterlands. As providers of employment and livelihood opportunities, cities sustain and nourish the economies of many countries. The bigger cities have been the centres of enterprise and innovation in India too. Mumbai, for example, is not just India's largest city but also generates 6.16% of the total GDP of the country. It also contributes 10% of factory employment, 25% of industrial output, 33% of income tax collections and 60% of the Customs duties. A Barclays Bank study of the contribution of urban areas to the total GDP of selected countries showed the figure for India at 62% and predicted that it would rise to 75% by 2020.

Urban centres, especially the larger ones, have evolved over a long period of time in acquiring their political importance, socio-economic stature and cultural identities. The continuous inward and outward migration of people for political reasons like conquests and colonisation in the past and for economic reasons in modern times have contributed to significant changes in the demographic, economic and cultural complexion of these centres. It is important to realise that our cities have evolved on the strength of migrants from villages and towns-near and afar-at various points of time in history. Yet, the role of urban centres is often taken for granted and they suffer conscious or benevolent neglect when resources are allocated by governments. As a result, most of our cities today have creaky and aging infrastructure ready to break down under pressure as the second wave of the pandemic has demonstrated. The pandemic has also exposed the fault lines of not just our economy but also our governance systems, especially of our urban centres. It is time to realise that there has been a collective failure to render justice to large sections of our population. It is, therefore, the most opportune time for us to rethink our urban policies and reset the priorities for the sector.

II

The Migrant Labour Crisis of 2020

Any discussion of our plans for the urban India of tomorrow cannot ignore the hard lessons we have learnt from the heart-wrenching saga of the migrant labour during the country-wide lockdown of March 2020 to contain the spread of Covid-19 infections. The suddenness of the move with just about 4 hours notice came like a bolt from the blue for most people. Since the announcement was at night, many who were not watching their television sets got to hear about it only the next morning when the orders were already being enforced. However, what happened thereafter in the larger cities was bizarre. Thousands of migrant labourers poured into the streets with their families including children in tow, all of them carrying some bagful of their possessions and many took the desperate decision to walk to their homes, hundreds or even thousands of kilometres away. Sadly, quite a few of them met with accidents, killing hundreds while many who were walking all the way under the harsh summer sun collapsed on the way from hunger and exhaustion. There were even more tragic stories of families sleeping on railway tracks presuming that no trains were operating, only to be run over by Goods Trains.

Yet, in less than a year after they left, we see that many of the migrant labourers are back in the cities - even if not the same cities or towns. Many more are expected to be back as the villages they had fled to would give them love and kinship but not money or work. Some State governments had opened works under the rural employment guarantee scheme but with limits on the total days of work and wages much lower than what they were getting in the cities, the workers realised that they stood a better chance to survive or prosper by taking a plunge into the urban alleys once again.

Economic Resilience of Urban Poor as a Development Objective

Many city administrators and urban planners recognise that making the cities resilient against natural or man-made disasters is an objective of their development programmes. Yet the discussions and plans for resilient cities are often limited to construction works- protective walls, bunds and drainage channels to ward off the threat of floods or creating emergency shelters and training of volunteers. The devastation caused by the pandemic has made us realise that a resilient city cannot be built by an army of hungry and malnourished citizenry ravaged physically and mentally by personal tragedies and unending financial hardships. Policy makers and planners have to wake up to the realisation that our cities and towns can become resilient only if we can ensure adequate and affordable housing in a hygienic environment to all citizens along with access to affordable healthcare, good quality education for the children and employment /livelihood opportunities. We certainly would need competent and committed urban administrators and city planners to make this happen who can deliver effectively only if they get support in the form of more funds and enabling laws and regulations from national and state level policy makers. Master-plan-related rigidities, zoning and land-use restrictions, unrealistic building bye-laws, are all issues which need to be initiated and tackled at the city level if plans to provide housing and civic amenities to the poor are to become a reality. Wherever the plans require any relaxation of the extant laws and regulations or inclusion of new enabling provisions, expeditious action from the State authorities would become necessary.

Dilemmas in Setting Goals and Priorities for the Urban Sector

Traditionally 'Urban Development' by government departments in the country were more about taking up infrastructural items like roads, bridges, storm water drains and sewerage lines, water supply works and waste-management units and similar construction or maintenance projects than about pursuing any overarching goals or priorities. These works are usually carried out as secular projects with no bias to any category of the population. Of what avail are cleanliness and hand washing campaigns or '*Swacch Bharat Abhiyan*', when even basic minimum quantities of water are not available to many who are surrounded by an unhygienic environment? Similar situations arise when extension of power lines or setting up of transformers are taken up. How do we promote education- conventional or online--- for the children if the homes-legal or illegal-- do not have power supply? No doubt, under the prevailing rules and regulations, municipal bodies and power companies cannot provide water or power connections to those living in illegal settlements. Digging new drainage and sewerage lines for regular settlements also get held up because of the problem of resettling occupants of houses / huts in their alignments. Even when city administrators and planners know that the problem calls for a resolution through regularisation of 'illegal colonies' and resettling any displaced/ affected families, all of them would say they are helpless unless 'political' decisions are taken from above. In many States, some of these problems get addressed on the eve of elections to the State or Central legislatures or to the municipal bodies when ad hoc 'political' decisions are taken to give some temporary facilities like common water taps/ hand pumps and streetlights (and from which supply lines it becomes possible to take illegal connections with total disregard for safety norms).

Even when some of them are convinced about the need for providing better civic amenities and housing for those living in slums or hitherto neglected areas of their urban area, they face other dilemmas like finding funds and more importantly additional land for such projects. In most of the Urban Local Bodies(ULBs) there is an unwritten agreement among the elected members or the Corporators that funds will be evenly distributed to all the wards irrespective of the special needs of any of the historically underserved ones. They oppose allocation of extra funds to any areas unless there are any expected electoral benefits to the political parties to which they belong. The returns in terms of property taxes for the ULB from projects for the poor would be negligible too in the eyes of some of them. Finding additional land in already congested colonies or near lands already under encroachments is not easy either. Any evictions or shifting of even a few to execute the projects, often meet with strong resistance from some of the beneficiaries too unless special efforts are taken to convince them that the benefits would far outweigh any temporary inconvenience to them. Providing alternate accommodation in a convenient location is the minimum they would insist on. It is clear that unless the State Government and the ULB agree on a common strategy with earmarked allocation of funds for priority areas along with time-bound targets, it is difficult to make any headway. If the Government of India can support these efforts with a national programme comparable in scale/financial allocation to the Jawaharlal Nehru Urban Renewal Mission (JNNURM) or the Smart City Mission, it will give a boost to make our cities more inclusive and livable.

A Place to Rest One's Weary Head

As early as in 1948, the United NationsUniversal Declaration of Human Rights (UDHR) recognised 'Adequate Housing' as one of the components of Human Rights. On the basis of the provisions established in UDHR, the human right to adequate housing was elaborated and reaffirmed in 1966 by the International Covenant on Economic, Social and Cultural Rights (ICESCR). India had ratified this Covenant in 1976. The 'Sustainable Development Goals (SDGs) 2015' formulated by the UN and adopted by India under Target 11 promises access to safe and affordable housing and basic services to all people. The specific indicator of progress is the fall in the proportion of urban population living in slums, informal settlements or inadequate housing.

Of all the areas where India's urban policies have proved inadequate and half-hearted, housing would top the list. Most available reports on surveys and estimates of housing needs of weaker sections are either out-dated or unreliable. Occasional news relating to the Prime Minister's scheme for urban poor talk about targets and completed numbers for the entire country and at times of particular States. It is difficult to get a sense or an update on the estimated number of people continuing to live in unsafe and unhygienic dwelling units or under tarpaulin sheets in illegal settlements or notified slums. UN Habitat estimated the percentage of urban population living in slums in India at 35.2 in 2018. Census of 2011 had put the figure for Mumbai at 42 percent. Surveys done in slum areas at State levels appear to have critical gaps. The Karnataka Slum Development Board's website shows the number of slums in Bangalore as 597 and the population living there as 3,69,711. This survey is part of the Census Report of 2011 and there is nothing to show that the Board has made any efforts to get it updated. A satellite imagery-based survey followed by ground verification done by Omidyar Network, India, and Duke University, USA, in 2018 showed over 2000 slums in the city. Similar discrepancies abound in surveys relating to other cities and towns too. While the percentage of the country's urban population living in slums is estimated to be about 30 percent in 2018 the number of people living in uninhabitable and unsafe dwelling units would be much higher.

All our current efforts including the Prime Minister's AwasYojana (PMAY) have not been able to make a dent on the ground situation as some of the reviews of the scheme have revealed. One important component of PMAY is the 'In-Situ Slum Redevelopment (ISSR)' which is a plan to assist building of houses through private participation on the land of the slum dwellers with a subsidy of Rs 1 lakh per unit which is too little to motivate even charitable trusts to get into the task of developing at least minimal infrastructure and construction of new houses. The scheme says that if either higher FSI/FAR or Transferable Development Rights (TDR) are provided to the private developer, even this Rs 1lakh will not be available. The second component is the Beneficiary-led Individual House Construction/Enhancement (BLC) scheme which provides for direct central assistance of Rs 1.5 lakhs to families belonging to EWS categories to either construct a new house or make additions and alterations to their existing house by themselves. Here again the subsidy is too low at current costs for an individual to make even basic improvements to their houses or ensure the minimum amenities as prescribed by the Ministry of Housing and Urban affairs (MHUA) in its description of the scope of the scheme. Some State governments have tried to give an additional subsidy from their budgets but overall, it has been difficult to see any visible improvements in the quality of the houses.

The third component is the 'Credit Linked Scheme (CLS)' which makes available loans ranging from Rs 6–12 lakh at low rates of interest, to both economically weaker sections and even other low income or middle income families for construction of new homes or renovation of their existing homes. One common difficulty faced by all potential beneficiaries in these three components of PMAY is that only those with land titles can avail of the scheme. Unless the State Governments and Urban Local Bodies regularise the slums and provide land titles to the residents they cannot get the benefit of the scheme.

There is a fourth component called the Affordable Housing in Partnership (AHP) which extends Central assistance of Rs 1.5 lakhs for affordable housing projects done by states, either through its agencies or in partnership with the private sector for the Economically Weaker Sections (EWS). As could be expected, the progress in the first two components, ISSR and BLC has been poor. While the latest progress of PMAY is not available in the website of MHUA, a study published in ' The Wire' an online journal in May 2019, has shown the progress in the two components at about 12 percent of the total. The other two schemes appear to have been more popular as comparatively better off sections of urban population rather than poorer ones find it easy to satisfy the eligibility conditions. The AHP scheme has been more attractive to both State agencies and private developers as the projects could cater to composite schemes including much higher income groups also.

If the flagship schemes of the governments suffer from conceptual problems, implementation of the projects on the ground face many more practical issues. In situ schemes cause disruptions in the day to day lives of the beneficiaries and in turn cause delays and cost overruns. Appropriateness of the design of the houses or layout plans of the projects also may cause heartburns and resentment among intended beneficiaries. Experience in some of the cities show that most urban poor are wary of moving into high rise apartment complexes as they are not sure about the reliability of common services like lifts, water supply and maintenance of common areas. Any breakdowns in these services could severely disrupt their lives especially if they have old family members or young school going children. Even in locations where land availability is a severe constraint, one plus three floors would be the maximum they would be happy to accept. It would be a good idea to hire the services of innovative architects to plan these housing projects.

Many States have addressed these problems in different and sometimes unique ways. Some States like Kerala have made available a large number of plots to the homeless over the years and also given them assistance by way of loans at subsidised interest rates in addition to subsidies (sometimes dovetailed with Central Government schemes) on the basis of progress of construction. In cities or towns where land is not available in areas acceptable to the beneficiaries, multiple storied complexes have been constructed but the nodal state agencies have been assisting the residents with maintenance support in the initial years.

One of the most radical steps taken by any State Governments in the country was the regularisation of all dwelling units in slum areas or in any other illegal settlements on all categories of urban land by the Government of Madhya Pradesh in 1985. The residents of these houses became title holders of the land on which their houses were located, limited to 500 square feet of land, overnight. Wherever the houses were obstructing public roads or drainage/sewerage lines, temporary land titles were given and the owners could be evicted only after alternate plots in nearby locations could be given to them with permanent land titles. The title deeds entitled the owners to get bank loans either for home improvements or other purposes making a qualitative change in the lives of those people. In this model the occupants on all the 'illegal' colonies and encroaches on other government lands became title holders of their homesteads something similar to the Kerala Land Reforms Act of 1969 which provided that all occupants of hutments on private agricultural lands would be entitled to 10 cents of land in rural areas and 5 cents in urban areas. Some other States have provided some ready built houses through Slum Development Boards or State Housing Boards/ Corporations. AP Housing Corporation of undivided Andhra Pradesh had constructed a large number of houses for the weaker sections of the population in both urban and rural areas. In recent years most State Housing Boards and Slum Development Boards have become lame-duck organisations with debt repayment/ default issues. The responsibility of making available developed plots or houses with basic infrastructure has thus come upon the Municipal bodies though many of them do not have qualified or experienced technical or accounting personnel. It is important that State Governments take a hard look at these issues and find appropriate agencies to plan and execute innovative projects that can provide safe and comfortable homes in a hygienic environment at low costs.

There is No Land in the City…for the Poor

Finding sufficient land within the city limits is considered the single biggest problem faced by civic authorities, State Housing Authorities and Slum Development Boards, when it comes to providing civic amenities or housing for urban poor. The fact, however, is that land for these uses are never considered by the governments as an important need, unlike land for construction of, say, new highways, ring roads,a metro line or even a stadium. Though land for resettling slums or to provide housing for the weaker sections is a continuing need in all urban areas, very few city or town master plans specifically provide for these uses. This also does not figure in the regular ongoing schemes of the local body. While the city needs construction labour (a good number of them are always migrants from within or outside the State), helpers, drivers, security staff, cooks, cleaners, and a host of other low-wage-earners, the need to provide for their housing seems to escape their attention of planners. Nor are the small traders/ vendors of grocery, fruits,flowers and vegetables or other small household items like pots, vessels and the like, able to find some 'legitimate' space to sell their humble wares.. The only option available to them is to become illegal occupants on public land of various descriptions since all other lands have already been cornered by richer classes and Government Departments.

A Bad Idea called Land Monetisation by Government Departments and Public Sector units (PSUs)

In the light of the above discussions, it is apparent that the natural claimants for any identified excess land in urban areas are the poor and homeless in particular, who never got their due in all these years. Many public bodies like Municipal Corporations, City Development Authorities and Housing Boards have over the years sold or auctioned the lands available with them or developed shopping centres and other commercial buildings with the aim of augmenting their ever-so meagre financial resources. Probably those heading these bodies never thought of land as a scarcer resource than money; nor perhaps would they have ever paused to reflect on the inadequacy of their exertions in making their cities and towns more liveable for large sections of its population. Individually, with their short tenures they may not be culpable for the visible collective apathy and negligence but each one of those working on the urban sector from the Ministry in Delhi to the town planners and Municipal counsellors in the field need to realise that we cannot afford to let the status quo continue any longer.

To start with, the Ministries of the Government of India and Departments of State Governments will need to revisit the ill-advised policy of monetisation of surplus land available with the Ministries/ departments or with the PSUs under them. A report in Times of India of March 22, 2021 mentioned the plan of Government of Karnataka to clear all encroached land parcels of land and sell them as a part of its asset monetisation plan. The report went on to say that in Bengaluru Urban District alone 16,149 acres of land were available for monetisation. In plain words it would mean that the poor will be evicted and the lands would be given to the rich and powerful. The report shows clearly that the claims of most State governments that they have no land to resettle urban poor or regularise areas currently occupied by them, are false. Since many of the encroachers are not poor, it would also mean that the government will evict them only to 'monetise' the lands and not for meeting the housing needs of the weaker sections.

In recent months we have also seen similar appalling reports of the Ministry of Defence and Railways preparing plans to monetise the excess lands available with them. Neither of these Ministries can pretend that it is not their role or duty to make available land for housing or resettling the urban poor. These lands were never earned or bought by them out of any revenues earned by them and were gifted by the country and the State Governments in particular at various points of time in public interest. All surplus lands of Ministries, Departments and PSUs should be placed with the State Government and in turn to the Local bodies for resettling crowded slums and for providing on priority, housing schemes on ownership or rental basis to the poor at costs they can afford. That would be one of the finest things that we as a country can do to atone for the collective neglect of urban poor over the years. Some of the most miserable urban poor are found on or near the Railway tracks of the country and they should not be evicted till they are resettled in the 'surplus lands' available with the Railways.

Why don't We have Rental Housing Schemes for Economically Weaker Sections in India?

A question that comes up frequently in this context is why India has not made any serious attempts to promote rental housing for the poor since it is known that the stock of housing for economically weaker sections is currently inadequate as neither real estate developers nor financial institutions invest in such projects. The simple answer is that no serious efforts were ever made in this regard. One normally gets to hear examples of rental housing schemes in Singapore, the US and the UK when this subject is discussed. No doubt, the definitions of urban poor or of affordable housing are vastly different in those countries but it may be possible to follow the broad features of those models in our country too.

The general belief is that without an efficient and a corruption-free agency, rental housing schemes cannot be implemented. It is known that migrant families and construction labour prefer rental housing as their workplaces are often temporary. It is also known that at any given point of time, a larger number of urban poor do pay rentals for their accommodation or for occupying a particular space for their huts, to someone or the other. While some of their landlords or slum lords are titleholders of the lands many others are merely illegal grabbers of Government/ public lands. Since the richer landlords or the real estate developers don't make houses at rental rates that the poor can afford, the tenants have limited options. The reason for the unaffordable rental levels is the high price of land in our urban areas.

In May 2020, Government of India announced an 'Affordable Rental Scheme' for urban poor. However, some of the guidelines that followed, like a common rental rate being fixed for the housing units created under the scheme anywhere in India could make it a non-starter. Even if some of the State Government agencies are able to follow these guidelines, no one is sure for how long they will be able to manage these projects satisfactorily. It would be a better idea to handover the constructed units to NGOs or Cooperatives on the basis of mutually acceptable terms and conditions.

In our urban areas, it has also been commonplace for many middle class or low income group families to rent out spaces from their existing houses or from additionally constructed extensions of their houses. Some of them also run what is popularly known as ' paying guest accommodation' or PGs. These landlords and ladies should be identified and given bank loans at rates subsidised by State or Central government to support their socially important initiatives. NGOs and Self-Help Groups could also be allowed to avail such concessional loans for Rental Housing projects. Governments should however avoid the temptation to fix limits on rental rates which should be left to market forces and rent laws prevailing in the States. At this stage it is more important to increase the stock of housing units for the poor, which alone will help stabilisation of rentals at more reasonable levels.

Another way to promote rental housing could be to persuade organisations like Associations of real estate developers, large contractors, and companies who supply staff/workers on contract basis to other companies to take up the responsibility of providing rental housing to the workers engaged by them. Individual developers who use their own or hired labour on contract, contractors and staffing companies who engage regular or temporary workers should be asked to contribute to a special fund created by their own associations which could be used to buy land and construct houses to be rented out to workers engaged by the member-companies. Payment of rent fixed by these associations can be paid directly by the tenants or the member-companies . If these associations do not take up this work voluntarily, Local Governments authorities should introduce suitable legislation to at least make them contribute to the fund and handover the responsibility of running the scheme to any other designated agencies.

State governments could also consider utilising a part of the substantial accumulated funds under the 'The Building and Other Construction Workers Act 1996' towards building rental housing complexes for construction workers in the city. These could also be managed by the Board created under the Act and rented only to genuine construction labourers working on live projects. Meanwhile, this Act needs updated provisions to include quality parameters relating to on-site accommodation given to the workers. The accommodation currently provided by most contractors to their workers have appalling living conditions.

Some States which take up land pooling or Town Planning Schemes (as they are described in Gujarat and Maharashtra) should instead of using the entire Government share of land for commercial, recreational or public facilities or even general housing projects, set apart some land for subsidised housing schemes including rental housing for the migrant labour and other economically weaker sections who are not able to buy houses from normal projects. Madhya Pradesh Government had in the 1980s a provision in the regulations for real estate development agencies by which 15 percent of the land being developed by them was required to be set apart and made available to Government agencies for developing housing schemes for the poor. However even when lands were made available by the developers, Government agencies could not utilise them for want of funds or their inability to raise funds exclusively for housing the poor (unlike composite schemes which get easier funding). In some cases, the land available in some locations was too little to promote viable schemes. Later the State Government amended the provision to say that the developers could instead of setting apart the land, pay the money equivalent of the 15 percent land to the designated government agency. However, this plan also didn't meet with much success. It should, however, be possible for many State governments to take up more pragmatic variations of such otherwise progressive ideas to promote housing schemes for the economically weaker sections.

Public Transport Can Make a Difference!

It would sound ironic that the Covid 19 has brought relief to at least some sections of the population in our cities who hailed some unexpected benefits of lockdowns: those who didn't have to move out of their homes to buy anything or go even to the bank, with virtually everything delivered home and payments made online. Services of all professionals and government offices and Law Courts could also be availed online. These sections of the population were delighted to note that air pollution levels had fallen and they were able to see the clear blue skies once again. However, the people delighted with the fall in pollution because of the lockdowns have been mostly users of their own cars or taxis for their commutes to work and seldom users of public transport. They in fact have been active contributors to the city's air pollution in normal times and they would be back on the roads as soon as the restrictions on movements are withdrawn.

Meanwhile, another larger section of the population was suffocating in their cramped homes or sitting outside their narrow streets unable to go anywhere with all public transport suspended for indefinite periods. Many families had exhausted all their savings in the early days of lockdown itself and their bread earners had to walk many kilometers everyday either in search of some odd jobs or to continue with their petty businesses or buy their daily essentials. Public transport has always been the first to close down and the last to restart whenever any restrictions were announced by Governments. Those with their own vehicles, even cycles, got a head start and went ahead as others missed the bus in a literal sense.

The above situation will have a huge impact on the prospects for public transport services as we trudge back to normalcy. Some sections of the population have become self-sufficient and are happy to avoid buses, metro services or suburban rail services. It is possible that congestion, traffic bottlenecks and resulting pollution could get much worse than what we have witnessed in pre-Covid times. Yet with some hard work and by following the basic canons of public transport like reliability, punctuality and safety while making extra efforts to make the journeys comfortable through better maintenance of the vehicles, we should be able to get public transport back on its wheels.

Some cities like Bengaluru had made extra efforts to promote bus transport with dedicated bus lanes in popular busy routes. Some cities like Ahmedabad , Indore, and Raipur have gone for Bus Rapid Transit Systems though currently for only on limited routes. Such initiatives will need to be copied/ multiplied by all our cities and larger towns. Metro and Suburban Rail authorities and public transport corporations will also need to coordinate on a continuous basis to help one another to serve the commuters better which will no doubt also help to serve their own financial interests in the longer term. Some cities have tied up with minibus and auto rickshaw operators, to resolve last mile connectivity issues. Bike renting facilities and even construction of better pedestrian pathways along roadsides leading to the bus stops can help the cause of public transport. Transport departments of State Governments, Metro Authorities and Bus Operators should however keep asking themselves whether their services are helping the segments of the population who need their services most.

Some States put harsh restrictions on private bus and minibus operators, not as much in public interest as to protect the State Bus Transport Corporations from competition. City authorities should conduct surveys for new bus routes and consider private operators in areas underserved by State Corporations. It would also make sense to incentivise use of private buses for transport of company workers or students by the managements of those organisations. Those buses should also be allowed to operate on dedicated bus lanes wherever such lanes are available. The services of innovative 'Start up' enterprises should be utilised for extending multiple services to the users of public transport once the operators are ready with their routes, timetables and tariffs. A big push to muti-modal public transport is necessary to persuade people to give up their individual vehicles and go for public transport options for their regular commutes to work.

As we have already noted, urbanisation is happening at a greater pace than in the past and Urban limits of many cities and towns are getting redrawn more often. Town Planners will need to plan for more efficient transport corridors and reserve areas along the corridors for housing of the weaker sections.

Social Infrastructure: For Whom, What and How much?

While planning and designing social infrastructure in urban areas, we need to ask once again the basic questions in any planning exercise: what, for whom and how much. Healthcare infrastructure is surely the most important area where we need to make up for the accumulated neglect of many years. We have been reading of many instances where in some States the Primary Healthcare Centres (PHCs) and Sub-Centres existed only on paper or there were only some dilapidated buildings without doctors or paramedical personnel. Though many of those reports relate more to rural areas, the situation is no better in the smaller towns. To start with, we need to find appropriate locations in under- serviced areas for new buildings to house healthcare facilities.

There is also the need to attend on priority to a related issue that will remain as a collective guilt in the minds of all Indians who have been fortunate to be alive today--the way our dead brethren were treated during the pandemic. The high cost of funerals, insufficiency of cremation and burial space led to a situation that made the dead suffer indignities and their relatives shame and pain for a lifetime. Providing for these inadequacies is the responsibility of city/ town authorities and they need to keep in mind that many from nearby rural areas also come to the cities to cremate or bury their dead. Existing facilities will also need modernisation to replace the use of wood to the extent possible.

It is known that women and children and those with physical or mental disabilities suffered neglect during the pandemic leading to long term adverse effects on their health. Services of many government departments for child care, nutrition of children and pregnant or lactating mothers had become non-functional during the pandemic. The proximity of the centres extending these services to the beneficiaries needs to be reassessed and more centres set up to serve slums and other areas where the vulnerable sections of the population live. Education of the school- going children is another area where we need to make many more improvements as many glaring inequalities and comparative disadvantages of children from families suffering economic hardships came to the fore. Online teaching and the consequent situation of children with laptops or at least smartphones alone being able to attend classes has added a new dimension to deprivation during the lockdown.

According to the Government of India's Unified District Information System for Education Report released on July1, 2021,only 22% of the schools in India had Internet facilities. Data relating to government schools show that less than 12% had the facility. Even in a state like Karnataka, nearly one-third of the students did not have access to any online devices during the 2020-22 academic year according to a survey conducted by the Directorate of Public Instruction reported in *The Hindu*. Equipping Government/Municipal Schools with smart class rooms and training of the teachers thus becomes a priority. Central and State Governments who are driving digital transactions and payments should take the help of smartphone manufacturers and Telecom companies to ensure availability of cheaper smartphones with connectivity to as many families as possible. Restarting midday meals with extra nutrition for the children rejoining the schools will also go a long way in getting the drop-outs to get back and stay.

The Challenge of Providing Employment, Incomes and Livelihoods

Cities have grown in size and prosperity on the strength of their ability to provide employment, incomes and livelihoods. In all these aspects cities received a battering during the pandemic. As we have noted, urban unemployment in India touched 17 percent in May 2021 and employees in many sectors faced pay cuts, layoffs, and retrenchment since the announcement of the nation-wide lockdown in March 2020. The Global Wage Report of ILO for 2020-21 shows that the wages of informal sector workers in India suffered a fall of 22.6 percent while salaries of formal sector employees went down by as much as 36 percent. Sadly, we have no estimate of the fall in incomes of other categories in the informal sector like street hawkers, artisans, and owners of micro enterprises. Nor do we have any reliable data on how many migrant workers had left the cities and towns during the pandemic and how many have come back. Even worse, we now learn that the official figures relating to deaths on account of Covid 19 are far lower than the real numbers. It should be obvious that the unreported cases can only be of people dying without property or insurance since otherwise the relatives of the dead would have ensured that the deaths were registered.

As business and industrial units plan the restart of their operations, local authorities will need to play a facilitating role, be it in renewing licences or permits, issuing fresh permissions and approvals wherever needed or may be in making available power and water connections. While Union and State governments have been wooing domestic as well as overseas investors, local governments like city corporations and Municipal bodies have often been perceived as unhelpful and dilatory in their dealings with business and industrial enterprises. A more proactive role from their side will help fresh investments in new or existing enterprises thereby helping creation of more employment and incomes for the people. Their supportive role is even more important for the informal sector units to restart operations. Making available space for informal markets, maintaining cleanliness and hygiene in such locations are important in giving a fresh start to those who had been forced to abandon their tiny businesses for long periods. NGOs and social workers should be supported in helping informal sector service units and vendors of fruits, flowers and vegetables in handling digital transactions and in availing credit from banks or micro finance institutions. State Governments will need to actively promote training and re-skilling of unemployed youth and labourers who have lost jobs in recent times.

III

Conclusion

While there is no way to make up for the lives lost to the Covid- 19 pandemic, we can do a lot more to save more lives being lost to disease, hunger and poverty. Creating cleaner and more hygienic cities is possible if we follow a clear set of priorities and focus our attention and resources on the people who need them most. The best of our town planners, science and technology institutions and young innovators should be involved in planning and designing improved settlements and housing, transport corridors, routes for public transport and preparing connectivity solutions. The first call for use of any vacant lands or excess lands available with government departments and PSUs should be for resettlement of slums, new housing colonies for weaker sections and for augmentation of civic amenities in underserved areas. Industry leaders, Social scientists, NGOs, MFIs and bankers should become partners in a collective effort to help those who lost jobs and livelihoods and the new job seekers in the market. Our urban areas have the strength and potential to lead our economic recovery and create a more sustainable and inclusive nation.

*P Joy Oommen is a former Chief Secretary of Chhattisgarh and currently an Adjunct Professor with Xavier Institute of Management and Entrepreneurship, Bengaluru. The author gratefully acknowledges the helpful comments and suggestions received from Dr Champaka Rajagopal of Azim Premji University, on the draft of this paper.

ENDNOTES

1. Pew Research Center: The Pandemic Stalls Growth in the Global Middle Class,Pushes Poverty up Sharply, Marsh 18, 2021

2. Vyas, Mahesh, Scroll.in, May 29,2021: '97% Indians have been left poorer by the pandemic'.

3. Praharaj,Sarbeswar; Vaidya,Hitesh, April 2020 :The Urban Dimension of Covid 19, National Institute of Urban Affairs, New Delhi.

4. Business Standard, March 20, 2014: Barclays Report-Urban Population to Contribute 70-75% of India's GDP by2020

5. Bhalotia,Shania; Dhingra,Swati;Kondirolli,Fjolla: City of Dreams no More: The Impact of Covid 19 on Urban Workers in India, Centre for Economic

6. Tripathi, Sabyasachi:'Why is the Rural to Urban Migration Rate in India so Low? An Empirical Analysis' Review of Regional Sudies, Volume 51,Issue1, September 28,2020

7. United Nations Human Settlements Programme (UN Habitat):Population Living in Slums, -India, 2018

8. Omidiar Network and Duke University: Studying the Real Slums of Bengaluru, 2018

9. Kanwar Shaguna in WIRE (the wire.in), May 14, 2019: How the PM's Affordable Housing Scheme Went from Promising to Dysfunctional

10. ORF Occasional Paper, March 2019: Housing Poverty in Urban India.

11. The Times of India, 29 June,2021: Land Sale; Karnataka Govt Plans New Asset

12. The Hindu, April 21, 2021, 'No Improvement in living conditions of metro workers in Bengaluru: Survey by Maraa, Media Collective.

13. The Hindu, July 2, 2021: Survey of Department of Public Instruction, Government of Karnataka

14. INTERNATIONAL LABOUR OFFICE, International Labour Organisation, December 2020 : Global Wage Report 2020-21: Wages and Minimum Wages in the Time of COVID - 19

15. Azim Premji University: Reviving Employment and Livelihoods in India, Covid-19 and After, February 25, 2021

7

COVID 19 AND COMPACT CITIES

Mis-aligned Institutional Goals, Policy Opportunism and Planning for Bengaluru, India

Champaka Rajagopal

Abstract: *At the root of the long-standing pre-occupation for decongestion in urban India is the historic bubonic plague, that inflicted most Indian cities in the early 20th century. More than a 100-years hence, the Covid-19 pandemic has only reinforced the fear of congestion in Indian cities. The City of Bengaluru poses an apt example. Aversion to congestion caused by Covid raises one immediate concern for urban planning. Increase in investments in real estate assets in the suburbs of Bengaluru may exacerbate urban sprawl and resource consumption in urbanisation processes, be it land, water, energy or finance. Spatial master plans for Bengaluru have over the last four decades inconsistently oscillated between decongestion and compact cities as an overarching paradigm to shape the city's future growth trajectories. This paper discusses how planning processes circumvent and navigate the governance of the city, manifested through mis-aligned values and goals of a variety of organisations involved in planning. By mapping inter-institutional tensions, public-public and public-private, the author highlights anomalies in urban planning as part of a wider process of State led legal and regulatory incentives for multiple markets that institutionalise urban sprawl. She discusses why sprawl-oriented development dissuades preparedness for uncertainties and concludes by underscoring the need for empowering local governments to orchestrate diverse institutions with divergent values, to frame shared goals and outcomes for Bengaluru.*

Key Words: Urban sprawl, master plans, uncertainties, risks, real estate, mobility, entangled markets.

Institutional Arrangements, Urban Policy and Planning

Stemming from the bubonic plague of the early 20th century, the historically rooted fear of crowding in Indian cities has preoccupied policy makers in their consistent efforts to promote outwardly movement of people from cities, for over four decades. Practitioners and scholars have previously questioned cities' sustained adoption of spatial planning paradigms that consciously promote decongestion. However, a limited body of work examines how weak political governance of cities in India and poorly coordinated heterogeneous organisations with divergent values, impact institutionalisation of urban planning paradigms that promote optimisation of resource consumption. Scholars and practitioners have underscored fundamental anomalies in the governance of urban planning as a cause for promulgation of unsustainable paradigms such as urban sprawl, for Bengaluru [Mohan and Rajagopal, 2011; Idiculla, 2014; Krishnaswamy, Idiculla and Rajagopal, 2017; Mohan, 2021; Krishnankutty, 2021]. The critical question is: how should we re-imagine urban planning as a process that aids reconciliation of divergent values and goals of public, private and civil society organisations, in order to promote judicious consumption of resources including land, and be better prepared for risks such as the Covid 19 pandemic? To respond to this question, this paper investigates contradictions in the responses of the State and local governments to demands of markets and civil-society organisations, in their promulgation of planning paradigms, laws and planning instruments for Bengaluru as a case in point for several other cities in India.

Planning authorities in Bengaluru have been oscillating between compactness and sprawl over the last several decades. Institutional arrangements in Bengaluru, involving a plethora of agencies, public, private and hybrid, often laden with mis-aligned values and goals, typify tensions in envisioning sustainable city futures through planning. The stakes to compactness or sprawl are held by multiple agencies of the government as well as markets. For example, on the one hand, public authorities advance compact or sparsely developed city cores and peripheries by using the master plan as a policy instrument, in order to exert and retain their own control over urban development and resources. On the other, regulatory incentives legitimise market driven agendas of realtors' who often partner with car-automobile dealers to promise images of good quality of life in sprawling gated communities occupying peri-urban areas, for the middle and upper classes. To counter the proliferation of sprawl, international and domestic non-profit organisations have consistently promoted compact cities.

Given this context of heterogeneity, the author analyses tensions and collaborative relationships between government organisations at different levels of governance (Centre, State, local) and between government agencies and allied sectoral markets involved in planning for Bengaluru. Two types of planning authorities, those entrusted with the regulation and governance of land and mobility, are studied. Using three regulatory processes: (a) the Draft Master Plan for Bengaluru 2031 (now revoked), (b) policies pertaining to Transit Oriented Development (TOD), Parking Policy and the Comprehensive Mobility Plan 2020, and, (c) amendments to the Karnataka Land Reforms Act 1961, this paper traces how competing organisations claim regulatory conditions causing contentious public purpose outcomes while drawing spatial development of the city in opposing directions.

The paper is structured in five parts. As a precursor to understanding the forces that cause urban sprawl, the second section below, establishes the context of urban governance and reiterates the question of who should plan for Indian cities [Krishnaswamy, Idiculla and Rajagopal, 2017]. The third section then explores and establishes the heterogeneous institutional context in urban planning in India involving organisations with divergent goals that steer spatial development. The fourth section shows how variety of agencies, government organisations, real estate and mobility markets opportunistically claim development stakes while steering through laws, policies, plans and regulations, in self-serving ways as opposed to in public interest, for Bengaluru. The fifth section discusses how flawed legal amendments, policy and regulatory incentives are at the centre of sprawl and how it has exacerbated multiple societal risks during the pandemic, particularly to the detriment of the poor. The paper concludes with urging the State and local governments to discard business as usual planning practices and instead, frame norms and practices that foster an ecosystem of mutual accountabilities, shared visions and goals among mis-aligned institutions.

Weak Governance of Cities, Ambivalent Ownership of Problems and Planning

It is 30 years since the 74th Constitutional Amendment Act was enacted (1992), with an aim to empower cities, politically, economically and financially, as a third tier of governance following the Centre and the States. The 12th Schedule of the Constitution entrusts urban planning functions with the municipal corporation. Notwithstanding Constitutional mandates to democratise planning processes under a Mayoral regime, urban planning has mostly remained vested with State governments and development authorities at the local levels. Despite repeated demands from civil society organisations, legal practitioners and academics, the landmark Central legislation remains pending implementation for almost all States and cities in India [Idiculla, 2017]. Using the case of Bengaluru, scholars and practitioners have underscored the problem of how weak municipal governments exacerbate anomalies of spatial-economic and social planning processes [Idiculla, 2014; Krishnaswamy, Idiculla, Rajagopal, 2017].

Despite constitutional mandates Members of the Parliament (MPs) and Members of the Legislative Assembly (MLAs) at the national and State levels respectively have continued to occupy territories of municipal legislation [Idiculla, 2015;

Mohan, 2019]. Further, they override municipal autonomy by virtue of performing executive roles in their constituencies [*ibid*]. With no local ownership, future imaginations of city centres are often captured by pro-business alliances between political and business elites [Mohan, 2020]. Incrementally developed peri-urban residential developments, also not free of the ownership conundrum, are often planned, developed, managed and governed in fragmented ways through semi-formal/ informal/ illegal networks between petty private developers, local community leaders, municipal, councils, village panchayats and local politicians, leaving their inhabitants poorly equipped with public health, education or civil amenities.

To compound the problem of weak municipal governance at the macro level, state level legislation for municipal functioning does not empower elected representatives at the lowest level of decisions, i.e., the Ward-level Corporator, to participate in strategic decision making with the State or local governments, leaving their domain of operation to mere execution of minor infrastructure projects. The problem of absent political engagement at the Ward level is inability of elected representatives to mediate contradictory goals of heterogenous groups, including businesses, communities, municipal officials and civil society organisations. Cumulatively, weak local governance plays a fundamental role in adversely impacting local- level planning and preparedness for dealing with emergencies.

On the administrative front, in the absence of a strong politically led municipal corporation, Commissioners of municipal corporations, generally from the Indian Administrative Services cadre, become instruments of political patronage [Jain, 2021]. Politically manoeuvred short-term tenures spanning one to a maximum of two years combined with extant staff imbued with accrued rigidity in bureaucratic operation often struggle to deliver rapidly changing demands of the public [*ibid*]. Senior bureaucrats rely on domain experts who are often technically inclined than strategic, tending to advance growth paradigms as an end in themselves. In times of duress, such as during this pandemic, the loss of strategic agility within municipal governments at the local levels and lack of political agency impedes planned flow of information, communication in locally relevant ways.

Complexifying the decision-making process at the local levels is an amplified set of actors, including international institutions such as International Finance Institutions, the private sector, banking, lending and finance institutions, civil society organisations, residents' welfare associations, which interact with public agencies in attempting to participate or influence decisions at the local levels [Kennedy, 2020] through new models and networks of governance involving 'competing views and interests rather than contestations' [*ibid;* Zérah, 2011 on Baud and de Wit, 2008]. Institutional variety exaggerates ambiguous ownership of public problems and coordination among institutions with divergent goals.

For Bengaluru, the impact of municipal weakness or its absence on planning and risk readiness exists on two fronts, internally within the jurisdiction of the BBMP and externally, areas that are permitted to develop beyond its limits. In a sprawling city such as Bengaluru informal urbanisation spatially transcends the BBMP's jurisdiction of 741 sqkm. Within the Bengaluru Metropolitan Area covering 1,309 sqkm, approximately 100 sqkm of urbanised territories in the peripheries of the city remain under multiple governance regimes, i.e., BDA for statutory planning, development of residential, mixed-use developments, Village Panchayats for village limits and Special Purpose Vehicles for infrastructure projects or Special Economic Zones delineated for manufacturing and services sector activities.

Decisions on whether to sprawl or contain spatial, social and economic development of cities navigates this maze of interests, producing and reproducing the perceived problem of congestion.

Mis-Aligned Institutions: Who Decides on the Question of Congestion

"Transportation technologies shape our communities, and modern sprawl is the child of the automobile." Edward Glaesar explains, in "The Triumph of the City". Transport infrastructure is thus integral to the future imagination of cities. He goes on to make a distinction, "Sprawl isn't the opposite of urban density;..." [Glaesar, 2011: 165-197]. For instance, localities developed distant from city centres may be designed for high density and have proximity to amenities. Sprawl occurs when places of living are substantially segregated from places of work, connected primarily by the private automobile/ the car [*ibid*]. The choice to live distant from place of work stems from a host of reasons including affordability, the price of property or rentals, hygiene, proximity to work sites such as manufactories, IT Parks located in peri-urban areas, social networks and the imagination of a personal good life. Owing to these factors, juxtaposed with the fear of congestion coupled with lack of infrastructure, Indian cities, large and medium, have promoted horizontal urban expansion as the paradigm for spatial development, for several decades now [WB, 2021: 26].

Planning authorities of rapidly growing medium-sized cities in India, such as Bhopal, Mysuru, Raipur or Bhubaneshwar or mega-cities such as Bengaluru, Hyderabad and Chennai have promoted outwardly spatial growth intensified by rapid growth in population[1]. The concern here is that public policy has institutionalised sprawl. Sprawling peripheries, such as at Chandigarh, Guwahati, Chennai and Patna and Ahmedabad are furnished with restricted elite access to public water supply, sanitation and transport [Narain, Banerjee and Anand, 2014]. Sprawl also escalates the city government's expenditure for infrastructure development and management as well as personal costs, threatening the overall need for optimisation in resource consumption [The Cost of Sprawl, 1974: pg 04]. During adversities such as the pandemic, inadequacies in the supply of scarce resources are further amplified with escalated costs of private provisioning of infrastructure, while also accompanied by loss of macro-economic growth, jobs and escalated inflation.

A key question therefore facing spatial planning in India is how much land should be opened up for future urban development. Critical planning practitioners and scholars have for more than a decade advocated compact cities in India [author's experience, 2003-21]. Central to the adoption of this paradigm is the intention to promote judicious use of land, economy in development and maintenance of compact infrastructure, supply of equitable amenities as well as affordable housing and cost-effective linkages between place of work and home.

However, this well-intentioned policy orientation is not bereft of the politics of multiple stakeholder claims. Elected and unelected officials, government agencies, private sector markets, civil society organisations and non-profit organisations each vested with conflicting goals use planning processes and instruments to claim stakes and strengthen their own legitimacy – government organisations to assert their power and control, private firms to enhance profits and market capture and influential communities to extract public resources, all jeopardising public interest in the process. To untangle these dynamics the section below discusses tensions in the roles of public-private and hybrid organisations in shaping urban sprawl or compactness.

Public organisations: Municipal Corporations

Given resistance from the State legislature to implement the 74th Constitutional Amendment Act 1992 and devolve power to local governments, planning legislation for cities in India mostly continues to be vested with State governments thirty years thence. Notwithstanding questions pertaining to their democratic legitimacy, urban development and infrastructure/ transport departments of State governments in-charge of land and mobility thus continue to be entrusted with the tasks of urban planning. At the same time municipal corporations have mostly remained in the periphery of strategic decision-making and planning, despite their status as the lowest level of democratic governance [Idiculla, 2014; Kennedy, 2020]. Decisions on urban growth strategy and infrastructure needs often circumvent municipal governments.

Public Organisations: Development Authorities and Special Purpose Vehicles

The decades of shifts in spatial development policy towards compact cities and intensification of city cores is hugely contested among public authorities. While the compact city approach is suited to roles and functions of some public organisations and markets, it works against the others. For instance, there are tensions between planning authorities entrusted with preparation of land use plans for cities and authorities in-charge of mobility. Development authorities often (dichotomously) assigned with a dual role also as planning authorities, obtain their revenues through spatial expansion of urbanisation through acquisition, subdivision and resale of agrarian land at subsidised rates and supplying affordable sub-divided land and housing for the economically weaker section (for example, city level development authorities such as the Bangalore Development Authority) [Mohan and Rajagopal, 2011].

In contrast, more recent forms of governance, such as Special Purpose Vehicles (SPV) involving shareholdings from national, State governments (and possibly private firms) governing mass transit facilities obtain their revenue returns through ridership [TOD Policy, Bengaluru, 2019]. Concentrating urban development in proximity to existing transit stations thus is a pre-requisite for mobility agencies to attract growth in ridership [ibid]. Multiple transit corporations including the Indian Railways Station Development Corporation at the national level, enterprises such as K-RIDE in Karnataka, created to modernise railway stations and metro rail corporations, are examples of SPVs involving shareholding between national and state governments. The issue is that the revenue models of the two institutions hinged on land and mobility require opposing spatial development paradigms. Development authorities require greater utilisation of land whereas SPVs governing mobility benefit from concentration of development in proximity to transit stations, including in the urban core.

Public-Private Partnerships and Special Purpose Vehicles

Given the paucity of government funding for industrial development and allied large scale infrastructure projects, post-liberalisation of the Indian economy, national and State governments institutionalised mechanisms of privatisation such as Public Private Partnerships (PPP) [Batra, 2009]. Modernisation of airports, railway stations, ports are governed using the Joint Venture (JV) or PPP models [Rajagopal, 2021]. Structured as mission led SPVs, PPPs are governed by Boards of Directors. PPP based SPVs are conceptualised as risk-free entities, ring-fenced from social movements or day to day involvement of political agents in decisions. Devoid of political representation, efficiency driven decisions by SPVs tend to conflict with democratically led municipal authorities which are ridden with the messiness of interactions between state and local level political agents [ibid]. While transit stations may be located in the core as well as the peri-urban areas, competing demands among them may tend to polarise spatial development policy orientations.

Entangled Markets

Multiple intertwined markets shape urban development: manufacturing, the services sector(s), real estate, the construction, infrastructure and energy, public and private transport service providers. Real estate markets involving international, domestic and local developers respond to Ready Reckoner or Guidance Value of land and property determined annually by the Department of Stamps and Registration at the state government level. Master plans for cities take cognisance of development dynamics in relation to the Guidance Value of land and property in cities. Real estate led spatial development thus navigates master plans and even shapes its regulatory conditions in formal and informal ways.

The governance of multiple modes of private transport also remains unaccounted for and uncoordinated. Private transport service providers in Indian cities account for a substantial number of trips made and are largely led by informal operations. Transporting daily commuters, transport of construction material or moving solid waste from city centres to landfills in urban peripheries are routinely controlled by a nexus of contractors and public officials forming petty and medium sized oligopolies that control private transport, truck, bus transport or cabs [interviews with transport contractors, Bengaluru, 2004-06; interviews with representatives of civil society organisation, Mumbai, 2014]. Compounding this complexity is newer platform aggregators for private services which remain weakly regulated [pending amendments to Karnataka Motor Vehicles Rules, 1989] advantageously for the private aggregators. The recent national and state government's policy initiatives for the Electric Vehicle Transition further exacerbates regulatory ambivalence in the governance of privately run mobility [Karnataka Electric Vehicle and Energy Storage Policy, 2017].

At the macro scale of cities and their relationships with mega-regions, PPPs as an institutional mechanism blurs the boundaries and complicates the relationship between government agencies and firms, as public transit organisations compete, collaborate, facilitate and even partner with private firms in this liberalised milieu [Rajagopal, 2021]. The tense structures of spatial, social and economic growth shaped through urban plans generally traverse this institutional ambivalence.

Non-profit organisations

Institutional heterogeneity entails non-profit organisations, including those stemming from corporate social responsibility wings of corporations, philanthropic initiatives and activist organisations. Non-profit organisations driving paradigms such as Transit Oriented Development (TOD) also endorse the 15-minute self-sufficient city as desirable and urgent policy reforms for Indian cities [Mehta and Behera, 2021]. A counterpoint is that the 15-minute self-sufficient city seems to defy pre-existing social and economic inter-dependencies between places and multiple larger ecosystems that a good city generically entails. For example, critics of the 15-minute city have argued that incrementally formed historical linkages between formal and informal sector activities developed over time across regions will get unevenly disrupted with greater consolidation of self-sufficient locales in areas with greater agency to capture scarce resources [Glaesar, 2021].

Another contention is gated forms of governance within which TOD Zones are structured. TOD zones are generally envisaged as Special Purpose Zones (SPZ), constituted as bounded companies under the Companies Act 2013. The governance structure of shareholdings in SPVs is anchored on financial models hinged on estimations of internal revenue returns (IRR) over a medium and long-term period, for shareholders. While non-profit organisations are rightly promoting urban design for gender inclusivity, child friendly cities and green mobility (walking, bicycling) at the local levels, it is imperative to remind ourselves that their realisation is currently envisaged primarily through exclusionary forms of governance that embed models such as SPVs, driven on financial criteria and structuring.

RWAs

The counterpoint to TOD, is decongestion, advocated by several elite Residents' Welfare Associations and civil society organisations stem from the fear of health hazards, but also from mis-trust in local government's fiscal, managerial capacity and political accountability to augment infrastructure apposite to high density-built environments. RWA's often 'nimbyist' attitude plays a dominant role in dissuading high density urban cores, tending to adversely impact revenue returns of SPVs and public transit authorities. At the same time, scepticism harboured by RWAs is a response to opaque deal-making between real estate developers, infrastructure markets, administrators and political agents in the framing of land use policy and prioritisation of public spending for infrastructure [engagement with community leaders, 2017 onwards]. Moreover, while the RWA is akin to the Area Sabha recommended in a government scheme (the Jawaharlal Nehru National Urban Renewal Mission, 2005), at the lowest level of disaggregation whose governance is mostly led by strong community leaders or registered Trusts, rather than through a democratically led electoral process. A governance arrangement hinged on the community leader's personal traits and vision tends to foster loyalty while bringing to question equitable representation, access to resources and collective readiness for risks at local and hyper-local levels.

A combination of forces including opaque deals that navigate weak municipal governments, organisational interests of development authorities, public agencies governing mobility, real estate/ mobility/ other markets, 'nimbyist' middle class, civil society organisations' pull the city's development densification of cities and compact cores in opposing directions.

Large metropolises such as Bengaluru in India, with its historical aversion to congestion, offer strategic cases in point for investigation, particularly because the policies they adopt set precedents for small and medium cities in the state of Karnataka, of which it is capital. During the course of the Covid-19 pandemic, Bengaluru has witnessed several policy amendments to its spatial development and serves as a strategic case. One, the Government of Karnataka revoked the Draft Master Plan for Bengaluru 2031, in June 2020, during the course of the pandemic, in favour of densification. Contrarily, a few months hence, the same government introduced amendments to conversion of agricultural land that negates intentions of shaping a compact Bengaluru. Below, are examined legal, regulatory and procedural contradictions and adverse implications of lack of shared visions, objectives and planned outcomes.

Bengaluru: Urban Governance, Institutional Variety and Development Stakes

In the absence of an overarching vision for development of the City, let us examine state-market forces behind contradictions and alignments among the Revised Master Plan 2031 for Bengaluru (RMP 2031), the Comprehensive Mobility Plan (CMP 2020), the policy for Transit Oriented Development 2019, the Parking Policy 2019 and amendments to land laws, passed by the Government of Karnataka, and its impact on the pursuit of a compact city.

Revoked in June 2020: Draft Revised Master Plan for Bengaluru 2031

In June 2020, amidst the onset of the Covid 19 pandemic and accompanying norms for social distancing, the Government of Karnataka (GoK) revoked the Revised Master Plan for Bengaluru 2031 [Bharadwaj, 2020], on the grounds that the plan disregarded Transit Oriented Development, and hence implicitly conveying that its regulations promulgated urban sprawl [*ibid*]. Preceding this stage, the Bangalore Development Authority had submitted the Draft Revised Master Plan for Bengaluru, 2031 (RMP 2031) to GoK in December 2016. Following a

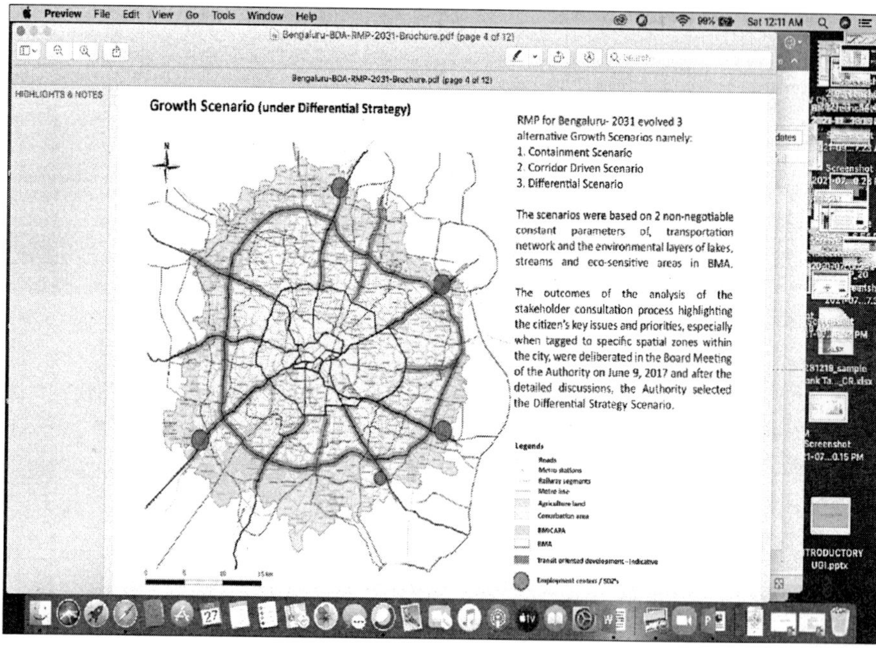

Fig. 1: Strategy for development, Draft Revised Master Plan 2031 for Bengaluru

Source: Bangalore Development Authority

provisional approval from the state government and prescriptions of the Karnataka Town and Country Planning Act 1961, the BDA invited suggestions and objections from the public for a 30-day period (extended on public demand)[2]. The BDA's Draft RMP 2031 proposed decongestion of the core while promot-ing higher intensification of development in the urban peripheries (see, Fig. 1.0). While the growth strategy claims to integrate land use and transport, the RMP 2031 demarcates Special Development Zones (SDZs) at the outer-peripheries of the urban agglomeration, with no explicit attention towards proximity to public transit. Given this disjuncture, a scrutiny of BDA's proposals by multiple public agencies in the city, particularly those concerning mass transit, i.e., the Director-ate of Urban Land Transport - GoK, Bangalore Metro Rail Corporation Ltd., Bangalore Metropolitan Transport Corporation, reopened the debate regarding the Plan's partial and selective adoption of the Transit Oriented Development model [CMP, 2020].

Recognising the need to prevent further sprawl, the preceding Master Plan, the RMP 2015 had proposed a dense core supported by secondary centres located in proximity to inter-modal transit stations. Several arguments were constructed then, to explain why a sprawl model is undesirable for a resilient city (see, Fig. 2.0). Digressing from this paradigm, rather than densify the core along mass transit/ public transit stations, the RMP 2031 had proposed restricted development in the city centres while intensifying development in the peripheries of the city. The RMP 2031 allocated gradually increasing development rights in a concentric pattern, forming Zone A (densely developed inner core), Zone B (moderately developed intermediate area), and, Zone C (sparsely developed peripheral area). Zone C was permitted consumption of higher Floor Area Ratios[3] (or development rights) of 3.5 as opposed to a permissible FAR of 1.0 in the core area.

To provide a backdrop to the logic of concentrically structured, Zone wise allocation of FAR, historically, the growth of Bengaluru City occurred in a concentric pattern, with dense historic centralities occupying the core. Land use plans of the 1980s and 90s for Bangalore thus proposed low density in the core, increasing towards the peripheries. The RMP 2015 however, shifted away from a zone-based development to instead recognise the diverse urban places of the city and infrastructure provisioning as key forces that must drive future proposed development of the city. The RMP 2015 thus recognised the traditional core, the Pete (16th Century A.D), ridden with poor natural light and ventilation, as a specific Zone for natural and planned urban renewal, advocated intensification of planned

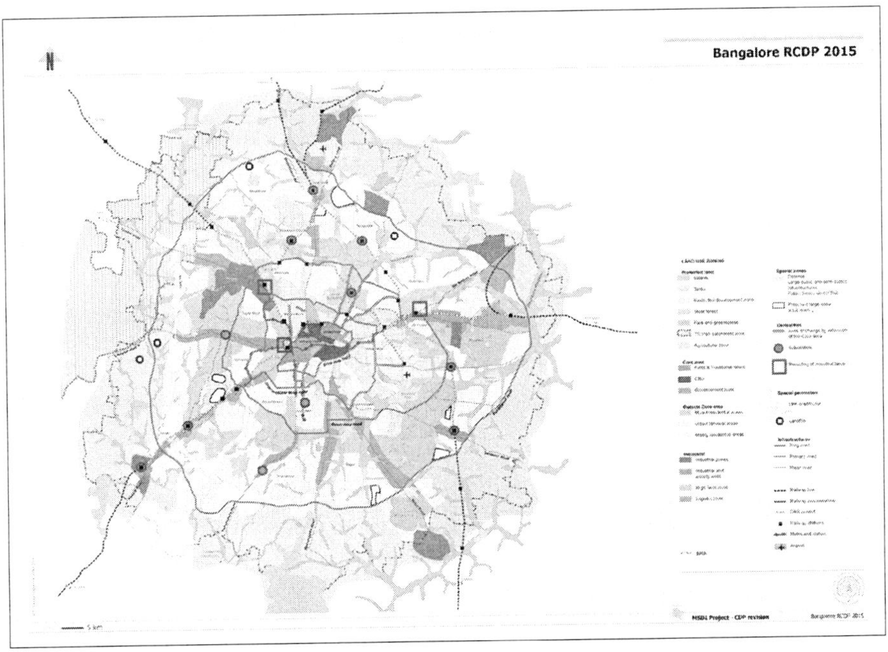

Fig. 2: Revised Master Plan 2015, Bangalore

Source: RMP 2015, Bengaluru

residential layouts such as Chamarajpete, Malleswaram and VV Puram, which were generously developed with infrastructure through substantial foresight by the erstwhile City Improvement Trust Boards (CITB) pre-independence (early 20th century A.D)[4], and, thereafter, Indiranagar, Koramangala (1970s), by the Bangalore Development Authority. The RMP 2015 proposed creation of secondary centres in the peripheries, at Yeshwanthpur, Baiyappanahalli (East), Kengeri (South-West), Bommanahalli (South), Whitefield (West) and Anjanapura (North) in proximity to transit stations.

Overall, the RMP 2015 proposed strengthening of linkages between residential areas and places of work (sites of manufacturing and services sector) as well as large and small-scale amenities such as schools, hospitals, municipal markets, transport hubs parks, through augmentation of city level infrastructure and urban design at local levels. By recognising diverse urban places, the RMP 2015 for the first time, legitimised mixed land use as a land use regulation, a condition integral to densification of the core. During the course of its implementation, unhappy with the spatial development and land use strategy of the RMP 2015, a few civil society organisations and Residents Welfare Associations (led by the Citizen's Action Forum, Koramangala) filed Public Interest Litigation against the proposals of the RMP 2015, in 2007, on grounds of engendering unliveable neighbourhoods [Kumar, 2018[5]].

Perhaps in response to contentions against the RMP 2015, the BDA reverted to the older paradigm of zone-based development and low-density core in the subsequent plan, the RMP 2031. A small segment of legal scholars and urban planners publicly expressed contentions about an unsustainable spatial development strategy [Krishnaswamy, Idiculla, Rajagopal, 2017; Mohan, 2017], giving rise to a plan that fell short of embracing liveability and inclusiveness [Sastry, 2018]. They underscored the benefits of high density (distinct from high-rise) development in the core areas, and the importance of integrating land use, transportation and other infrastructures. They argued that ease of affordable mobility increased livelihood opportunities for the economically weaker sections of the population, enhanced access to affordable housing, infrastructure and amenities. Predictable and affordable mobility provided through public/ mass transit options helped economise on time taken to commute, reduced green-house gas emissions, helped mitigate climate change and improved public health of inhabitants in the long term. Proximity proffered by dense localities also augmented flow of information and enhanced collective action among inhabitants of the city while reinforcing resilience.

Notwithstanding these societal benefits, the imagination of the city as a low-density, mono-use core seems welcome to middle-class inhabitants of planned residential areas in the city's centre [engagement with residents welfare associations, Bengaluru, 2017]. Particularly, BDA's proposal to allocate higher development rights in the peripheries was presumably attractive to real estate developers who could acquire and develop on land priced at lower rates than in the core areas [ARCP, 2009]. Areas outside municipal limits in Bengaluru are dispersed with more than 75,000 apartment buildings developed as gated communities, most of which are serviced by private amenities [Prashanth, G.N, 2013[6]].

Moreover, developers in Bengaluru benefit from the Joint Development model, incentivised by the state government to attract investors. Information Technology (IT) Parks, incentivised by the state government as Special Economic Zones in public interest for employment generation and economic growth, are developed through the Joint Development model involving land contribution by the state government and development and operations by private, real estate parties [informal discussions with urban planner, Smita Singh, 2021]. The peri-urban areas of Bengaluru are thus strewn with about 18-20 IT Parks, each covering 75 to 500 acres of land area, designed as gated, mixed-use, residential cum office and commercial use campuses [Nestaway, 2019[7]]. Here, the state as a partner to the real estate and IT markets becomes central to promulgation of urban sprawl for Bengaluru.

Expanding urbanisation into the peripheries would need to be supported by road infrastructure and private transport, considering development of mass transit lines to new locations would take atleast a decade to reach, if not longer, providing them access to private ridership. Other allied markets including those in the transport and construction industries thus find the possibility to expand services into larger regional/ inter-city terrains lucrative [Philip, 2021[8]].

However, the proposal to sprawl clearly did not suit all stakeholders of the city. Public sector organisations in-charge of mass transit, such as the Bengaluru Metropolitan Transport Corporation (BMTC), the Bengaluru Metro Rail Corporation (BMRCL) and Directorate of Urban Land Transport (DULT), managing bus fleets/ routes, metro rail services and surface transport for sustainable mobility, seemed adversely affected by a spatial development strategy that selectively adopted the TOD model.

Competing with the RMP 2031: the TOD Policy 2019, the Parking Policy and the Comprehensive Mobility Plan 2020

The BMRCL fundamentally disagreed with the BDA's Draft RMP 2015. It seemed to hasten the preparation of the Draft Bengaluru Transit Oriented Development Policy 2019 in the period the Draft RMP 2031 was being finalised by the BDA. The Bengaluru TOD Policy boldly negates the RMP 2031:

> The current developments in Bengaluru are guided by provisions of Revised Master Plan-2015 (RMP-2015). To replace RMP-2015, Revised Master Plan-2031 (RMP-2031 Draft) has been prepared and is under consideration of state government for approval. RMP-2015 advocated high density, compact development of mixed use by introduction of ancillary use in development control regulations. However, it could not materialize as envisaged. RMP-2031 (draft) has adopted a divergent approach. As per approach, the area within outer ring road (i.e. Planning Area - A) has less scope for growth and high densities and crippled by congestion and pollution and therefore requires strategies to stabilise growth and interventions that discourage commercialisation of economic centres. Therefore, RMP-2031 has not proposed enhanced FSI in TOD Zone in Planning Area-A and enhanced FSI of 4 is proposed within 150 m on either metro in Planning Area-B (Area beyond ORR and upto conurbation area). RMP-2031 also proposes to add another 80 sq.km for urbanisation and thus encouraging urban sprawl.

Source: Draft Bengaluru Transit Oriented Development Policy 2019; 6.0 Need for a Bengaluru TOD Policy.

The collective demand of mobility related public organisations for complete adoption of TOD in the RMP is a relatively recent dynamic in the imagination of the city's resilient future. Previously, the governance of use of urban land in Bengaluru was primarily controlled by the Urban Development Department at the state level, through the municipal corporation, the BBMP and autonomous authorities such as the BDA. However, faced with high population, employment growth rates, including in-migration [RMP 2015][9] the crisis of climate change and imperatives to reduce carbon emissions, the last decade witnessed increasing demands for public transport as a key determinant of sustainable development of cities. Traffic congestion combined with poor travel time of 4-5 km per hour and long commuting hours caused increased emissions, decline in air quality and respiratory health of inhabitants, stress and mental health, efficiency and productivity concerns [Draft RMP 2031].

In the decade that passed between 2007 and 2017, the alignment and integration of multiple modes of mass and public transit networks became central to sustainable development for Bengaluru. Following the imperatives of the National Urban Transport Policy, 2009 (NUTP) for promotion of mass transit, TOD, last mile connectivity and soft mobility (walking and bicycling), the role of public organisations charged with developing and managing mass transit started to assume greater importance in deciding where development in Bengaluru needs to be concentrated in cities.

Aligned with the need for concentration, the Draft TOD Policy for Bengaluru strongly advances advantages of TOD as a strategic paradigm that promotes compact city development, opens up avenues for inner city natural urban renewal process and land value capture for urban renewal in city cores, while preventing indiscriminate expansion into agricultural lands for urbanisation. The policy further argues that the adoption of TOD for the city will increase ridership in public transport modes and enhance financial viability of transit. Greater use of public transit fosters walking and bicycling, reduce pollution, improves public health and efficiency, reduces carbon emissions and make the city more liveable, the policy argues. In tandem, the Comprehensive Mobility Plan (CMP, 2020) for Bengaluru highlights the urgent need for integration of land use, zoning and transport infrastructure. The TOD paradigm and public transit is central to the CMP.

The CMP 2020 also desirably promotes the adoption of a demand management approach to parking, which categorically treats private parking as a payable service, negating BDA's regulatory treatment of car parking as a public amenity rather than a luxury commodity. Drawing on Donald Shoupe's tenets, the parking Policy 2019 argues in favour of restricted permissible rights for onsite parking,

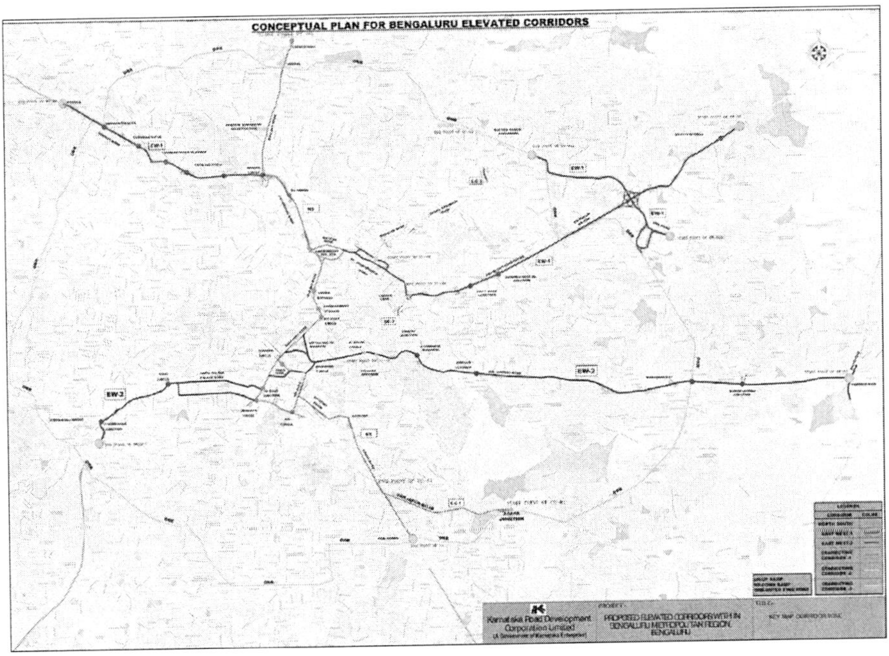

Fig. 3: Elevated Expressway Project, Bengaluru

Source: Scroll.in, Karnataka Road Development Corporation

paid on-street parking and in doing so promulgates the creation of a market for privately developed and operationalised multi-level car parking units, preferably located in proximity to transit stations, inturn supporting the TOD.

And yet, almost contradicting its own advocacy of public transit, and notwithstanding civil society protests[10], the CMP does not betray multiple mobility markets. The CMP continues to support the private automobile, transport services, infrastructure, construction and engineering markets by situating the Karnataka Road Development Corporation's city-wide, 100 km-elevated expressway as a key project to promote the city's economic growth impetus [Fig. 03]. There are other anomalies. Some researchers argue that given the current structure of Bengaluru, the CMP's promotion of TOD along mass transit, such as the metro rail network, which plies into peri-urban areas of the city only enhances the problem of sprawl [discussions with Mathai, 2021].

Going beyond regulatory incentives, at the heart of arguments for BDA's promotion of sprawl into agricultural lands or the BMRCL and DULT's aggressive advancement of a compact city, I speculate, also lies their respective misaligned revenue generation models. Aligned with its role as stipulated in the BDA Act 1976, the BDA tends to use the RMP as a policy instrument to advance its own legitimacy through horizontal expansion of urban land into agrarian territories while the BMRCL, true to its own functions, demands intensification of the core and transit alignments, in order to meet its targets for revenue returns and managing commitments on debt with central, state and international institutions.

The tussle between land and mobility related organisations for steering the shape of the city was further complexified with other incentives that the state government offered to industrialists.

More Law and Policy Amendments Post Covid-19

The pandemic radically disrupted economic growth. 2019 had already witnessed a slowing down of the economy from annual growth rate of 6.6% in the preceding year to 4.4%. The major metropolitan cities including Delhi, Mumbai, Bengaluru, Pune, Chennai and Kolkata accounted for almost 60% of all cases of Covid 19 in India, within the first six months, only to cross 70% during the second wave.

Urban economies were severely affected as medium and small sized economic activities closed operations. During the first lockdown and thereafter (23rd March 2020), some industries completely closed down including the hotel industry, railways, airlines and other transport services. Manufacturing suffered economically by about 40%. Retail and real estate sectors remained stagnant during the first lockdown. Allied industries such as the construction industry faced among the worst circumstances of a 50% slump, initially. Karnataka State, regis-

> Atmanirbhar Bharat demands reduced dependence on imports by manufacturing such products locally together with inculcating a citizen led movement towards using locally produced products.... Urban areas that are manufacturing hubs, regional growth centres, transport hubs or ports, tourism destinations, capital cities, economic zones or evolved as a financial, education, IT hub and more, are going to lead this change. Atmanirbhar Bharat shall also include enhancing our capacity, creativity, and skills. Therefore, to become a manufacturing economy, we need to shift our focus from 'Make in India' to 'Make for world' by importing raw material and exporting value-added products.

Source: NUPF, 2020: 09

tered revenues of over 1 lakh crore INR in October 2019, which a year later, in October 2020 had fallen by a quarter and stood at Rs. 78,232 crore [Deshpande and Shaha, 2020[11]].

In a desperate response, state and local governments introduced several policy measures to address economic crisis. The Ministry of Housing and Urban Affairs published the National Urban Policy Framework 2020 (NUPF, 2020 (undated)), calling for urgent measures to deal with problems of urban development, now exaggerated by Covid 19. The National Government's protectionist policy for economic self-reliance, 'Atmanirbhar Bharat', was extended to cities. In its chapter on economic growth, the strategy states:

Apparently taking cognisance of the national mandate, while discussions on contentions of urban sprawl promoted by the BDA's Draft RMP 2031 were still underway at the office of the Chief Minister for Karnataka, through the early part of the year, in May 2020, the Government of Karnataka amended the Land Reforms Act 1961 to precisely facilitate greater urbanisation in the peri-urban areas, this time, in the interest of the economy. As a response to and anticipation of further slump in the economy, the state government allegedly, hastily permitted industrialists desirous of promoting agri-based industries, to now buy land directly from farm land owners[12]. Previously, the same law ascribed the power to acquire agricultural land for industrial purposes only to state government agencies (such as the Karnataka Industrial Area Development Board, KIADB), which would acquire and allot agricultural land to industrialists through an elaborate process.

News reports show that as early as November 2019, the state government had been considering the amendment as a means to attract more investments in the agro-industrial sector. Media reports also indicate that the GoK was contemplating amendments to Section 109 of the Land Reforms Act, which permitted ease resale of land for industrial purposes earlier in January 2020 [Bopanna, 2020].

Reports show that this amendment was tabled by the state legislature already in March 2020 and passed later on July 13, 2020 [ibid], presumably capitalising on the drastic decline in growth rates during the pandemic.

The amendment now reduced the original three year long process of obtaining access to land to a rapid 30 day period. While the amendment brought relief to private business entities of agro-industries, allied real estate and construction markets, civil society activists resisted the move, albeit with little impact given relatively limited access to decision making spaces during the pandemic [*The Hindu*, 2020[13]]. While the concerned state department clarified that land allotment would be hastened only on restricted uses, the larger issue was that the amendment, made primarily through discretion of the government and the office of the CM, would bear an immediate impact to sprawling cities.

In a parallel occurrence, in October 2020, the BBMP tabled an amendment to the BBMP Act, involving specialised conditions of governance for Bengaluru. While several scholars and practitioners critiqued measures undertaken in the amendment to retain the weakness of municipal governments, an amendment that caught less attention was the provision of expansion of municipal limits by 1km in the peripheries. In the absence of a systematic decadal review of the BBMP's boundaries, this increase in the municipal corporations limits was allegedly, opportunistically persuaded by a select few Members of the Legislative Assembly at the state level in order to capture development potential on the outskirts of the city.

Markets' Response: 2020-21

Entangled markets responded to the pandemic in unpredictable ways. Bengaluru is dominated by the Information Technology and Information Technology Enabled Services (IT/ ITeS), which inturn shape demand for real estate and mobility infrastructures. The Draft RMP 2031 [Master Plan Document, RMP 2031: pg.44] states:

There is a steep growth in Real estate sector, Business & Legal Services from 2001 to 2011 with its sectoral share increasing from 4.3% to 22.7% during 1991 to 2011. However, the share of manufacturing has reduced from 34.2% to 21.1% during 1991 to 2011. The other important sector – public administration reduced during the same period from 6.1% to 1.2%. Further, the contribution of construction (~8%) and other services (~23% to 25%) have more or less remained constant during past three decades.

Media reports and interviews have indicated that markets pertaining to the IT and finance sectors have seen a surge or remained stable during the pandemic [Kumar, 2021[14]].

Immediately after the first lockdown, the city's real estate markets recovered, but not without government led incentives. The moratorium period on home loan EMIs was extended, interest waiver introduced, Stamp Duty reduced, funding options enhanced for stalled projects, among others. The Chairperson of the Confederation of Real Estate Developers Association of India (CREDAI), Bengaluru, confirmed a rise in demand for all categories of residential uses, including the luxury sector [Govind, 2020[15]].

While real estate companies anticipated corresponding increase in demand for hybrid work spaces, large IT conglomerates holding real estate portfolios on 100 - 300 acres of land behaved contrarily. Corporate giants such as IBM [Pramanik, 2021[16]] and Tata Consultancy Services [Poovanna and Nandi, 2020[17]] have opted to consolidate their assets in the peripheries of the city and reoccupy its compact core areas [interviews, Khalil, 2021; Regunathan, 2021]. Real estate markets initially unsurprisingly witnessed a drastic fall in sale of land and property. However, the rapid spread of Covid 19 (particularly in the second more devastating wave) saw the resurfacing of the old psychological resentment to the problem of congestion in Bengaluru. Middle-class inhabitants from within the city and other metropolises have opted to invest in homes in the peripheries, to escape congestion. My interviews with real estate professionals revealed that purchase of second homes in gated communities has not been uncommon during this time. The market witnessed a surge in December 2020 – January 2021, only to experience a downturn again during the second wave [Khan, 2021[18]].

In the face of these cyclical uncertainties in markets, political agents who amended BBMP's limits justified their opportunism by arguing that the BBMP's amendment to the BBMP Act on expansion of its urban limits, would restore buyer's sentiment and market demand [Shankar, 2020[19]]. Lower state determined land and property prices in the peripheries (almost at half the rate[20]), accompanied by state led subsidies and incentives for buying property in the peripheries rather than renting in the core, would bring some relief to losses, they substantiated. In addition, continued tax subsidies for purchase of four wheelers when accompanied by extension of urban infrastructure, they persuaded, would boost the hard hit real estate sector [*ibid.*].

On the other hand, public and particularly mass transit options were closed during the first and second lockdowns and waves of Covid 19. The Bengaluru Metropolitan Transport Corporation (BMTC) underwent revenue losses of about 1 crore INR per day during the time of the pandemic [Navya, P.K, 2021[21]]. The Bangalore Metro Rail Corporation (BMRCL) experienced substantial loss of 904 Crores INR, i.e. 80% of its revenue [Kidiyooor, S, 2021[22]]. Cab aggregators witnessed a downturn. Ola experienced 95% loss in revenue during the fiscal year and Uber laid off over 600 employees in India[23]. Unsurprisingly, private automobiles, particularly the four-wheeler witnessed a two-fold excess increase in sales, potentially escalating Bengaluru's congestion ranking from No. 06 to higher [Pandey, 2021[24]]. The BBMP's amendment in its jurisdiction, I speculate, will also contribute to greater congestion.

The core issue is one of government led incentives in the form of laws, policies, regulations and procedures that institutionalise sprawl. Regulatory amendments made during the course of a health emergency such as a pandemic diminishes the possibility for consultation. Amendments to land reform legislation and the BBMP Act, at different scales of decisions, the state and the city government, suddenly disrupted the compact city agenda that the BMRCL and DULT had advanced. Rather than taking cognisance of compact city visions that the same state government had championed in the RMP, presumably persuaded by real estate, mobility and other market driven lobbies, it now used the pandemic as an opportune moment to legitimise long pending contentious amendments to open up agrarian land for direct acquisition by agri-industrialists.

Mixed policy initiatives promulgated by the same state government and state legislature point towards uncoordinated, mis-aligned objectives. At risk is a city that grossly neglects public interest. Once holding major promises of a good quality of life, Bengaluru continues to remain devoid of adequate social amenities and infrastructures, while promoting vested, opportunistic interests of select markets and their unscrupulous nexus with government agencies laden with mis-aligned goals. A state government with no cohesive vision for Bengaluru, driven by decisions suited mainly to political and business elites, poses greater threats to post Covid futures.

Why Sprawl is Undesirable, Especially During a Public Emergency

Researchers and practitioners have explained how governments, not people, are at the centre of sprawl. In his response to the question, 'What's wrong with sprawl', Ed Glaesar expands on multiple reasons. Through the late 20th Century, cities such as Dallas, Houston, Atlanta and Phoenix in the United States of America attracted more people than other cities in California, because their governments were friendlier to new development, despite their inherently productive characteristics [Glaesar, 2009: 193]. Cost of living space and government subsidies on home ownership in the peripheries incentivised people to move out of cities into the suburbs, as in the case of Bengaluru. At the same time, regulatory conditions for use and governance of land use do not incentivise either holistic or natural urban regeneration in the core areas of the city.

In Bengaluru, policies and regulations that cater selectively to separate demands of public institutions and markets cause open inter-dependencies between them to diminish. Endless urban regions in the making may support Development Authorities. However, extant public institutions, such as BMTC or BMRCL which are dealing with mobility, do not respond quickly enough to changing commuting needs of people. Moreover, infrastructure engineering projects such as for metro rail require periods of time for construction that generally far exceed the pace of urban expansion. The middle class thus resorts to car/ cab-based commuting while those needing affordable transport to commute long distances suffer from inadequate access to quality mobility infrastructure. Paradigmatic preferences of organisations and motivations for territorial control from political agents on the question of concentration of people in cities end up exacerbating long standing gaps in institutional coordination, ultimately jeopardising societal interest.

Studies conducted during the preparation of RMP 2015 for Bengaluru showed that a sprawl scenario of development would require five to seven times higher allocation of annual budgets for development and maintenance of all trunk infrastructure. Lower per capita access to consumption of infrastructure translated directly into high per capita carbon foot print. Generally, areas located outside of municipal jurisdictions in the peripheries suffer inadequate infrastructure. Gated enclaves tap into public infrastructure networks in proximity to their development and mobilise private access to ground water, electricity, sanitation and solid waste management. Privately run mixed use gated enclaves thus contribute negligible or no revenues to municipal authorities or parastatals while consuming services they deliver upto a certain extent [Kennedy, Sood, 2016].

The middle class's psychology of fear of congestion stemming from Covid 19 only legitimises governments mistaken incentives that threaten to disproportionately exacerbate urban sprawl in Bengaluru. Skewed incentives for urban sprawl only promote a select group of public organisations and private firms as opposed to markets as a whole. Smaller realtors and individual land owners in city centres have no regulatory provisions or market conditions to initiate parcel level regeneration. The result is disproportionate concentration of high-end development, commercial, office, recreation and residential in clusters or belts. In Bengaluru, Whitefied, Sarjapur and the Electronics City represent such sites of distorted accumulation [RMP 2005-2015; Goldman, 2010, 236; Rouanet and Halbert, 2015]. Other forms of fragmentation also result.

Researchers working on impact of large-scale infrastructure on urban-rural transitions have shown how poorly thought through conversion of agricultural land use and relocating agrarian communities gives rise to uneven development in the peripheries [Kennedy, 2014; Kennedy, Sood, 2016; Gururani, 2020]. Disadvantaged communities, they argue, stagnate outcomes and hide governments own failure to meet its welfarist goals for enabling equitable distribution of resources. At the same time, the absence of decentralised urban governance and political accountability at the local and hyper local levels leaves the urban poor in core areas of cities also disadvantaged as supply of vital civic amenities and transport infrastructure seldom meets demand.

The problem is compounded since Bengaluru, by virtue of being capital to one of the more progressive states in the country becomes a default precedent for other cities in India competing for investment, such as Hyderabad, Chennai, or Pune and more than 40 medium sized cities such as Bhopal, Raipur, Nagpur or Chandigarh, Guwahati, Chennai and Patna and Ahmedabad [Narain, Banerjee and Anand, 2014].

Towards an Ecosystem Approach for Institutionalising an Outcomes Driven Planning Process

The problem of multiple contradictory regulatory incentives on part of the same government agencies for Bengaluru's development futures brings us to the questions we set out with: how should we re-imagine urban planning as a process that aids reconciliation of divergent values and goals of public, private and civil society organisations, in order to promote judicious consumption of resources and be better prepared for risks such as the Covid 19 pandemic? Building a risk ready state means a politically led local government that is capable of orchestrating shared visions for cities across agencies with divergent uncompromising goals and values, at multiple scales of decisions. Dealing with the problem of urban sprawl is a key component of such a vision.

To address the long pending issue of urban sprawl, I reinforce four key measures advanced by critical urban planner's cohort. Macro level structural reforms and strategic shifts are both essential.

One, urban governance and planning must be entrusted with the municipal government, under the aegis of the Metropolitan Planning Commission at the regional level, as mandated in the 74th CAA. Institutional linkages across sectors, between the city and the region is an imperative given the larger set of economic and social transitions underway, as the case of Bengaluru clearly shows.

Two, the state legislature must empower and capacitate the municipal government to coordinate urban planning processes and negotiate competing demands forged by mis-aligned institutions, public, private and the civil society. The municipal corporation must be capacitated to orchestrate multiple institutions with divergent goals. This means mediating mis-aligned goals such as in the case of the BDA and the BMRCL. Participation in the context of an emergency such as the pandemic would go beyond grievance redressal or expressing demands to actually crafting partnerships involving mutual accountabilities geared to accomplishing shared goals.

Three, planning experts must comprehend the nature of markets and business cycles of companies in order to craft growth strategies that accommodate market's needs as well as welfarist goals of the State.

Four, state and local governments must craft regulatory incentives the outcomes of which do not deviate from accomplishment of shared visions and goals. In the case of Bengaluru, any amendments to laws, policies or regulatory processes, including the Land Reforms Act 1961, the RMP 2031, TOD Policy 2019, CMP 2020, the Parking Policy and Ready Reckoner Rates for land and property in the city must incorporate conditions that prevent urban sprawl.

Decisions in normal course, whether to consolidate compact cities or channelling revenues for ubiquitous access to infrastructure, when conducted through democratically led processes at State, region, city or local levels will establish robust channels for communication between elected representatives, administrators and local communities. Only democratically led channels at multiple scales will build collective ownership of public problems and solutions, while helping all groups – public, private and inhabitants of cities to deal with crises more effectively.

Annex

Summary of Key Development Cost Considerations [The Costs of Sprawl, 1974: pg 04].

SUMMARY OF KEY DEVELOPMENT COST CONSIDERATIONS

Cost or Effect Category	Sensitivity of Cost to Development Patterns	Sensitivity of Cost to Housing Densities	Sensitivity to Site and Regional Location Factors	Incidence of Cost	Sources of Information	Availability of Cost Data
Land	Prices more orderly in planned development, with less speculation compared to sprawl. Not clear what differences are in overall magnitudes.	Costs decrease per unit and increase per acre as density increases.	Variation in cost at least 10% above and below average cost.	Land developer purchases originally; cost passed on to builder then to purchaser of property. Government obtains most rights-of-way by dedication, buys most other public sites.	Appraisals, case studies, FHA reports, HUD studies, land use inventories for particular communities.	Factors determining value and their relative importance not well documented. Information on land values scattered, not comprehensive and must be assembled.
Housing	Little or no inherent cost differences because of development patterns per se, however planning could entail higher standards and, thus, higher costs.	Costs per unit decrease as density increases: smaller units, fewer garages, less appliances.	Colder climate increases costs, also severe site conditions increase costs.	Builder pays, passed on to owner in purchase price and renter in monthly rent payment.	U. S. Census, HUD-FHA, NAHB studies.	Data on multi-family relative to single family data.
Transportation and Utilities	Linkage costs greater in sprawl, duplication, upgrading and replacement also more likely. Costs occur earlier in larger increments in planned development.	Distribution and collection system costs decrease per unit and increase per acre as density increases.	Roads and sanitary sewer costs affected somewhat; storm sewer and water affected greatly, electricity, telephone and gas not significantly influenced.	Developer provides some facilities, passed on to builder, then to purchaser of property. Utilities provide facilities and services; costs reimbursed by user fees. Government pays part of roads, sewer, and water.	DOT studies; utility company records; case studies; cost-revenue, fiscal and economic impact studies at state and local levels.	Data are either on unit or per capita basis, difficult to relate to housing types and development patterns. Data on sprawl lacking and/or disaggregated.
Public Facilities and Services	Probably greater and earlier costs attributable to more and better facilities in planned development, more likelihood of duplication and replacement in sprawl.	Uncertain and irregular; some variation due to population only, some to area differences.	Minimal: similar to variations among all buildings.	Local governments or non-for-profit corporations. Paid by taxes and user fees.	Fiscal and economic impact studies; planning standards from recreation, educational, health care, governmental organizations; case studies from particular localities; national statistics from federal agencies.	Not related to housing or development types; standards based largely on per capita, not area, basis. Data on sprawl lacking and/or disaggregated.
Environmental	Air, water, noise pollution impacts somewhat mitigated by planned development, preservation of unique areas and natural features more likely and land uses are more related in planned communities.	Generally become more adverse as overall density increases - clustering at same density is beneficial.	Considerable variation in environmental effects; severe site or climatic conditions may prohibit development.	Local governments and owner-occupant.	EPA studies; environmental impact analyses; planning documents for some state and local areas.	Small amount related to housing types and development patterns, not comprehensive in many instances.
Personal	Generally more favorable in planned development.	Discretionary time increases with density increases. Safety, privacy, comfort vary, but tend to decrease as overall density increases.	Not directly related to densities or development patterns to a significant extent.	Household and individual.	Traffic analysis from Highway Research Board; crime statistics from Dept. of Justice.	Usually not considered as part of development; deficiencies in some areas; in general not related to development patterns or housing types.

REFERENCES

1. Asia-Pacific Network for Global Change Research. (2009). Peri-Urban Development and Environmental Sustainability: Examples from China and India. https://www.apn-gcr.org/wp-content/uploads/2020/09/6bce404fc002fc548031e7203e5b1ac2.pdf. Accessed on 29th July 2021, at 1300 hours, IST.

2. Batra, L. (2009). A Review of Urbanisation and Urban Policy in Post-Independent India - Working Paper Series, CSLG/WP/12. Centre for the Study of Law and Governance, Jawaharlal Nehru University, New Delhi.

3. Bengaluru Development Authority. (2015). Draft Revised Master Plan, 2015, Bengaluru (RMP 2031).

4. Bengaluru Development Authority. (2017). Draft Revised Master Plan, 2031, Bengaluru (RMP 2031).

5. Bengaluru Development Authority. (2017). Volume-3, Master Plan Document. Draft Revised Master Plan, 2031, Bengaluru (RMP 2031).

6. Bengaluru Metro Rail Corporation. (2019). Draft Bengaluru Transit Oriented Development Policy, February, 2019. http://urbantransport.kar.gov.in/Draft%20Bengaluru%20ToD%20Policy%20with%20Annexure.pdf. Accessed on 01 August 2021, at 1600 hours, IST.

7. Bharadwaj, A. (June 27, 2020). BDA withdraws draft Revised Master Plan - 2031, to Review and Rewrite. https://www.thehindu.com/news/cities/bangalore/bda-withdraws-draft-revised-master-plan-2031-to-review-and-rewrite/article31929610.ece. Accessed on 29th July 2021, at 1300 hours, IST.

8. Bopanna, A. (2020). How Does Karnataka's New Land Reforms Amendment Impact the State? https://vidhilegalpolicy.in/blog/how-does-karnatakas-new-land-reform-ordinance-impact-the-state/. Accessed on 01st August 2021, at 1300 hours, IST.

9. Deshpande, R.S and Shaha, K. (2020). A devastating year as soon as it began. The Indian Express. https://www.newindianexpress.com/states/karnataka/2020/dec/30/a-devastating-year-as-soon-as-it-began-2242920.html. Accessed on 29th July 2021, at 1800 hours, IST.

10. Directorate of Urban Land Transport. (2020). Parking Policy 2.0 for Bengaluru. http://www.urbantransport.kar.gov.in/parking/Parking_Policy_2_Bengaluru_Final.pdf. Accessed on 01 August, 2021, at 1615 hours, IST.

11. Directorate of Urban Land Transport and Bengaluru metro Rail Corporation Ltd. (2020). Comprehensive Mobility Plan for Bengaluru, 2020, (CMP, 2020), http://www.urbantransport.kar.gov.in/docs/CMP%20Bengaluru%20-%20Final%20Report.pdf. Accessed on 01 August, 2021, at 1450 hours, IST.

12. Glaesar, E. (2011). *Triumph of the City*. Penguin.

13. Glaesar, E. (May 28, 2021). The 15-minute City is a Dead End — Cities Must be Places of Opportunity for Everyone. London School of Economics Blog. https://blogs.lse.ac.uk/covid19/2021/05/28/the-15-minute-city-is-a-dead-end-cities-must-be-places-of-opportunity-for-everyone/. Accessed on 29th July 2021, at 1500 hours, IST.

14. Goldman, M. (2010). Speculative Urbanism and the Making of the Next World City. International Journal of Urban and Regional Research. https://doi.org/10.1111/j.1468-2427.2010.01001.x. Accessed on 29th July 2021, at 1300 hours, IST.

15. Govind, R. (2020). Bengaluru was not down even during lockdown; https://www.thehindu.com/life-and-style/homes-and-gardens/bengaluru-was-not-down-even-during-lockdown/article32522981.ece. Accessed on 01 August 2021, at 1330 hours, IST.

16. Gururani, S. (2020). Cities in a world of villages: agrarian urbanism and the making of India's urbanizing frontiers, Urban Geography, 41(7): 971 989, https://doi.org/10.1080/02723638.2019.1670569.

17. Idiculla, M. (December 08, 2014). Who decides where your city ends? Citizen Matters. https://bengaluru.citizenmatters.in/who-decides-where-your-city-ends-6994. Accessed on 29th July 2021, at 1300 hours, IST.

18. Idiculla, M. (2015). Who Governs the City? The Powerlessness of City Governments and the Transformation of Governance in Bangalore. Paper presented at the RC21 International Conference on "The Ideal City: between myth and reality. Representations, policies, contradictions and challenges for tomorrow's urban life" Urbino (Italy) 27-29 August 2015. http://www.rc21.org/en/conferences/urbino2015/

19. Idiculla, M. (February, 16, 2017). Planning for the People. The Hindu. https://www.thehindu.com/opinion/op-ed/Planning-for-the-people/article17308011.ece. Accessed on 29th July 2021, at 1300 hours, IST.

20. Idiculla, M. (2021). Full citation of the references?

21. Jain, D. (March, 18, 2021). Bureaucratic Reforms are Difficult but not Impossible. https://www.livemint.com/opinion/online-views/bureaucratic-

reforms-are-difficult-but-not-impossible-11616000635649.html. Accessed on 29th July 2021, at 1400 hours, IST.

22. Jana, R and Sinha, A.K. (2019). Changing Pattern of Urban Land Use in Raipur City (Chhattisgarh State, India): 1976-2011. IOSR Journal of Humanities and Social Science (IOSR-JHSS) Volume 24, Issue 9, Series. 1 (September. 2019) 43-49 e-ISSN: 2279-0837, p-ISSN: 2279-0845. http://www.iosrjournals.org/iosr-jhss/papers/Vol.%2024%20Issue9/Series-1/G2409014349.pdf. Accessed on 31st July 2021, at 2100 hours, IST.

23. Karnataka Town and Country Planning Act 1961; http://dpal.kar.nic.in/11%20of%201963%20(E).pdf. Accessed on 01 August, 2021, at 1450 hours, IST.

24. Karnataka Electric Vehicle and Energy Storage Policy, 2017. https://kum.karnataka.gov.in/KUM/PDFS/KEVESPPolicyInsidepagesfinal.pdf. Accessed on 29th July 2021, at 1300 hours, IST.

25. Karnataka Motor Vehicles Rules, 1989.

26. Karnataka Land Reforms (Second Amendment) Bill, 2020; Passed by the Karnataka Legislative Assembly, Fifteenth Legislative Assembly. https://prsindia.org/files/bills_acts/bills_states/karnataka/2020/Bill%2042%20of%202020%20Karnataka.pdf. Accessed on 01 August 2021, at 1300 hours, IST.

27. Kennedy, L. (2014). The Politics of Economic Restructuring in India Economic Governance and State Spatial Rescaling. New York. USA: Routledge. Special Indian Edition.

28. Kennedy, L and Sood, A. (2016). Greenfield Development as Tabula Rasa. Rescaling, Speculation and Governance on India's Urban Frontier. Economic & Political Weekly, 2016. ffhalshs-02001520f. pp. 41-49.

29. Kennedy, L. (2020). Actors and shifting scales of urban governance in India. Danielle Labbé; André Sorensen. International Handbook on Megacities and Megacity Regions, Edward Elgar, pp.101-118, 2020, 978 1 78897 269 7. 10.4337/9781788972703 . halshs-03044381

30. Khan, S. Second Covid Wave slows down residential property sale, construction activity in Bengaluru; The Economic Times; https://economictimes.indiatimes.com/industry/services/property-/-cstruction/second-covid-wave-slows-down-residential-property-sales-construction-activity-in-bengaluru/articleshow/82308433.cms?from=mdr. Accessed on 01 August, 2021, at 1400 hours, IST.

31. Pandey, K. (2021). Bengalureans buy double the number of vehicles in COVID-19 pandemic year, thumbs down for public transport. Timesnow news. https://www.timesnownews.com/bengaluru/article/bengalureans-buy-double-the-number-of-vehicles-in-pandemic-year-thumbs-down-for-public-transport/733036; Accessed on 01 August 2021, at 1550 hours, IST.

32. Kidiyoor, S. (2021). Pandemic Fallout: BMRCL suffers INR 904 Crore loss. The Hindu. https://www.thehindu.com/news/cities/bangalore/pan-demic-fallout-bmrcl-suffers-904-crore-loss/article35138231.ece; Accessed on 01 August, 2021, at 1400 hours, IST.

33. Krishnankutty, M. (2021). Mumbai's Orphan Plan: How the EDDP 2014-34 was Conceived, Crafted and Abandoned. Book chapter in Politics of Planning. Pattaroni, Bhide and Lutringer eds., forthcoming.

34. Krishnaswamy, S. Idiculla, M. Rajagopal, C. (2017). Planning for Benga-luru, A Five-Part Series. The Hindu.

35. Kulkarni, C. 2021. Losing 82% in pandemic times, BMRCL looks to Karnataka Government for loan. Deccan Herald. https://www.deccanher-ald.com/city/top-bengaluru-stories/losing-82-revenue-in-pandemic-times-bmrcl-looks-to-karnataka-govt-for-loan-1000465.html. Accessed on 01 August 2021, at 1550 hours, IST.

36. Kumar, M.P. (2018). What saved your neighbourhood from becoming a messy, commercial hub. Citizen Matters. https://bengaluru.citizenmatters.in/caf-pil-bda-master-plan-2015-land-use-koramangala-28237. Accessed on 01 August, 2021, at 1455 hours, IST.

37. Kumar, S. (2021). Bengaluru Real Estate, A Post-Covid Snapshot. https://www.constructionweekonline.in/business/17863-bengaluru-real-estate-a-post-covid-19-snapshot. Accessed on 01 August 2021, at 1515 hours, IST.

38. Mehta, P. and Behera, A. (2021). Alternative Mobility – A Must Have for Indian Cities. https://wri-india.org/blog/alternative-mobility-—-must-have-indian-cities. Accessed on 29th July 2021, at 1450 hours, IST.

39. Mohan, A (April 19, 2021). Bird's Eye View of City Planning is Full of Blur. India Together. http://www.indiatogether.org/bird-eye-government. Accessed on 29th July 2021, at 1300 hours, IST.

40. Mohan, A. (2020). Bangalore needs Elite + Mass Activism to be Effective. https://www.integrateddesign.org/bangalore-needs-elite---mass-activism-to-be-effective. Accessed on 31st July 2021, at 2300 hours, IST.

41. Mohan, A and Rajagopal, C. (2011). Outsourcing Governance? Revising the Master Plan of Bangalore, 46th ISOCARP Congress 2010.

42. Ministry of Housing and Urban Affairs. (2020). National Urban Policy Framework, Strategic Intent. https://iica.nic.in/images/Articles/NUPF_Final_Oct%202020.pdf. Accessed on 29th July 2021, at 2100 hours, IST.

43. Narain, V. Banerjee, P, Anand, P. (2014). The Shadow of Urbanization: The Periurban Interface of Five Indian Cities in Transition. Environmental Change, Vulnerability, and Governance, East West Centre, Working papers, No. 68, January 2014.

44. Narayanan, N. (2019). Why Bengaluru's proposed mega elevated road corridor has sparked protests. Scroll. https://scroll.in/article/916777/why-bengalurus-proposed-mega-elevated-road-corridor-has-sparked-protests. Accessed on 01 August, 2021, at 1520 hours, IST.

45. Nair, J. (2005). The Promise of the Metropolis. Bangalore's Twentieth Century. Oxford University Press, New Delhi.

46. Navya, P.K. (2021). Low ridership, high fares: COVID nudging BMTC into vicious circle. Citizen Matters. https://bengaluru.citizenmatters.in/bmtc-covid-reduced-services-informal-workers-58496. Accessed on 01 August 2021, at 1700 hours, IST.

47. Nestaway. https://community.nestaway.com/info/tech-parks-in-bangalore/. Accessed on 01 August, 2021, at 1300 hours, IST.

48. Philip, M.C. (2021). Bengaluru: Hit hard by Pandemic, Cab Operators Focus On Inter-City Routes. Times of India. http://timesofindia.indiatimes.com/articleshow/77619955.cms?utm_source=contentofinterest&utm_medium=text&utm_campaign=cppst. Accessed on 29th July 2021, at 1300 hours, IST.

49. Poovanna, S and Nandi, M. (2020). Work from home transforms Bengaluru's IT Clusters. The Mint. https://www.livemint.com/news/india/work-from-home-transforms-bengaluru-s-it-clusters-11596375108870.html. Accessed on 01 August, 2021, at 1400 hours, IST.

50. Pramanik, A. (2021). IBM plans to reduce office space by nearly half in India; The Economic Times. https://economictimes.indiatimes.com/tech/software/ibm-plans-to-reduce-office-space-by-nearly-half-in-india/articleshow/76447772.cms?from=mdr; Accessed on 01 August, 2021, at 1400 hours, IST.

51. Prashanth, G.N. (2013). Rise of the gated Community. Deccan Herald. https://www.deccanherald.com/content/370253/rise-gated-community.html. Accessed on 01 August, 2021, at 1500 hours, IST.

52. Rajagopal, C. (2021). An Entrepreneurial State in India? Investigating Public Private Partnerships Incomplete Contracts and Risks in the Transport Sector. University of Amsterdam.

53. Real Estate Research Corporation. (1974). The Costs of Sprawl: Environmental and Economic Costs of Alternative Residential Development Patterns at the Urban Fringe. Portland Regional Planning History Oregon Sustainable Community Digital Library.

54. Rouanet, H and Halbert, L. (2015). Leveraging Finance Capital: Urban Change and Self-Empowerment of Real Estate Developers in India. Urban Studies. https://doi.org/10.1177/0042098015585917. Accessed on 29th July 2021, at 1300 hours, IST.

55. World Bank. (2020). COVID-19 Crisis Through a Migration Lens. Migration and Development Brief,no. 32;. World Bank, Washington, DC. © World Bank. https://openknowledge.worldbank.org/handle/10986/33634 License: CC BY 3.0 IGO. Accessed on 29th July 2021, at 1300 hours, IST.

56. World Bank. (2021). Lall, Somik V.; Lebrand, Mathilde Sylvie Maria; Park, Hogeun; Sturm, Daniel Marbod; Venables, Anthony J. Pancakes to Pyramids: City Form to Promote Sustainable Growth (English). Washington, D.C. : World Bank Group. http://documents.worldbank.org/curated/en/554671622446381555/City-Form-to-Promote-Sustainable-Growth. Accessed on 29th July 2021, at 1300 hours, IST.

57. Sastry, B. 2018. Bengaluru's draft master plan: A myopic approach to urban design. Citizen Matters.

58. Shankar, S. (2020). Realty sector may gain from Bengaluru city limits extension. The Times of India; https://timesofindia.indiatimes.com/city/bengaluru/realty-sector-may-gain-from-bluru-city-limits-expansion/articleshow/79727579.cms. Accessed on 01 August, 2021, at 1425 hours, IST.

59. Zérah, Marie-Hélène. "I.S.A. Baud and Joop de Wit (eds.), New Forms of Urban Governance in India: Shifts, Models, Networks and Contestations ", South Asia Multidisciplinary Academic Journal [Online], Book Reviews, Online since 18 January 2011, connection on 19 April 2019. URL : http:// journals.openedition.org/samaj/3109

ENDNOTES

1. For example, Bengaluru city experienced a doubling of population between 1991 and 2001 and again between 2001 and 2011, with a corresponding near-doubling of urbanised area [RMP 2015]. Raipur, a medium-sized city doubled in spatial expansion between 1976 and 2011 [Jana and Sinha, 2019].
2. 22 January, 2018, The Hindu. RMP 2031: BDA gets 8,869 suggestions and objections. https://www.thehindu.com/news/cities/bangalore/rmp-2031-bda-gets-8869-suggestions-and-objections/article22492350.ece. Accessed on 01 August, 2021, at 1445 hours, IST.
3. See, Section 12(g)(ii) of the Karnataka Town and Country Planning Act 1961 for definition of Floor Area Ratio (FAR). "Floor Area Ratio" means the quotient of the ratio of the combined gross floor area of all the floors, excepting areas specifically exempted under the regulations, to the total area of the plot." Greater the FAR, greater the potential to build on a parcel of land.
4. See, Idiculla, 2021 for the origins of the CITB in the bubonic plague, early 20th century, A.D.
5. October 23, 2018, Citizen Matters.
6. Nov 22, 2013; Deccan Herald.
7. February 12, 2019.
8. August 19, 2021, The Times of India.
9. See, RMP 2015: 3.5% annual growth rate for population and 3.7% for employment; (https://www.statista.com/statistics/886982/india-employment-growth-rate-by-city/). Accessed on 01 August, 2021, at 1510 hours, IST.
10. March 16, 2019, Scroll.
11. December 30, 2020, The Indian Express.
12. See, The Economic Times, September, 28, 2020; 'Karnataka assembly passes amendment to land reforms act, makes it easy to buy farm lands' - "...the reforms passed repeals Section 79 (A) that sets a limit on non-agricultural income at 25 lakhs to buy agricultural land, section 79(B) that bars non agriculturalists from purchasing agricultural lands and Section 79(C), that deals with penalty for falsely claiming eligibility to holding agricultural land; https://economictimes.indiatimes.com/news/politics-and-nation/karnataka-assembly-passes-amendment-to-land-reforms-

act-makes-it-easy-to-buy-farm-land/articleshow/78336440.cms?utm_source=contentofinterest&utm_medium=text&utm_campaign=cppst. Accessed on 31st July 2021, at 1400 hours, IST.

13. September 22, 2020; Changes to land reforms opposed at 'people's session' in Karnataka
https://www.thehindu.com/news/national/karnataka/changes-to-land-reforms-opposed-at-peoples-session-in-karnataka/article32672073.ece. Accessed on 01 August 2020, at 1300 hours, IST.

14. May 27, 2021, Construction Week Online.

15. September 22, 2020, The Hindu.

16. June 19, 2020, The Economic Times.

17. August 02, 2020, The Mint.

18. April 29, 2021, The Economic Times.

19. December 15, 2020, The Times of India.

20. See, Magic Bricks; Malleswaram (city centre) at 11,387/- INR per Square Foot versus Whitefield (peri-urban, prime IT area), at 6,052/- per Square Foot; https://www.magicbricks.com/Property-Rates-Trends/ALL-RESIDENTIAL-rates-in-Bangalore. Accessed on 01 August, 2021, at 1430 hours, IST.

21. April 27, 2021, Citizen Matters.

22. July 04, 2021, The Hindu and June 23, 2021, The Deccan Herald.

23. July 14, 2020, The Economic Times. https://economictimes.indiatimes.com/mobile/how-the-pandemic-has-hit-ola-uber-hard-in-india/articleshow/76956369.cms; How the pandemic has hit Ola, Uber hard in India. Accessed on 01 August, 2021, at 1530 hours, IST.

24. March 16, 2021, Timesnow News.

8

OPPORTUNITIES AND CHALLENGES TO E-GOVERNANCE DURING COVID-19 AND AFTER

Krishna Mohan

Abstract: *Covid-19 pandemic pushed the limits of India's e-governance infrastructure, mobile networks and smart devices. Technology adoption has increased to a new height not only by Central Government but also by State & Local Governments and tech-savvy citizens and by many who were not active technology users earlier. Post-Covid, the importance of e-governance initiatives in the lives of citizens at large has witnessed a paradigm shift. It has been a slow movement towards a contactless world. Thus, it is important for the Government to proactively plan for the new reality and emerge stronger from the crises by further accelerating the digital transformation of Governments service delivery and engagement through e – Governance. If leveraged correctly, this situation can help India attain new heights in terms of e- Governance adoption and utilization.*

Key Words: E-governance, good governance, contactless, information technology, digital India, e-courts.

Introduction

The emergence of Covid-19 has brought devastation to people all over the world. Everything from the death of loved ones to the shutting down of small businesses, these are all crises that people have had to accept and find ways to move forward. The road to recovery and building back a sense of normalcy comes a little easier for some more than others.

The coronavirus has certainly made its mark on 2020, for better and or worse. But there's no denying the positive economic impact it has made on certain industries. Sure, some industries are suffering more than others while certain industries are thriving. As countries are firefighting the Covid-19 pandemic, one thing is becoming clear, the post-coronavirus world will be different in many ways economically, socially and health- wise. No one will come out of this crisis without losing something. Previous threats to individual and social freedoms could not change our way of life but now this important asset of our civilisation is seriously threatened. In a post-Covid-19 world, a new international order will be redrawn by the powerful countries taking into account the lessons learnt in dealing with the current pandemic.

Information Technology will play a major role in all aspects of life in education, e-governance, commerce, health and artificial intelligence. Use of tracking devices to monitor citizens would conflict with human rights concerns in favour of security and safety. The lesson from Covid-19 is poignant. This pandemic has attacked one thing most precious to modern civilisation, which is human liberty. In most parts of the world, our way of life has been characterised by individual and social freedoms for which countries have gone to wars and won them after making costly sacrifices. But now this important asset of our civilisation is seriously threatened by a coronavirus and its aftereffects.

The 2020 pandemic came like a bolt from the blue and knocked our civilisation's complacency. Such disruptions are rare for they involve a combination of impact, speed and scale. They force us to reflect upon our position and velocity as an intelligent species and make us introspect on some flawed designs upon which our society casually reclines. No doubt, such difficult times require our priority on containing the menace, but oftentimes it also provides an opportunity to adopt long-term sectoral reforms. There is no doubt that this pandemic has forced us to move towards a contactless world, hence e-governance has taken a quantum jump to ensure delivery of public services to the citizens confined to their homes.

Every time the government uses an e-governance technology, it results in more efficiency, lesser costs, lesser manpower requirement and lesser physical presence of humans in the job at hand. The last advantage is indeed of concern in the lockdown and social distancing practices of the present pandemic situation. It is also worth mentioning that if hardware automation and artificial intelligence are added to e-governance, it can reduce manpower requirement and their physical presence in every possible job/economic activity. If this pandemic would have struck a century later, the world would have been far better equipped to absorb the shock. But, nobody can predict the timing of a catastrophe — one can only predict its impact and prepare in advance. The present paper focuses on e-governance possibilities in India in the wake of this crisis.

I

Governance, Good Governance and E-Governance

From the pre-Independence to the post-Independence era, the system of Governance in this country has undergone a transition - from colonial system of governance to a citizen-centric system of governance. The focus has now shifted to the citizen while formulating public policies. Now, the objective of the Government is to make a systematic effort to focus on the commitment of the Government towards its citizen in respect of standard of services. It is now expected to do so through an efficient system of information, consultation, non-discrimination, responsiveness, courtesy and realizing the value for time & money for the citizens. The actors in governance now comprise the State, Civil Society and Market. The State's aim is to create a favorable political, legal and economic environment, the market is expected to create opportunities for people and the Civil Society's function is to mobilize people's participation. The Governance now has become too important to be left to the Government alone.

Improvement in the delivery of the government services is an important issue for countries like India, as the largest cost of inefficiency is borne by the poor. India is home to a large number of pilots of electronic services delivery in different sectors. Public has indeed benefitted a lot from these projects. One of the key challenges has been to adopt the successful and best practices at a nationwide level. The Central Government has already developed an ambitious e-governance programme under the umbrella of Digital India which has impacted the service delivery mechanism in a variety of departments. Having said that, it must be mentioned that there are always advantages as well as challenges to be faced when adopting a new technology in an existing system. A lot of project management, business process re-engineering techniques, and skillful change management were required to successfully implement the projects. The most significant challenge in implementing, ICT applications in India came in overcoming resistance from Government employees, who were directly affected by implementation of e-governance. ICT application can result in reducing discretionary power of a civil servant and bring more transparency to decision making process and information. This results in loss of power and authority to favour some citizens at the expense of others. Besides, there was also an inherent opposition to capacity building and training in these new ICT techniques.

In spite of all this opposition from some of the stakeholders, developments in the Information and Communication Technology fields have been taking place throughout the country. Some of the Central Ministries and many of the States were keen implementers of e-governance for bringing improvements in the public service delivery. The push given by successive Central Government as well as many State Governments led by e-savvy Chief Ministers has helped India emerge as a major initiator in e-governance adoption. This is despite the challenge arising out of conditions related to awareness literacy, infrastructure, bandwidth issues and multilingual and cultural issues pervading the country. If the STD/ISD/PCO booths and mobiles phone have revolutionized the communications sector by making deep inroads into the rural India, e-governance with ICT techniques has indeed made the lives of the citizen of the country a lot better by timely and easy availability of public services.

Good Governance: The paradigm shift from Government to Governance with the citizen as its focus required the governments world over to shift to a new system of governance. This new system came to be called as "Good Governance". Good Governance aims at providing an environment in which all citizens irrespective of class, caste or gender can develop to their full potential. In addition, good governance also aims at ensuring the delivery of public service effectively, efficiently and equitably to the citizens. The four pillars on which the edifice of good governance rests in essence are Ethos (of service to the citizens), Ethics (ensuring honestly, integrity & transparency), Equality (treating all citizens alike with empathy) & lastly but not the least important, Efficiency (speedy & effective delivery of services).

With Good Governance as the foundation for ensuring citizen-centric administration with improved public service delivery, Information Technology was thought of as an enabler and an effective tool for bringing about the reforms. Information Technology gave an added feature to the way information can be stored, processed and transferred within an organization - public or private. With increasing awareness about Information & Communication Technology (ICT), information systems continue to proliferate all over the world at breathtaking pace. The emergence of web-based delivery systems has increased the relevance of these tools for collecting, collating and sharing information at low cost. This Technology has helped social sectors like health, education, rural development and other areas to reach out and deliver the goods & services to distant consumers. In effect, IT has given freedom to the citizen from People, Place and Time.

The gradual penetration of ICT in all facets of human existence is leading to multidimensional changes. It is changing the way individuals interact with each other and with the society. The way of governing a country is no exception to this emerging and changing scenario. India is one of the few countries where this trend has caught on in a good measure.

Information Technology facilitates Government to explore innovative ways of creating knowledge and citizen's involvement in the decision making process. The last few years have witnessed a much more responsive, transparent and inclusive governance pervading the remotest parts of the country due to increasing reach of IT-enabled services. The Prime Minister summed up India's transformation exercise in the form of an equation:

IT (India's Transformation) = IT (Information Technology) + IT (India's Talent)

The emerging Information and Communication Technologies have made significant contribution towards achievement of Good Governance.

Evolution of E-Governance: E-Governance is in essence the application of Information & Communication Technology to Government functioning in order to create Simple, Moral, Accountable, Responsive & Transparent (SMART) Governance. The "e" in E-Governance stands for electronic. Thus, e-governance is basically associated with carrying out the functions and achieving the results of governance through the utilization of ICT. The reason why countries around the world including India are increasingly opting for e-Governance is because now Governance has become more complex and people's aspirations are also rising. Now, the citizen expects to have the best delivery channels of public service available to him as are prevailing world over.

ICT has indeed helped in efficient storage and retrieval of data, instantaneous transmission and processing of information as compared to the earlier manual system. It has also resulted in speeding up government processes, taking decisions expeditiously and judicially increasing transparency and enforcing accountability. The system has become more robust and the reach of the Government has increased both geographically & demographically.

The system of e-governance is supported by 5Cs which may to termed as its pillars. These are:

I. Computers

II. Connectivity

III. Content

IV. Consumer, and

V. Confidence Building.

The e-Governance aims to make the interaction between Government and Citizen (G2C), Government and Business enterprises (G2B), Government to Government (G2G) & Government to employer (G2E) more friendly, convenient and inexpensive.

E-Governance in India and its earlier trends: Recognizing the important of ICT, the Government of India established National Information Centre in 1977 making it an important milestone towards adoption of e-Governance in India. By late 1980s, a large number of government offices had computers but they were mostly used for word processing. Various ministries, department, etc. started adopting ICT for both internal (payroll processing, etc.) and business requirement (monitoring of development work, report generation, MIS, etc.). In 2006, the e–governance initiative in India was named as National e-Governance Plan (NeGP). The NeGP started with 27 Mission Mode Projects (MMPs) and four more MMPS were added in 2011. Thus, with the passage of time, e-governance in India has developed from the introductory stage in which the citizen is informed about the existence of Government websites and their usefulness to the stage of focusing on transactional & participatory type services. Some of the success stories include pioneering efforts made in the realm of Railway Ticket reservation, air ticket bookings, e-commerce, net banking, income tax, e–procurement, passport, etc. The Government of India Ministries were much more proactive in implementing e-governance initiatives. Subsequent to that, various State government like Andhra Pradesh, Karnataka, Gujarat adopted e–Governance measures in computerizing & digitizing land records, treasuries, commercial taxes, education, police, transport and health sectors.

E-Governance is implemented by government in almost every field. From urban to rural areas and from politics to teaching, Governance has spread its root everywhere. Whether it is public or private sector, common man or businessman all are largely dependent on e-governance. Some of these are:

i. Transportation: Services provided by e-governance in this area are Issuance of Time Table of buses, Provision of booking facility for Interstate transport, Transportation Improvement Programme, Regional Transport plans, Congestion Management Process, Transportation Demand Management.

   a. CFST: Citizen Friendly Services of Transport Department by Andhra Pradesh government to provide services such as Issue of learner licenses, Issue of driving licenses, Renewal of driving licenses, etc.

   b. *Vahan* and *Sarathi*: The backend applications Vahan & Sarathi help in speeding the overall work flow in the transport department of Tamil Nadu govt.

iii. Online payment of bills and taxes: Services provided by e-governance in this area are Online Transaction, Payment of Bill, Payment of taxes, Payment of house EMIs.

   a. FRIENDS: This project is started by Kerala Government for its citizens to make online payment of electricity and water bills, revenue taxes, license fees, motor vehicle taxes, university fees, etc.

   b. E-SEVA: Electronic seva by Andhra Pradesh government to pay utility bills, avail of trade licenses and transact on government matters at these facilities.

iii. Municipal services: Services provided are as: House Tax Assessment, Billing and Collection, Maintain records of Land & property, Issue of Death Certificates, Registration & Attorneys of Properties, Review and approval authority for site plans.

iv. Agriculture: Following are the projects used in Agriculture:

a. Gyandoot: In the State of Madhya Pradesh it is an Intranet-based Government to citizen (G2C) service delivery initiative.

b. BELE: It is a web-based application with 3-tier architecture for capturing and monitoring the major activities and services.

c. AGMARKNET: It is a project approved by Department of Marketing & Inspection (DMI), Ministry of Agriculture, Government of India.

v. Public Service Delivery and Redressal of Grievances:

a. E-JanSampark: Services & Information accessible to the common man in his locality to meet his basic need. This project is started by Chandigarh.

b. Prajavani: it is started by the Government of Andhra Pradesh.it is a Web based On-line Monitoring of Public Grievances.

c. Police: It is designed by Hyderabad, developed and hosted with many exciting public utility features like Safety tips for all citizens, verification status of Passports, Stolen vehicles, etc.

vi. Land record management: By facilitating e-governance service in this area, millions of land records can be maintained in a very short time span.

a. *Bh*oomi: It is the first e-Governance land records management system project which is successfully implemented for the benefits of the common man by the Government of Karnataka.

b. Comprehensive Modernization of Land Records (CMLR): This project is started by the Government of Andhra Pradesh. It allows integrating functions of property registration, mutations and updating of field survey maps.

c. E-*Panjeeyan*: It is started by Assam government to deals with the computerization of the Document registration work at Sub Registrar Office.

vii. Health: Service provided by these projects are availability of medicines, Special health camps, Facilities at Anganwadi centers.

a. Online Vaccination Appointment for International Travellers: Citizen-centric application for the purpose of vaccination of the persons proceeding abroad and issuance of International Health Certificate.

b. SMS-based Integrated Disease Surveillance System: It is an SMS based Integrated Disease Surveillance System. It facilitates to report the occurrences of disease, number of persons affected from the area of occurrences immediately to the concerned authority.

c. Hospital OPD Appointment: Hospital OPD Appointment System is another welfare measure undertaken by Chandigarh Administration to make life of citizens simpler.

viii. Education: Providing basic education (elementary, primary, secondary) to children, Providing computer education to children, Results for 10th & 12th classes, Information on eligibility for "Distribution of books" scheme

a. Online Scholarship Management System: It is meant for the purpose of distribution of scholarships and fees reimbursement.

b. AISES (All India School Education Survey): this project is started by Assam government. This project is used for surveying the number of schools in district Census.

Challenges faced: There are various challenges for the implementation of e-government in India. These challenges are like low literacy, lack of awareness, low broadband penetration, lack of system integration within a department, etc.

This can be largely attributed to various front-end and back-end challenges that the government continues to face. Front-end challenges relate to user-specific issues such as, high illiteracy levels, non-availability of user-friendly interfaces, inadequate power supply in rural areas, low broadband penetration and most importantly, lack of awareness of e-Governance initiatives.

On the other hand, back-end challenges relate to technical, process or human resource issues within the government. These issues include lack of systems integration within a department, lack of integration across government departments, limited knowledge of using computers at various levels of bureaucracy and deployment of technology without proper process re-engineering.

Digital India: In 2014 the Government of India announced an investment of Rs. 1 Lakh crore for the Digital India programme. The initiative includes plans to connect rural areas with high-speed internet networks. Digital India consists of three core components. These includes the creation of digital infrastructure, Delivery of services digitally & Digital literacy. The focus is on making technology central to enabling change.

Aadhar: India's digital governance revolution got a further push with a biometric identification scheme known as "Aadhaar". Since then, a 12-digit unique identity number has been issued to Indians who present valid proof of identity and register their biometric data, including fingerprints and iris scans. Banks, telecom companies and a host of government agencies are now able to verify Aadhaar numbers online, while Aadhaar accounts can be stored on the cloud. Building on the Aadhaar unique ID system, authorities have rolled out Aadhaar-based direct benefit transfers and a remittance system that allows government agencies to transfer benefits ranging from pensions to short-term relief, directly to Aadhaar-linked bank accounts.

Pradhan Mantri Jan Dhan Yojana (PMJDY) – Vehicle for Social and Financial Inclusion: The Aadhaar-supported financial inclusion scheme, Pradhan Mantri Jan Dhan Yojana (PMJDY), aims to bring low-income households into the banking system. This forms the backbone of a brand-new social security delivery system and is also promoted as a vehicle for social inclusion for the marginalized and disadvantaged. Under the Jan Dhan Yojana scheme, bank accounts accessed with Aadhaar identification are used to distribute direct benefit transfers, wages under the Mahatma Gandhi National Rural Employment Guarantee Act (NREGA) and other poverty alleviation and welfare delivery schemes, like the food and public distribution system. PMJDY also provides life and health insurance coverage to eligible beneficiaries. About 400 million PMJDY accounts had been opened as of August 2020.

First proposed in India's *Economic Survey of 2014-15*, the Jan Dhan-Aadhaar-Mobile (JAM) initiative links bank account numbers, Aadhaar numbers and mobile phone numbers to make cash transfers and other benefits available to beneficiaries via their mobile phone. The JAM trinity thus promises to connect the Aadhaar system with the government's database of bank accounts, including PMJDY accounts, and a database of more than 900 million mobile phone accounts.

India's e-governance and digitalization drive harnesses 'smart' technology in an effort to generate new economic opportunities, boost economic growth, govern more efficiently with less corruption, and distribute relief and benefits to the poor and disadvantaged more effectively. The Covid-19 pandemic has presented a monumental challenge to India's emergent e-governance and digital welfare infrastructure, while also putting the Central Government's capacity for technological innovation to the test.

II

Dynamics of E-Governance in post- Covid era:

When the virus struck the entire world, it led to scare all around. People hid themselves with fear. Anxiety was writ large on all faces. Fear of death loomed large. Jobs were lost, people lost wages, Earnings came down. Restrictions on movement through lockdown, Curfews became the order of the day; people had to remain confined to their respective homes. The virus harassed us to no end. It led to enhanced hygiene requirements - Masks, washing of hands, sanitizers, social distancing. Restrictions on delivery of food & other articles from outside had to be imposed. Gyms, swimming pools, malls, shops all were closed. Mental peace was taken away. The question before everyone was "Can I survive??" We had no control over the virus - No vaccine. There was acute anxiety over what was in store for future! Everyone was angry over what was happening. There was a feeling of taking revenge. Even though the virus was not visible to us we started hating it. There was a feeling of retaliation against the country which gave birth to this virus.

Way back in 2015 in one of his Ted talks, tech giant Bill Gates had predicted that viruses pose the greatest risk of global catastrophe; when compared to other threats of humanity. If anything kills over 10 million people over the next few decades, it's most likely to be a highly infectious virus rather than a war or missiles, he warned. Five years later, Coronavirus, brought the world to its knees. Businesses were shut, schools and colleges were closed, travel banned.

After the detection of Covid-19 in India in early 2020, health authorities launched intensive monitoring of cases and hospitalizations across the country, watching with alarm as the disease continued to spread. On 24 March 2020, at 8:00 PM, India's Prime Minister declared a nationwide stay-at-home order. Issuing curfew guidelines from the Union Ministry of India, initially for twenty-one days the PM announced that all Indians must stay at their residence to prevent the spread of Covid-19. The guidelines imposed unprecedented restrictions on mobility. As workplaces came under lockdown, migrant labourers had to leave for their original homes, while all public transportation was suspended.

The pandemic has no doubt put the fabric of Indian society to the test, and has taken a heavy toll on the population, especially on informal workers, the rural poor and other marginalized groups. The pandemic has also pushed the limits of India's e-governance infrastructure and accelerated the Indian population's dependence on the digital infrastructure, mobile networks and 'smart' devices.

E-Governance in Post-Covid India: Opportunities and Challenges: As Albert Einstein once said "In the middle of a difficulty lies an opportunity." This has again been proved by the rapid emergence of innovative technology solutions across the globe as a response to the Covid-19 outbreak. Challenges do create opportunities. Covid-19 may have turned our lives upside down but it has certainly provided an opportunity for all of us to rise to the occasion during these testing times.

Post-Covid the importance of E-Governance initiatives in the lives of citizens at large witnessed a paradigm shift. The enforcement of social distancing by central as well as local Governments in the last one and half years led to enhanced role of E-Governance initiatives in delivering critical to common services/facility to the citizen at large. Due to the ongoing Covid-19 pandemic, which was declared a pandemic by the WHO on March 11, 2020, E-Governance initiatives gained interest among the Governments across the world at unprecedented levels, especially in case of a large country like India which had to cater to a population of almost 130 crores.

Covid-19 has engendered unprecedented disruptions across sectors. From suspending flights and trains to restricting the movement of people and vehicles, it has had a large-scale impact on the Indian economy. However, some sectors are also considering this hour of crisis as an opportunity to innovate their existing business models and create solutions.

Health: In its fight against Covid-19 India has leveraged e-Governance for various kinds of information dissemination, tracing and monitoring activities. One such notable initiative is the *Arogya Setu* app which is a contact tracing, syndrome mapping and self-assessment digital service.

This mobile app, was rolled out by the Government of India and uses a combination of Bluetooth, global positioning systems (GPS), artificial intelligence (AI) and data analytics for contact-tracking and contact-tracing.

The usual features of healthcare and medical management related applications being used at the state level include (a) tracking the geographical spread of the pandemic on a real time basis using GIS-linked tools; (b) features for real-time patient and related data upload by healthcare professionals, municipal officials, Covid-19 call centre operators into a single central database; (c) monitoring of availability and utilization levels of hospital facilities and beds; (d) managing the demand, availability and utilization levels of equipment like ventilators as well as essential medical items, including N95 masks and PPEs.

Many of these solutions are also providing a layer of data analytics with simulation and predictive functionalities for further spread of the disease in a particular geographic area, including identification of potential hotspots, demand for hospital beds, associated equipment and consumables.

The launch of CoWIN web portal helped in vaccination registration. It displayed booking the slots of covid -19 vaccine available in the nearby areas. Booking can then be done on the website. It has been created for real time monitoring of Covid-19 vaccine.

As people adopt better personal hygiene practices in the post-Covid-19 world, the consumption of nutrition and wellness products is expected to see a rise. At present, products like disinfectants and sanitisers are recording the highest sales – a trend that seems likely to continue and become deeply ingrained in consumer behaviour. Fitness products like fitness tracking gadgets and apps are also seeing a surge in demand.

This shift in mindset towards healthier living opens the door for collaborations between fitness product manufacturers and healthcare providers, creating a positive impact on the country's GDP in the coming years. Moreover, as people turn to the online medium, provisions like online medicine delivery and teleconsulting – which is already seeing stellar growth owing to the lockdown – will rise even further in the future.

We might also see more healthcare-oriented investment from private and public sectors as the country enhances its healthcare infrastructure in the wake of the ongoing pandemic. This will have a two-fold impact on the Indian economy. Firstly, essential healthcare services will become more accessible, available and affordable for the mass consumer. Secondly, and just as importantly, the number of employment opportunities will explode. In a country that has been facing some challenges with the high level of unemployment of late, this will be a major shot in the arm.

Education: Among the most-affected sectors is education. Since the first phase of the lockdown in March, educational institutions have been working hard, looking for new ways to reach out to the students.

Covid has given a huge lift to online learning both in the metros and non-metros. Online education, has got a major boost. Educational institutions, business organisations among others, have taken online education to a new level by offering classes, coaching and courses in an innovative way to keep their audience busy at these times of lockdown. In India, students and professionals are signing up for online classes- from entrance exams like JEE and NEET or for upskilling, the demand has grown manifold. Several schools across the country have started online classes. Students are attending classes virtually. Schools have ensured that virtual classroom looks like normal classrooms with hours filled with activities and homework.

With institutes closed and regular classes on hold during the lockdown period, online learning has emerged as the most viable tool for educators looking to ensure that the pandemic's impact on their learners' academic progress is minimised.

Even before the Covid-19 outbreak, the Indian online education market was expected to grow appreciably by the year 2022. The pandemic has only served to accelerate this growth by making it essential for educators and learners to adopt more efficient digital processes and tools. As the economy normalises, the disruptions and innovations coming to the fore during this phase will become key industry growth drivers in the future.

Challenges: The sudden and nearly complete shift to online education due to closure of schools amid the novel coronavirus disease (Covid-19) pandemic has thrown up many challenges. Virtual learning has made learning difficult for them. Some of the challenges are discussed below:

Without eye contact and personal interaction, teaching has become challenging: As far as communication is concerned E- learning is helpful. But the big question is : How much knowledge is being actually received by the receivers? Since there is limited or no personal interaction in these online classes, one of the most alarming problems arising out of this set-up is the continuous use of mobile phones and computers by our students.

This is not only affecting their eyesight but also their bodies and mind. Students are complaining about headaches, back pain and stiffness in their legs. With movement being restricted, physical ailments are on the rise. Apart from concerns over physical health, students have also been sharing how their mental health is getting impacted. Many are going through a phase of anxiety and hypertension. The same goes for teachers as well.

Parents are also facing several challenges. Foremost among them is the issue of affordability. Many parents are feeling awkward that their children's education is hanging precariously on these smartphones without which their kids would lag behind in the learning process. The inability to afford, for the internet is not free after all, are depriving several students from receiving information. This has raised the issue of exclusion and many fear that such issues of access and affordability may enhance the gap between the "haves" and "have-nots", even though education is supposed to be a universal right. Many parents have witnessed increased negative behavior and the children experienced changes in their behaviour. These include an increase in anger and irritability as well as lack of concentration.

Specially abled children: Specially abled children require routine and emotional support as well as therapy and personal attention for their overall development. Physically attending school before the pandemic helped them learn effectively. But the progress has largely been undone with the online mode, according to experts. Commonly used technology platforms like WhatsApp, Zoom or Google Meet being used in schools are not designed to keep inclusivity in mind. They require assistive technology — products and related services that enhance inclusion for people with special needs — to study online.

Some schools, especially the private ones, have been able to leverage technology to teach them. However, under-resourced schools are unable to leverage these for their students. They compound the already existing challenges for children with autism or low-vision. Virtual classes for children with autism and other behavioural disorders are still a challenge.

Social-emotional development: Lack of physical interaction with teachers and peers has stunted the socio-emotional development of such children.

Preparedness for Exams: Educational learning has been an unusual victim of the ongoing novel coronavirus pandemic. Continuity of learning has been impacted adversely — so has the students' overall satisfaction regarding preparedness for exams via digital means.

Network Quality: The student-satisfaction level has been found to be highly correlated to network quality; when the network was fairly good, satisfaction levels were also high. With a fall in internet continuity, the satisfaction level fell appreciably.

For both students and teachers residing in remote rural locations, the challenges are found to be immense, with some teachers having to walk long distances across the mountainous terrain to connect to the internet.

Problem in evaluation: Another major issue with the online medium was with the checking of assignments. The previous system of checking excercises was less cumbersome and teachers had more liberty to share comments. Now, since the comments were being shared via WhatsApp, a messaging service, it was almost impossible to give a holistic feedback on the submitted assignment covering all points.

Practical Work: Practical work, an important aspect of education, has stopped completely. Many initiatives were taken to address this issue. Through this, sharing of videos was done to impart knowledge to the students. These little measures have definitely been helpful but can't match the first-hand experience students used to get via laboratory work.

E-Retail: While most Indian households still rely on their neighbourhood stores for grocery, many have lately been switching to online retail platforms. This is to ensure compliance with social distancing. And players in the space are capitalising on this trend to establish themselves as an integral part of the daily grocery fulfilment value chain.

Given the rise in demands, most players are witnessing a 20 percent to 80 percent surge in their order volumes despite challenges like order delays and cancellations. In a way, the lockdown is gradually changing the mindsets of consumers and encouraging them to switch to online grocery shopping. This indicates that online grocery will be a sunrise sector in the long term, even after the Covid-19 chapter comes to a close.

Local Governments have also been quite innovative and leveraged these solutions to provide livelihoods in their locations. For example, there have been instances of hand- cart vendors or rickshaw pullers (who register on the app) being paid on a daily or a monthly basis by grocery and other outlets in local markets to make doorstep delivery to customers in a particular locality, with the customer directly making payment to the local market shop through the app without having to physically visit the outlet.

While the above Apps and technology solutions were developed as part of the response to the Covid-19 pandemic, they have also provided a number of additional benefits. First, they have led to increased technology adoption by Government and municipal officials, citizens /households, grocery / retail outlets, unorganized street vendors, and handcart / rickshaw pullers, many of whom were not active-technology-users earlier.

The large sections of new users like grocery / retail outlets in the local market, handcart pullers, and street vendors who have hitherto been a part of the informal unorganized sector have now been somewhat formalized through adoption of online payment mechanisms and featuring in a database maintained by the local government, which can be subsequently used for other Government schemes and initiatives.

BFSI : The Indian banking industry witnessed unprecedented growth since the 2008 financial crisis up until about a couple of months before the COVID-19 outbreak.The crisis, however, is also providing the BFSI space with an unparalleled opportunity to bring about a fundamental change in the way that it functions. India is a cash-driven economy that, despite large-scale measures such as demonetisation, has not been outgrowing its dependence on cash. This seems to be changing, as the viral nature of the novel coronavirus has made Indians circumspect of cash.

The time is perfect for players in the BFSI space to reinvent themselves and test newer business models that are more digitally-driven. By leveraging advanced technologies and digitising their existing set of offerings, they can supplant legacy processes with newer, more optimised workflows.

E-Courts: E-courts were launched as a part of the National e-Governance Plan (NeGP) way back in 2006. However, the sudden and unexpected advent of Covid-19 crisis has provided a greater fillip in bringing about a rapid transformation in the manner of court administration in the country. As physical appearances by lawyers and litigants were discouraged in courts due to the strict safety protocols of the Covid-19 crisis, greater use of technology, already put in place, came in handy in justice and court administration.

An important step towards the digitization of the justice administration system which was already taken prior to the onslaught of the Covid-19 crisis was the introduction of the Supreme Court App.

This official mobile App of the Supreme Court of India, is free to download and provides useful information on pending and decided cases with a personalized dashboard containing Cause Lists, Case Status, Daily Orders, Judgments, Latest Updates, Office Reports, Circulars and much more. All these can be accessed, downloaded and shared in a user-friendly interface.

Even before the Covid-19 crisis made its appearance, , the E-courts Services mobile application was launched in 2017. The E-Court Services App provides information related to cases filed in the Subordinate Courts and most of the High Courts in the country. It can be exclusively used for District Courts or High Court or both. The App provides several useful features to digitally assist the lawyer or the litigant Further, the E-Court Services App also provides numerous other services. This includes anyone viewing entire case history of a lawsuit through this App; Case status, cause list, next date of hearing and so on. There is also a provision for lawyers and litigants to e-pay court fees. The App provides scanning of QR code to access the entire case status. The App is also connected with all 18,000 District and Subordinate Courts and 21 High Courts with more than 3.2 crore case statuses available on the App. Some useful features include that the History of Case Hearings option in the App shows entire history of the case from the first date of hearing to the current date of hearing.

The Courts' Responses to Covid-19 – A Speedier transition of E-courts to E-judiciary in the Post-Covid-19 Crisis Era: E-judiciary is a step beyond E-courts. E-judiciary involves not only filing of cases online, but also includes, among other things, avenues for online interaction between the judges and advocates, online proceedings, online examination and cross examination of witnesses and finally passing of online judgements. Prior to Covid-19, after the success of E-courts, there was no urgency in moving forward and things had been moving at their own bureaucratic pace in the implementation of E-judiciary in India.

The Covid-19 crisis, due to its safety protocol norm of social distancing, started nudging the judicial administration to take a quicker leap from the existing stage of E-courts and jump to the next level, i.e., E-judiciary. In fact, as a direct consequence of the Covid-19 crisis, after E-courts we are now witnessing a new impetus to move from E-courts to E-judiciary as a preferred mode of justice administration in courts at various levels.

As a result of these measures, virtual court hearings are becoming more and more common by the day. Normally, virtual proceedings were being conducted in the pre-Covid-19 crisis era generally in criminal cases where the accused could not be produced physically before the court due to security reasons. However, due to the strict Covid-19 crisis safety protocols, the courts have started hearing even the normal cases through video-conferencing.

On the infrastructure front, with the Covid-19 pandemic dangers in view, the Government is also speedily providing video-conferencing rooms in courts across the nation in order to facilitate E-judiciary mode of justice administration during the Covid-19 crisis period.

FASTag: FASTag, an inclusive technological tool for toll collection on highways, is ensuring safety of commuters during Covid-19 times. Huge number of FAST-ags were issued across the country.

FASTags not only prove useful now but would be more practical and beneficial in the coming times post- Covid-19.

Smart Cities: Smart Cities Mission (SCM) is actively providing support for rapid response in Covid-19 management. These practices were around gathering information, rapid communication, active management of Covid- infected areas and people and take proactive steps in avoiding spread of the pandemic.

Smart cities would not just have an easy to access to infrastructure but also be technology advanced in govt. -citizen interaction. Technologies like AI, IoT, radio frequency identification, cloud computing and many more would be used by govt. to offer smarter solutions.

Using social media and electronic media to increase engagement and build a strong online brand community: Social media activities are being increasingly used to help and entertain customers while they are stuck at home. Creating helpful content to show customers how they can get by at home until they can use your products again, is one of the best says to strengthen customer relations. Doordarshan went ahead and telecast old TV serials like Ramayan and Mahabharat to keep people glued to their television sets during lock-down. Many ministries of Government of India (Railways, for example) used social media extensively to remain engaged with citizens to have first hand knowledge about their problems and grievances.

Telemedicine: Following the outbreak of Covid-19, India's government launched *new telemedicine guidance* to help healthcare professionals and the ICT industry provide medical services to the population during lockdown , though there are many challenges .

One of the key challenges in resource-constrained settings is the skewed distribution of healthcare delivery infrastructure. While a large proportion of the population live in rural areas, healthcare establishments are located in urban settings. Telemedicine has the potential to play the bridging role in overcoming these infrastructural challenges.

The Covid-19 pandemic has highlighted the importance of robust and reliable data systems. Countries with robust health data infrastructure have leveraged real-time data, informing key strategic and public health responses. The Covid-19 pandemic has demonstrated the potential telemedicine offers in augmenting health systems capacity in India.

Even as the health systems transformation envisaged through establishing primary care networks and health and wellness centres under Ayushman Bharat are being established, the Telemedicine Guidelines 2020 provide the opportunity to leap frog and invert the healthcare delivery paradigm.

Large-scale telemedicine practice in India would also facilitate adoption of electronic health records and thereby realize the grand vision for the digital health backbone as envisaged in the National Digital Health Blueprint and strategies outlined by NITI Aayog in Health Systems for a New India: Building Blocks—Potential Pathways to Reforms.

Drones (Co-Bot) Indian states are using the Covid-19 opportunity to further spread the use of technology – whether it is use of Collaborative Robots (Co-Bot) by the government in the eastern state of Jharkhand or the municipal corporation of Bengaluru, India's tech hub, using drones to spray disinfectants, survey areas, monitor containment zones and make public announcements.

Payment of online bills: Another useful experience from the coronavirus pandemic was the way governments adjusted to the requirement of citizens paying their household and business bills and accessing other government services through e-government portals. In a post-Corona world, countries will focus on expanding e-government services to enable citizens to pay utility bills, rates and taxes, obtain official documents and receive government notifications directly in their mailboxes, as these are issued. Banks had already integrated IT in their services at a high level of customer interaction. These will be further developed to reduce cyber-crime and eliminate the need to have bank branches located in every village and town. Banks are likely to become more invisible to the public with only head offices located in major cities. Biometric and voice identification is already being used by banks to identify clients electronically. In the future credit cards could be replaced by iris recognition or embedding smart chips in human bodies.

Work From Home: Work from Home (WFH) is another major change that has become a part of our lives. Many IT companies in the West and even in India has been practicising it with perfection. Covid-19 has taken it to another level with almost all companies asking its employees to WFH.

The culture has seeped into our living rooms with people especially, women, shuttling between cooking, parenting and working at the same time!

Public Distribution System: Relief in the form of cash payments to those in need and rations of food supplies through the public distribution system have been provided during the lockdown. The JAM delivery system has served as the Indian government's main vehicle for the distribution of Covid-19 financial assistance and relief. A relief package under the Pradhan Mantri Garib Kalyan (PMGK) scheme was announced only two days after the lockdown, on 26 March 2020. The PMGK relief package ordered the transfer of INR 500 per month for three months to all female PMJDY account holders, and INR 1,000 in three instalments to senior citizens.

E-pass: Another such e-Governance initiative was the e-pass service delivered through the service plus framework and was used by 17 states of India to provide movement e-pass services during covid 19 pandemic.

OTT Platform: When Covid-19 shut down the Box office, over the top streaming platforms came to Bollywood's rescue. Industry and Internet search data show viewership on OTT platform indeed increased considerably. The shift from conventional media particularly during the locked down period has resulted in a war between streaming service providers to attract and retain customers.

Public Private Partnership: E-governance also facilitated formation of interactive channels for collaboration between various stakeholders. Many organisations especially Non-profit were encouraged to join such e- governance initiatives thereby leading to delivery of public services through Public Private Partnership (PPP).

Some Initiatives taken by different states:

a. Arunachal Pradesh: Arunachal Pradesh Chief Minister Pema Khandu launched the State Wide Area Network (SWAN) providing secure digital connectivity to all district headquarters and local administrative centres.

Under this scheme, digital connectivity is being provided between the state headquarters and block-level administrative centres via district and sub-divisional headquarters, in a vertical hierarchical structure with a minimum bandwidth capacity of 2 Mbps per link.

It will reduce the cost of communication between government departments at different locations and will provide secure network infrastructure to enable electronic transfer of sensitive data, payments, etc.

b. Delhi: The Delhi Transport Department has launched "faceless services" Under the scheme, 33 major transport-related services such as driving licence, registration certificate, permits and termination of hypothecation among others have become online and people would not require to visit MLO offices. Applicants now will only require to visit transport offices to undertake driving test for permanent driving licenses and for fitness test of vehicles.

The faceless services scheme has received a very encouraging response. The data shows that the scheme has become popular among masses as it provides many important services online. The process is Aadhaar-authenticated and fees can also be paid online.

The document will be dispatched to the applicants through speed post. They can also download it through a link sent to them through an SMS on their registered mobile number.

In another such use of E-Governance information on availability of hospital beds, related to covid -19 treatment has been made available by Delhi Government. The said initiative was coupled with a helpline number to raise grievances

c. Karnataka: The government has a target of connecting all Indians through the Internet by 2025 mostly through broadband of BharatNet, simplifying cyber-law for ease of doing business and focusing on high technology like Quantum Computing and Artificial intelligence. Districts which have never had any contact with the Government in months could get direct financial transfer in the accounts during the pandemic.

Digital infrastructure, governance and services on demand and digital empowerment of citizens are the cornerstones of Digital India initiative.

d. Madhya Pradesh: The Madhya Pradesh police has launched an initiative on an experimental basis to allow people to get FIRs registered online regarding thefts of vehicles or theft of cash and items up to Rs 1 lakh.

Any aggrieved person who has suffered a vehicle theft (up to Rs 15 lakh) and simple (monetary) theft which can be of any thing like cash, jewellery, mobile, equipment (up to Rs one lakh) is free to lodge an e-FIR.

Under the initiative, citizens will be able to register FIRs without going to the police station. Necessary instructions have been given to all police stations in this regard across the state. The e-FIR registration facility will be available round the clock.

e. Himachal Pradesh: An initiative called the "Harghar pathshala" (school at every house) has been started in Himachal Pradesh (HP). Under the initiative, state authorities in-charge of education-related issues shared videos for each subject and class with the principal of the school and these were then shared with the rest of the teaching staff.

The "Swayam sidham" portal, an initiative of the HP government, helped students get access to study material. Lesson indicators, lesson plans, question banks, MCQ tests and e-books are available for download at this portal. Although the word "sidham" has multiple meanings in Hindi, the word that corresponds to portal's name is "self-accomplished".

The new normal: remote working leading to a contactless world: The Covid-19 pandemic disrupted labour markets globally during 2020. The short-term consequences were sudden and often severe: Millions of people lost jobs, and others rapidly adjusted to working from home as offices closed. Many other workers were deemed essential and continued to work in hospitals and grocery stores, on garbage trucks and in warehouses, yet under new protocols to reduce the spread of the novel coronavirus.

Perhaps the most obvious impact of Covid-19 on the labour force is the dramatic increase in employees working remotely. This has resulted in individuals and companies shift out of large cities into suburbs and small cities. It was found that some work that technically can be done remotely is best done in person. Negotiations, critical business decisions, brainstorming sessions, providing sensitive feedback, and onboarding new employees are examples of activities that may lose some effectiveness when done remotely. Remote work and virtual meetings are likely to continue, albeit less intensely than at the pandemic's peak.

Remote work may also put a dent in business travel as its extensive use of videoconferencing during the pandemic has ushered in a new acceptance of virtual meetings and other aspects of work. While leisure travel and tourism are likely to rebound after the crisis, it is expected that the entire share of business travel, the most lucrative segment for airlines, may not return. This would have significant knock-on effects on employment in commercial aerospace, airports, hospitality, and food service.

Covid-19 may propel faster adoption of automation and AI, especially in work arenas with high physical proximity.

III

Learnings from Covid-19

We have come to learn that Covid -19 is actually a blessing in disguise. Lot of learnings have emerged out of common sense to hedge against the virus. Social distancing has actually brought the families closer to each other. Staying confined to homes, we spend more time with family. Our needs have come down. We have come to learn that we can live without too much of consumerism.

There is a shift now from materialistic to non-materialistic way of living. So we should actually thank Mr. Covid for bringing about a change in our life style. We have become more empathetic eg. donations made to PM Care fund, worry & care for the migrants, for domestic helps and workers in the factories. We have slowly started getting rid of ego, greed, anger, attachment and jealousy. These have been replaced with new managers taking control of us – Compassion, kindness, love, togetherness, forgiveness, empathy etc. We are becoming better human beings and human spirit is ultimately prevailing. Suddenly there is no urge to buy anything more than our needs, hence in many households the savings have also increased. People have started doing the household chores by themselves. There is less dependence on domestic help. We are now giving vent to our hidden talents - our culinary skills, our hobbies etc. We have started realizing that cleanliness is Godliness. New hygiene regime has come to occupy our lives. – Sanitizing, washing hands, distancing, masks etc. Downturn in economy is worrisome, but actually we are managing well. Fear of COVID is ensuring less visits to malls, hotels, unnecessary shopping. Since the world is slowly turning into a contactless world there is a great use of modern gadgets - smartphones TV, laptops, for working from home. We now manage things with technology - virtual platform. As scare of covid-19 starts receding, as medication/vaccine becomes available - people's fears/scares are likely to drift away. Vocal for the Local rather than imported stuff is gaining ground. We are now maintaining placid lifestyle – we now experience happiness without much reason. So during lockdown people remained indoors & car keys gathered dust. Skies began to breathe - Nature started repairing itself. People started smiling, & clapping to say thank you to health workers. So much so about our lifestyles but let us now see what the future scenario is going to be like in the post covid era which will lay greater stress on technology.

There are many assessments going around as to what kind of world we will inherit in the next decade. These are based on evolving hypotheses, as countries are still busy firefighting the pandemic. There is, however, sufficient material to sift through and put together a construct of what the future may look like for humanity in the coming months and years when life gets back to a new normal.

As a result of the global economic downturn, which may prove worse than the financial and economic crisis of 2008–9, nationalism will dominate any future discussion on international cooperation. Although globalisation cannot be eliminated, it will take a back seat, as countries will vie to care for the well-being of their citizens first before helping others.

The IT sector will see the highest growth. Heavy reliance on the internet during Covid-19 forced major IT giants to adjust their public websites to allow clients access to increased cyber communication. Companies such as Zoom and

Skype, which provide web-based conference servicing saw their shares rise in the stock market. Home entertainment giants Netflix and Disney gained new subscribers in millions. Google and Apple joined hands to compile statistics on coronavirus. In the post-corona phase these giants are likely to invest more in IT services to meet rising demand.

The controversial 5G broadband is likely to advance to support artificial intelligence in industrial and social applications. Hospitals and defence industries will find it more cost effective to use robots and drones to avoid human exposure to hazardous situations. Health professionals may stop seeing patients face-to-face in routine appointments unless they have gone through the first stage of initial consultation through video link. Medicines will be approved by Doctors for patients online and delivered at home without the recipient having to go to the pharmacy for collection.

Mobile and fixed broadband data will acquire the same importance as gas, electricity and water for every household and individual. Advancements in IT will ensure that citizens will have access to free public WiFi hotspots at airports, hospitals, train stations, shopping centres and other public places.

Coronavirus will disappear over a period of time but its effects will be around for a long time. Covid-19 in a global tragedy but it is a historic one and it will change our lives, our jobs, our offices and our countries forever Even when we find a cure, we will prefer to stay with the world we have found, than what we left behind. Old habits will become extinct. Covid is going to change the lives of most of us both individually and collectively. Some of the anticipated changes are discussed below:

A. Office: The office will become less & less relevant. In a lockdown it was even illegal to open them – So importance of office will gradually wither away. Already companies have started realizing they don't need an office. Consequently, they don't need to pay huge amounts of rent for the office when all the employees can easily work from home. Once we realise that our jobs can be done remotely, we will not want to be stuck in traffic, paying huge rents for both office and apartments just to get to the office. This means this is the time when we need to get a stronger Wi-fi! Working from homes will lead to greater flexibility both to the employer and the employees.

B. Jobs: Many jobs can be done remotely. You just need an internet. So when Covid-19 hit, millions of people drove out of New York back to their homes to be with their family. They realized --- why do I need to pay huge amount of rent for an apartment just to live in cities.

C. Cities: Cities will no longer be the same; people have started realizing that they don't like the traffic, the noise and the pollution. They can now work close to a very exciting nature. So, in future, millions of people will immigrate from cities to suburbs/ farms / beaches / small towns. So after Covid 19, Delhi, New York and even other major cities will not be the same. They will have a lot lesser traffic. Work will be attended to remotely through online means.

D. Talent: If you don't need to be in office, Companies can hire you wherever you are in the world. Therefore, if you are a genius sitting in India, Indonesia, Iceland or Zimbabwe, you can be hired straight from your bedroom. All you require is lot of talent. You don't need U.S. visa, you don't need to immigrate, you don't need to go to office. People will be hired without even meeting them in person. It will all be done online.

E. More Tech Savvy: There will be greater reliance on digital modes working from homes would necessitate the people to become more tech-savvy. Processes will therefore become more robust.

F. Less visits to Big Gatherings: People will avoid big gatherings - visiting concerts, rallies, malls etc. Online meeting & conferencing will become the new normal. Most of the decision making will now result through virtual online mode.

G. New Skills: People will learn new skills to pursue different means of livelihood. Some of the Skills which will gain prominence will be:

i. Coding Skills

ii. Digital marketing skills

iii. Closi–g - Sales over phone

iv. Project management

v. Copywriting for content marketing/ advertising.

H. Industries Which Will Boom after COVID -19: The following industries are likely to boom post COVID 19

* E-Learning – Learning opportunities from home.

* Medical Products - Masks, Sanitizer, Delivery services/ online shopping- Stuck at home, buying online -Delivery at home.

* Home Entertainment Industries– YouTube, Netflix -Keep Creating Content Online Gaming.

* Software – Zoom, WebEx, MST- connecting people for meetings, video conferencing. Online coaching /consulting.

* Supplement Industry- people will become health conscious.

* Take care of the body- with vitamins, supplements.
* Online fitness class–s - Big demand for home gym equipment, physical trainers, home trainers will be in demand.
* Super markets - Groceries booming - People will buy & hoard.
* Cleaning industry - Offices, hospitals, homes – Cleaning/disinfecting.

The pandemic placed the whole world at a standstill with nations going into lockdown to stall the virus's relentless march. Still, there is no specific data on when situations will stabilize. What is certain is that the people are learning valuable lessons through this global crisis, and life after Covid is sure to change for the better. Aristotle, the celebrated philosopher, taught, "It is during our darkest moments that we must focus to see the light." Thus, this is perhaps the right time to look ahead at expected improvements in the post-Covid world.

I. Sustainable Lifestyle: People have learned to live with the bare essentials during the lockdown. Healthy home-cooked meals replaced junk food. Closed shopping malls highlighted the futility of mindless consumerism. As pollution levels went down and nature flourished, people have realized the necessity of a sustainable lifestyle for the health of the planet. In the future, more environment-friendly ways to operate will undoubtedly emerge, like remote working to save fuel and online paperless transactions. The people are more likely to give priority to a simple yet rewarding lifestyle, reducing consumption, increasing savings as precautions against future income uncertainties. The protection of the earth and the next generation is going to drive a majority of life-choices.

J. Upgraded Healthcare System: The pandemic has stressed the need to prepare the healthcare system for handling rapid surges in the volumes of patients. Steps are underway for creating adequate capacity in hospitals to cope with emergencies better. Digital health technologies like the use of contactless thermometers are on the rise, improving patient care. The contagion has raised awareness among the masses about adequate cleanliness. People are forming habits of wearing masks and washing hands frequently, practices that are certain to develop overall hygiene. Increased use of telemedicine is making access to medical assistance convenient. Since the protection of their family's health has become everyone's primary concern, the improving face of hygiene and healthcare will relieve anxieties.

K. Digitally Restructured Education Sector: Even after the curve of coronavirus spread flattens, the virus will probably continue to exist. Wearing masks, using hand-sanitizers, and maintaining physical distances are going to be the new normal. In this situation, to reduce the chances of contamination, educational institutes will need to modernize their teaching techniques with smart technologies. During the lockdown, parents are home-schooling their children efficiently, and schools are taking classes online. As parents will prefer to shield small children from exposures until the coronavirus threat passes, virtual classrooms might take over conventional teaching methods.

L. Centric Work Culture: Excessive workloads and long commutes to workplaces robbed modern society of family-time, until the lockdown. In the current scenario, social distancing cannot be fully relaxed until a vaccine helps build up immunity in the majority of the population. Thus, a vast portion of the workforce may not be able to return to the office soon. Work-from-home, meetings through video-conferencing will become the new work culture. People will spend more time with their family when they seek breaks from work-pressure, nurturing closer family-ties.

M. Protection to Garner 'New' Mind Share: Perhaps the most vital lesson that Covid-19 has taught people is the need to protect their loved ones from the uncertainties of life. The time for living in denial of the inevitable is now past. Covid-19 has shown that irrespective of socioeconomic background and age, eventualities can strike any time. Nobody could predict such havoc, and now people are far more aware of securing their families against unforeseen risks. Until recently, people viewed term life insurance largely as a tax-saving tool. Now people realize its importance as valuable financial buffers for their loved one's economic conditions in their absence. Demand for life protection will inevitably increase after the pandemic. People start to place the protection of the family first over every other consideration. Get a Covid-19 insurance along with your life protection now!

IV

How will be the world be different after Covid-19

In the words of James Manyika who is the Chairman and Director of the McKinsey Global Institute, "the world after Covid-19 is unlikely to return to the world that was. Many trends already underway in the global economy are being accelerated by the impact of the pandemic. This is especially true of the digital economy, with the rise of digital behaviour such as remote working and learning, telemedicine, and delivery services. Other structural changes may also accelerate, including regionalization of supply chains and a further explosion of cross-border data flows.

The future of work has arrived faster, along with its challenges—many of them potentially multiplied—such as income polarization, worker vulnerability, more gig work, and the need for workers to adapt to occupational transitions. This acceleration is the result not only of technological advances but also of new considerations for health and safety, and economies and labour markets will take time to recover and will likely emerge changed".

Jean Saldanha, Director of the European Network on Debt and Development, has remarked that "In *The Pandemic Is a Portal*, Indian author Arundhati Roy writes, Historically, pandemics have forced humans to break with the past and imagine their world anew. This one is no different. It is a portal, a gateway between one world and the next.

The way multilateralism operates will have to change to reflect this very different world. The Covid-19 pandemic has been testing the limits of global cooperation. Support for developing economies in particular remains inadequate. They were hit early by the global economic downturn, including through record capital outflows and tightening financial conditions. Facing the worst humanitarian crisis since World War II, these economies are experiencing unprecedented pressure on their already limited fiscal capacity to tackle urgent public health and social needs. Choices made now will have far-reaching consequences. Reliance on more of the same is untenable and ignores the scale of human suffering unleashed by the pandemic."

Sharan Burrow, General Secretary of the International Trade Union Confederation, is of the view that "the world after the first wave of Covid-19 must be more inclusive, resilient, and sustainable. Today, we live in a world in which inequality between and within countries has grown as a result of businesses' race to the bottom and working poverty among a vast portion of the global workforce. Too many countries suffered the external shocks of Covid-19 without universal social protection, robust public health systems, a plan to reach net-zero carbon emissions by 2050, or a sustainable real economy with quality jobs."

Sergio Rebelo, Professor of International Finance at the Kellogg School of Management at Northwestern University, feels that "Covid-19 will leave a lasting imprint on the world economy, causing permanent changes and teaching important lessons. Virus screening is likely to become part of our life, just like security measures became ubiquitous after 9/11. It is important to invest in the infrastructure necessary to detect future viral outbreaks. This investment protects economies in case immunity to Covid-19 turns out to be temporary. Remote work is likely to become more common. We had some evidence that working from home is at least as productive as working at the office. However, many companies were reluctant to embrace remote work. Now that many have tried it with good results, remote work might be here to stay. The pandemic crisis has accelerated the pace of digital transformation, with further expansion in e-commerce and increases in the pace of adoption of telemedicine, videoconferencing, online teaching, and fintech".

V

Conclusion

It is fairly well accepted now that the pandemic is likely to continue for some time at least and Governments across the world including in India have stated that "we have to learn to live with the virus."

Given the significant economic costs associated with a lockdown, it has also become imperative for the Government to facilitate a calibrated resumption of economic activities and delivery of Government services to citizens. The new normal is therefore likely to see continued usage of both categories of apps and technology solutions. Till now, the ecosystem behind this new set of e-Governance solutions has been driven largely by separate initiatives taken by stakeholders at the Central Government, State Governments and Local Governments. However, the time may have now come for Government to consider national and state level initiatives for (a) sharing best practices towards improving features and functionalities of the apps / solutions and also bring in an extent of standardization; (b) streamline and strengthen the existing policy and regulatory mechanisms around delivery of Government services, data privacy issues, technology and data standards. This may help facilitate sustainable adoption and maximization of benefits both to citizens and the economy at large.

The lesson from the coronavirus disease is poignant. It is a new struggle for the survival of the fittest in humanity's post-modern evolution. It implies that if you haven't got the strength as an individual or as a nation to beat the economic, financial and social pressures that confront you, the lease on your survival in a highly competitive world is due to run out soon. Humanity demands that in the march of civilisation we take our weak and vulnerable along with us, even if we have to carry them on our shoulders.

As the economy starts to open up, the new reality is unravelling across dimensions , impacting the way businesses function , including the delivery of Government services to the citizens. Challenges and uncertainties are expected to persist in the near future. We are slowly moving towards a contactless world. Thus it is important for the Government to proactively plan for the new reality and emerge stronger from the crises by further accelerating the digital transformation of Governments service delivery and engagement through e – Governance. Technology adoption has increased to a new height not only by Central Government but also by State & Local Governments and technology savvy citizens and by many who are not active technology-users earlier. If leveraged correctly this situation can help India attain new heights in terms of e- Governance adoption and utilization. It took a virus to make us understand each other & bring people together. Sometimes you have to become sick to become better. We call it a Great Realization.

REFERENCES

1. Challenges and Opportunities in the post Covid-19 world – insight report – World Economic Forum.
2. Challenges of Global Governance amid the Covid-19 Pandemic – Council on Foreign Relation May, 2020.
3. E-Governance Project Life Cycle – National E-Governance Division, Government of India
4. How Covid-19 has pushed companies over the technology tipping point – and transformed business forever – Survey October, 2020
5. E-Governance possibilities in India for the post Covid-19 era – ORF by Raman Dutta
6. The complexity of managing Covid-19 : How importance is Good Governance – Alaka M. Vasu, Kaushik Basu and Jose Maria U. Tapia
7. Governance and Institutions - Covid-19 response resources – The World Bank
8. How will the Corona virus reshape Democracy and Governance globally – by Frances Z. Crown, Suskia Brechenmacher, Thomos Carothers
9. Webinar on Covid-19 and prospects and challenges of e-Governance in Nepal – AIDIA – Webinar series
10. How would the Covid-10 pandemic reshape retail Real Estate and High Streets through acceleration of e-Commerce and Digitization – Journal of Urban Management June 2021
11. Governance an Institutions Covid-19 response resources – World Bank Group
12. The Economic Times Markets – Sectors that will be the worst affected by Covid-2.0
13. Post Covid-19 e-Governance challenges : A case study of Anganwadi Services by Tabrez Alam and Md.Afroz
14. The role of e-Governance in combating Covid-19 and promoting sustainable development – A comparative study of China and Pakistan by Atta Ullah and others
15. Embracing e-Government during Covid-19 pandemic and beyond – insights from the Gambia by Lamin B. Ceesay and Malang B.S.Bojang
16. Are we ready for the post Covid World by Paul Laudi Gina
17. E-Governance: A change Management Tool – P. Panneervel
18. Internationally Monitory Fund : Life post Covid-19
19. Dynamics of e-Governance in post Covid era : India by Upmith Singh, Kamlendra Rawat and Ashim Raj Singhla

CONTRIBUTORS

Aditi Mehta

Aditi Mehta did her undergraduate education from Delhi University's Miranda House in Economics Honours and went on to Smith College, Northampton, MA. to complete a second BA degree. She returned to Delhi to do her MA in economics from the Delhi School of Economics in 1977, and after a brief foray in journalism with the Times of India, joined the Indian Administrative Service in 1979.

Aditi's most distinctive career highlight is the long period spent in the field, from the inception of the career, as a Sub-Divisional officer, to the period of when she was Secretary, Health and Family Welfare, in Rajasthan. This has given her a rich perspective grounded in field realities. Her main professional interests have converged on issues of the social sector, including health and education, but specially issues of social justice and the empowerment of marginalised peoples, the de-notified and nomadic tribes and issues with respect of the self-expression of Dalit, tribal and other marginalised groups. After super-annuation from the IAS in 2013, Aditi has been involved in NGOs that deal with the issues of her particular interest. She is currently completing a documentation and analysis of the Gavri, a votive dance form of the Bhil tribals of southern Rajasthan.

Aditi lives between New Delhi and Udaipur, Rajasthan and has three daughters and three grandchildren.

Champaka Rajagopal

Champaka Rajagopal is an independent practitioner and researcher in urban policy, planning and governance. She brings over twenty years of experience of having worked with national, state and local governments in India and abroad. She is faculty at the School of Public Policy & Governance, Azim Premji University, where she is Coordinator, the Hub for Law and Policy. Prior to joining Azim Premji University, she was Head, Urban Development at Egis India Consulting Engineers Pvt. Ltd., During this time she co-led and worked on several large scale public sector projects including the Development Plan for Greater Mumbai 2034, with the Municipal Corporation of Greater Mumbai and the Revised Master Plan for Bengaluru 2015, with the Bangalore Development Authority. Champaka holds a doctoral degree in Planning and International Development Studies from the University of Amsterdam, a Masters' Degree in Urban Design from University of California at Berkeley, USA and an undergraduate degree in Architecture from Centre for Environmental Planning & Technology, Ahmedabad, India. Champaka is a recipient of Oxford University's PhD Grant in Global Challenges in Transport Studies. She trained at the Haas Business School at UC Berkeley on Leadership Skills for Women Executives in 2015.

Dr. C K Mathew

Dr CK Mathew is an IAS officer of the 1977 batch from the Rajasthan cadre and was Chief Secretary of the State before retirement. He has served as District Collector in two districts and was Secretary to the government in various departments such as Irrigation, Energy, Mines, Education, Information Technology and Finance, besides serving as Secretary to the Chief Minister for five years. After retirement he has worked as Senior Fellow in the Public Affairs Centre at Bangalore and was also Special Rapporteur in the National Human Rights Commission for the southern states. Currently he is Visiting Professor in the Azim Premji University. Dr Mathew holds a Ph D in English literature and is the principal author of three annual reports called the *Public Affairs Index* on the quality of governance in the states of India. He has also compiled and edited a series of essays by retired Chief Secretaries titled In *The Rear-View Mirror.* He is an avid blogger and author of three novels.

Gopalan Balagopal

Gopalan Balagopal had his education in Kerala and Delhi and started his career as an Executive Trainee with Fertilizers & Chemicals Travancore (FACT) a Central Public Sector undertaking in Kerala in 1969. After working there for five years he was selected to join the Indian Administrative Service in 1974. He served in West Bengal as Collector of two districts and the Ministry of Information & Broadcasting of the Government of India. His services were loaned to the United Nations Children's Fund in January 1994 and he worked with UNICEF as Chief of Child Protection in Bangladesh; as a Senior Adviser, Child Protection at UNICEF Headquarters in New York and as UNICEF Representative in North Korea. After his retirement from UNICEF at the end of 2009, Mr. Balagopal has been extensively consulting in Africa for the Economic Commission of Africa and partners in strengthening government systems for Civil Registration and Vital Statistics at the continental level and by helping several African countries on the ground.

K Narayanan Unni

Born in Thodupuzha, Kerala in 1955. Obtained Bachelors degree in Mathematics and Master's degree in Statistics from University of Kerala. Joined Indian Statistical Service in 1979. Worked as Deputy Registrar General (Civil Registration) in the Office of the Registrar General, India during 2001-06. Also worked with the Ministries of Agriculture and Statistics & Proramme Implementation. Also worked as Technical Adviser with UNFPA for Inter Censal Population Survey 2012 in Ethiopia. Was engaged in consultancy projects relating to Civil Registration and Vital Statistics with the United Nations Economic Commission for Africa, Unicef (Zimbabwe) and Unicef India. Was a member of the team that prepared a report on strengthening Civil registration and Vital Statistics (CRVS) with the support of support by Unicef, India. Was a member of the Technical Advisory Committee for 2011 and 2021 censuses.

Dr. Manju Menon

Dr. Manju Menon is Senior Fellow at the Centre for Policy Research, New Delhi. Her main areas of work are resource politics, environmental law and regulatory decision-making. She has published popular articles and papers on environment, law and development for over two decades.

Ms. Kanchi Kohli

Ms. Kanchi Kohli is Senior Researcher at the Centre for Policy Research, New Delhi. She works on environment, forest and biodiversity governance in India. Her research explores the links between law, industrialization and environment justice. She has authored various publications, research papers and popular articles.

Krishna Mohan

More than thirty seven years of rich experience in all aspects and crucial sectors of public administration as an officer of the Indian Administrative Service (Haryana Cadre – 1977 Batch) with multiple core competencies in a complete range of sectors and departments through several key appointments in the State of Haryana and the Union Territory of Chandigarh as Head of the Department, Managing Director and Administrative Secretary (1977 to 2013). His last posting was Addl. Chief Secretary, Revenue & Disaster Management, in the rank and scale of Chief Secretary. After this he was further re-employed as Advisor to the Chief Minister, a post which he held till October 2014. Some of the most challenging assignments were Home Secretary, Chandigarh Administration (2004 to 2008) & Deputy Commissioner-cum-Estate Officer, Chandigarh Administration (1986 to 1991). While serving for almost 9 years in these two assignments he carried out pioneering development works in the city of Chandigarh. Additional prominent positions which he occupied were MD Hafed, Excise & Taxation Commissioner, Registrar Cooperative Societies, Director Agriculture, Health Secretary, Home Secretary, Agriculture Secretary, Cooperation Secretary, Transport Secretary & Forest Secretary in the Govt. of Haryana.

Shri Krishna Mohan is a certified National Trainer and Facilitator on Ethics. He has been selected by DoPT in collaboration with UNDP to be a part of the National Pool of Trainers on Ethics. Shri Krishna Mohan has also been certified as Recognized Trainer on e-Governance duly certified by NeGD (National e-Governance Division) under the Ministry of Electronics & Information Technology, Government of India.

Shreelata Rao Seshadri

Shreelata Rao Seshadri is Professor, Ramalingaswami Centre for Equity and Social Determinants of Health, Public Health Foundation of India. She has been involved in research, practice and teaching in the field of public health for almost three decades. She has had a range of professional engagements, including with multilateral agencies, global research initiatives and grassroots NGOs. Her research interests include health systems policy and governance, public health nutrition and mental health, with a special interest in program implementation and evaluation. Shreelata has published widely on a variety of public health issues, including nutritional challenges faced by primary school children, traditional food systems and their transformation, and governance issues associated with access to health and nutrition services in both urban and rural settings. Shreelata has served on several government committees and as well as President of the Indian Health Economics and Policy Association and on the Board of the Center for Budgeting and Policy Studies.

Joy Oommen

P Joy Oommen is a former Chief Secretary of the Government of Chhattisgarh. He was a member of the 1977 batch of Indian Administrative Service. He also served as the founder Chairman of Naya Raipur Development Authority which planned and developed the new Capital City of Chhattisgarh. Other positions he held include: Chairman of Chhattisgarh Electricity Board, Additional Chief Secretary, Chhattisgarh, CEO and Member Secretary, Central Silk Board, Bangalore, Managing Director of Madhya Pradesh Textile Corporation, Secretary to Governor of Madhya Pradesh, Secretary Finance, Madhya Pradesh, Joint Chief Controller of Imports and Exports Chennai and Collector and District Magistrate of Dewas District, Madhya Pradesh. After his retirement he also served Government of Kerala as Chairman and Managing Director of Kerala Financial Corporation. Currently he is Adjunct Professor in Economics with Xavier Institute of Management and Entrepreneurship, Bengaluru.